THE DANCE OF DEATH

THE DANCE OF DEATH:

NIGERIAN HISTORY AND CHRISTOPHER OKIGBO'S POETRY

DUBEM OKAFOR

Africa World Press, Inc.

P.O. Box 1892

Trenton, NJ 08607

P.O. Box 48

Asmara, ERITREA

Africa World Press, Inc.

P.O. Box 1892

Trenton, NJ 08607

P.O. Box 48

Asmara, ERITREA

Copyright © 1998 Dubem Okafor

First Printing 1998

Book & Cover design: Jonathan Gullery

Library of Congress Cataloging-in-Publication Data

Okafor, Dubem.
    The dance of death: Nigerian history and Christopher Okigbo's poetry /
Dubem Okafor
        p.   cm.
    Includes bibliographical references (p.) and index.
    ISBN 0-86543-554-5 (cloth). -- ISBN 0-86543-555-3 (pbk.)
    1. Okigbo, Christopher, 1932-1967--Criticism and interpretation.
    2. Nigerian--In Literature. I. Title.
    PR9387.9.0378Z63   1997
    821--dc21   97-15056
                                                          CIP
PRINTED IN CANADA

CONTENTS

To the Living Memory of My Uncle
Christopher Okigbo: Poet, Prophet, Warrior;
To My Daughter and Sons
And All Sons and Daughters of Nigeria —
the Bird that Devours its own Young —
that their Future may Coruscate
with Sunshine, Laughter, Full Stomachs;
that they may be Spared the Giddy Agony
of the Dance of Death and Carrion;
that they may know Sanity, Harmony, Stability, Progress, Peace.

ACKNOWLEDGMENTS

I wish, first and foremost, to express my immense gratitude to Professor John Mowitt, the Director of my doctoral dissertation at the University of Minnesota, where this book had its genesis. Easily one of the most amiable and erudite of scholars and teachers, John was able, very early, to discern the profound articulacy behind the wall of reticence which shielded the poet and student. He became my academic advisor, mentor and (naturally) my supervisor, in which last capacity, despite his diverse commitments, he saw me through to the successful completion of my doctoral work.

I am also beholden to the other members of my doctoral committee, who together constituted a formidable team of scholars. Professors Richard Leppert, chair of the Department of Cultural Studies and Comparative Literature, was also the chair of my doctoral committee. Lisette Josephides of the Anthropology Department made sure that I did not feel "homeless," so far away from home. Charlie Sugnet, director of the Creative Writing Program of the English Department, and Prabakhara Jha of the Comparative Literature Program, two intellectual luminaries, facilitated my doctoral work.

I am grateful to the Graduate School, University of Minnesota, for the grant which supported my work while I sojourned there.

But I must also mark the importance of the following scholars and teachers of mine, whose conspiracy, witting or no, produced me. The grateful student in me, thus, remembers: Professors Peter Nazareth, University of Iowa; Mary Ann Caws, Amy Mandelker, Fred Nichols, and Vincent Crapanzano of the Comparative Literature Department, Graduate Center-C.U.N.Y.; Tony Boxill and Barry Cameron of the University of New Brunswick, Canada; Gerald H. Moore (now in Trieste University,

Italy), with whom, at the University of Sussex, I began the long journey of initiations into academic mysteries; Edward Okwu, now at Alvan Ikoku College of Education, Owerri-Nigeria; Kalu Uka of the University of Calabar, Nigeria; Chinua Achebe, Emmanuel Obiechina, and M.J.C. Echeruo, emigrants now from the University of Nigeria, Nsukka, where they first sowed the seeds of curiosity and inquiry.

I'd like to recognize my friends whose faith in me and continued moral support have always encouraged me: Professors Xiuwu Liu, Molefi Asante, Barbara Harlow, Bernth Lindfors, Chris Odionu, Lawrence Ocho, Okechukwu Umeh, Nnadozie Inyama, Innocent Dozie Ezigbalike, Uzo Esonwanne, Emeka Okeke-Ezigbo, Emeka Nwadiora, Tanure Ojaide, Houston Baker, Jr., Emmanuel Enekwechi, John Allman, Obi Nnaemeka, Chimalum "Spirit" Nwankwo, Tess Onwueme, Jare Adeniran, Everett Green, Alfred Prettyman, Kevin McCloskey, George Muugi, Kate Clair, Francis Imbuga, John Ruganda, Arnold Newman, Jim Applewhite, Bette Reagan; Dr. Joseph Amprey; Hose Artiles; Uju &Victor Anyakwo, Frank Ikwueme, Ifeanyi Alex Araka, and Tony Okolo.

My immense thanks go to Kristina Rolin, Doctor of Philosophy of Science, whose companionship and productive conflicts sustained me during the birthing of this work.

I must also recognize Professor Chinwe Christiana Okechukwu, accomplished writer and scholar herself, whose magic has transformed my dolor into ebullience, and brought sunshine and laughter into an erstwhile somber existence.

My eternal gratitude goes to my Uncles: Dr. Pius Nwabufo Charles Okigbo, world-renowned economist; Chief Lawrence Chukwuemeka Okigbo; and Chief Okunwa Isaac Nwamuo Okechukwu; and to my aunt, Mrs. Susana Anakwenze. Their faith in me, as well as their unstinting moral and financial support, has always kept me going.

Finally, I'd like to remember and express my appreciation to Nneka, that noblest of women and greatest of wives, who has so gallantly held the fort all these years, and our children, Ikenna

Chukwuka, Adaiba Ifeanyichukwu, and Dubem, Jr. Anyaegbuna, as well as my first son, the "Heir Apparent," Nnaemeka Chukwudi—they have all endured the pangs of my long absence.

In the end, this work could not have been accomplished without the painstaking and meticulous labor of project editor Frank Blisard and all the rest of publisher Kassahun Checole's team of dedicated professionals at Africa World Press.

PREFACE

This book is a bipartite intervention in the sense that it is both a long-overdue book-length study of Okigbo's poetry and a loud reminder to the mis-managers of the Nigerian nation-state of the warnings and prophecy of Okigbo's oracles against national insanity and suicide. It is, therefore, at once a scholarly and a patriotic duty. But it is also an offering of love and homage to my late uncle, the poet, with whose socio-political concerns and progressive readings of the historico-political tendencies of Nigeria I fully identify.

This total agreement with my visionary uncle explains, in part, my engagement in the tradition of "the man and his works," which is still a very valid and illumining critical approach. My sojourn in the Western world has exposed me to a whole array of exciting theories and critical practices, but unlike the more fashionable -isms, "the man and his works'" approach is favored here because it enables the critic to place the writer squarely within the complex socio-historical-cultural-political milieu, for the better elucidation of the writer/his works and the total social formation. Because I believe that the African signifiers / signifieds are still firmly rooted in the cultural soil, the kind of socially useful criticism which I here engage in, that which foregrounds the social-political, cannot be enabled by a fascination with decentered and decentering -isms.

This identification with the politics of my uncle, as well as my exilic location as a postcolonial scholar in the "First" World, which has afforded me a clearer perspective on the cultural-political-historical lineaments of Nigeria, also explains my own impatience with the "selfish self-seekers," the comprador political elite, whose primary interest has continued to be the spoliation of the "national cake" at the real risk of destroying the already precarious statal edifice. In this gastrocentric scramble, the ten-

sion between ethnic sectionalism and nationalism gets exacerbated and made almost unresolvable. But an optimistic reading
of Okigbo's poetry, itself a succinct capsulization of the cultural-
political history of Nigeria from the first days of imperialist penetration into the country to the present, asserts that "the
repetitive cycle of human stupidity"(Soyinka) and doom could be
averted if only those in charge of the affairs of the country would
listen. Okigbo's optimism, his "divine rejoicing," as well as his
total identification with the generality of Nigerians—"the quadrangle, the rest, me and you"—assures us that we can all not only
get along but together begin to build a Nigerian nation.

For, as it is, nationness has eluded Nigeria, while its history,
since the Amalgamation of 1914, has been a protracted mediation and attempted containment of primordial centrifugalities.
The mediation and containment have not always been successful, as a concatenation of bloody eruptions attests. Consequently,
the concerted and often half-hearted attempts at political and ter-
ritorial consolidation became a precarious exercise in ethnic balancing, political destabilization, economic stagnation, unequal
sharing of resources and loot, lopsided development, and brazen
opportunism. The result of all these was a labyrinthine detour
through thirty long months of dismembered limbs and rivers of
blood, against which Okigbo had very loudly warned.

Bullets and blood have thus remained a permanent factor
in the tortuous trajectory of Nigeria. But they have not succeeded
in inculcating in the citizenry a national consciousness and sanity, without which a "national" movement becomes, never
progress, but only a circular race which always ends where it
started and always begins again. But the situation need not
remain dizzy. We only need to listen to what the writers have
been telling us. Apart from Okigbo, Achebe, Soyinka, and the
first-generation writers, a salutary development is the influential
emergence of a new brand of "national" writers, including the
market poets, who have begun to reach the generality of
Nigerians because they have tended to valorize the people's lingua franca, which I have called Nigerian English, and which has

the ability to transcend ethnolinguistic disparities, and facilitate the transition from localism to nationalism, from fractious divisiveness to harmonious co-existence.

Let us give our writers the respect they deserve, and our ears. Let us look again at the pages of Okigbo's prophecy, and stop the dance of death which the latest political saviors are determined to prolong. Then poet-prophet will have died for a noble cause.

CHAPTER I

DISCOURSE, BLOOD, AND NATION: NIGERIA 1914–1996

I. INTROIT OR MAPPINGS

The "Introit" or "Mappings" is a kaleidoscopic panorama of the cultural-political history of Nigeria, undertaken here to underline the importance of primordialism as the bane of Nigerian politics, and to show how, in a precarious anti-structure, a mere political breeze, an ordinarily trivial, everyday event, can trigger off actions whose consequences are unpredictable, cataclysmic, and far-reaching. I will begin then with a detour, a rough translation and brief analysis of the lyrics of a song which became so popular and so ill-fated during the crisis-ridden period, 1966-1970, especially among "foreign" (that is, nonindigenous) elements in Northern Nigeria. Its importance in the political equation of Nigeria may not be immediately apparent, but will become so as my elaboration proceeds. The "Introit" will be followed by extended reiterations of the major salience already indicated, in the form of tripartite periodization which will not only foreground the deep roots of ethnicity in the evolution of the Nigerian nation-state, but will also provide a vindicating backdrop for Okigbo's prophecy of the tumultuous unfolding of the third (that is, present) period, 1970-1996.

The goat is bleating,
yes, the goat is weeping;
the dog is yelping,
yes, the dog is barking;
the donkey is neighing,
yes, the donkey is groaning.

Decontextualized, this rough translation of a verse from the song "*Ewu na Ebe Akwa*" ("The Goat Is Bleating"), by the late Cardinal Jim Rex Lawson, a famous musician from Southern Nigeria, nominates a bestial guttural commonplace. It does not represent poetry, or any such serious thing. As the verse stands, it can only, at best, qualify as clap-trap jingle. But in the context of the musical composition, when played, the rhythmic resonance of these lines captivates even the musicologist. Yet, that is not what makes the lines important. Read within the context of the conflagrant moment, 1966-1967, in the political-cultural history of Nigeria, these lines assume an allegorical significance far-reaching in the consequences that followed their performance. I will attempt in the following paragraph a simple and brief analysis of the major words, the nouns and the verbs, of the lyric whose implications will be kept in view as the discussion proceeds.

The goat and the dog are domesticated animals characterized by stupidity and blind fidelity, respectively, while the donkey is a stupid, docile, and long-suffering beast of burden. The latter is also a favorite means of transportation, especially for lepers, in Northern Nigeria. Bleating is a normal goat-sound; but it is also a cry emitted in anguish by humans before the flashing sword. Weeping is lament, occasioned by bereavement, loss, and mourning. Yelping is normal dog-sound, while barking is associated with anger, rage, fury, rabidity, derangement, and dementia. Finally, the donkey neighs ordinarily and for different significatory purposes, but groaning indicates excruciating pain, as when bones, on being mangled and broken, crack!

This interpretive simplification could have been considered quite innocuous—that is, in ordinary circumstances; but in the extraordinary circumstances of the 1966-1970 conjuncture in Nigerian history, the lyrics had much wider cultural and political ramifications. For the musical composition was performed by a famous southern Nigerian musician in Muslim Northern Nigeria, at a time when the North was still licking the fresh wounds of the loss of its political and religious leaders in the military coup of January 1966. Thus, as I read it, that musical, everyday event, which ushered in a flood of other events of national/international implications, was not only not just one of several events, nor was it only a mere trigger of these other events; that everyday event became both a paradigmatic and microcosmic exemplification of the national debacle in the sense that it adumbrated the confliction and disjunction of the biographical and the symbolic, the diachronic and the systemic axes: the famous musician (together with his largely Southern fans) was a single individual whose cultural practice and production did not proceed as part of, or contribution to, the total Northern Regional cultural ensemble. Rather, as it became interpreted and disseminated by the civil/religious society of the North, that cultural performance was flagrantly disruptive of the civil/religious/cultural/political order of the Northern cultural section. For the allegorical pejoration of the lyric was directed at the bereaved and bewildered Muslim population of the North. This mockery of the Northerners would appear to vindicate the late Prime Minister Balewa, a Northerner and first victim of the January 1966 coup. As far back as 1948, Balewa had observed that "the Northerners looked upon the Southerners living in the North as invaders who do not mix with the Northern people" (Nnoli 1978:231). In the eyes of the Northerners, therefore, the musical provocation, illustrative of the insensitivity of the Southern "invaders," was enough justification for the concerted and collective extirpation of the infidels from the sacred cultural space of the North.

After the foregoing preamble, the discussion that follows will attempt a traditional narratological typology in that the story of the Nigerian debacle can be constructed in terms of a beginning which will quickly scan the cultural political history of Nigeria from the colonial period to 1966, and attempt to provide an explanatory backdrop for subsequent events; a middle which will examine the crises of the 1966–70 conjuncture; and an end which will complete the narrative cycle and return us to the *status quo ante bellum* in which the concept of nation in Nigeria remains not only not yet "imagined," but an oneiric imaginary.

What came to be known as Nigeria was a conglomeration of different ethnic groups, or what reactionary Anthropology used to designate as tribes, but which, following Post and Vickers (1973), I will call "cultural sections" (17), or nations. For that is what they rightly are—unless, that is, such collectivities as the English, the French, the Spaniards, and the Hungarians are also to be similarly designated as tribes. Prior to colonization, these sections were relatively autonomous and isolated. When England established the two Protectorates of Northern and Southern Nigeria, they governed the administrative centers located in Lokoja, Lagos, and Calabar. At first, these centers administered their territories largely independently of each other. But after the amalgamation of the two protectorates in 1914, these separate sections were brought under one central administration. It must be stressed, however, that the acquisition and incorporation of these sections were piecemeal, that even with Amalgamation, effort was made to keep the North distinct from the South, and that the subsequent "development" of the sections was consequently uneven. This differential incorporation did not mitigate the relative isolation to which these groups had been accustomed; instead, it exacerbated the situation by pitting the groups one against another and by widening the already existing chasm of cultural differences, thus adding to the stress and tension. It is this tension that I see as the abiding feature of Nigerian cultural-political history. For the imposition of the European modular-state structure on the incipient "country" did nothing to counteract the determinative power of primordialism in the attribution and exercise of loyalty (Davidson 1992). Put differently, Nigeria's cultural-political history has been a study in primordial tensions and conflicts.

During the slave trade, brother was set against brother, community against community, and cultural section against cultural section. The resultant drift of human populations, in which millions of able-bodied Africans were translocated to the New World, left profound fissures on the psyche of the Black person. The African, as much as the Arab and European slavers luxuriated on this traffic with the result that when the trade was officially declared illegal in 1807, both classes of traders were infuriated and continued, albeit clandestinely, to supply the Portuguese and other merchants who rushed in to fill the vacuum created by the British exit from the trade.

The British withdrawal from the slave trade, which was "necessitated" in the first place by economic needs and was subsequently rationalized in economic terms, was not so much a humanitarian and altruistic gesture as it was a compelled obedience to the economic imperatives of the Industrial Revolution, which now created wants in other than human materials. Attention was now directed towards such raw materials as palm produce and cotton. Astute and foresighted local entrepreneurs, forerunners of present-day comprador business elites—that is, indigenous businessmen who are content to serve as commissioned agents of Western exploiters of their countries—went over to this new and legitimate trade and became the middle-men between the local farmers and the European traders. The cut-throat competitiveness that had characterized trade in slaves continued, and some of these comprador traders became tremendously wealthy (Dike 1962:1; Miyoshi 1993:729).

Meanwhile the masses toiled on, but got very little benefit from their sweat. Their lot was not ameliorated by the appointment of direct buying agents by the Royal Niger Company, for the same pattern of inhuman exploitation continued. It is clear that as early as this, there had already developed very serious socio-economic tension and rivalry within and among the new powerful and influential comprador elites from the different cultural sections (Collis 1970:4-6).

To consolidate and enhance British economic interests, it was necessary to establish direct political control over these territories. And it was also expedient to coin a name that would embrace the different cultural sections over whose territories the Royal Niger Company had already been, for some time now, exercising economic suzerainty. As the *London Times* of January 8, 1897 put it:

as the title "Royal Niger Company's Territories" is not only inconvenient to use but to some extent is also misleading, it may be permissible to coin a shorter title for the agglomeration of pagan and Mohamedan states which have been brought, by the exertions of the Royal Niger Company, within the confines of a British Protectorate, and thus need for the first time in their history to be described as an entity by some general name. To speak of them as Central Sudan, which is the title accorded by some geographers and travellers, has the disadvantage of ignoring political frontier lines. . . . The name "Nigeria," applying to no other portion of Africa, may, without offence to any neighbours, be accepted as coextensive with the territories over which the Royal Niger Company has extended British influence. (Coleman 1958:44)

Officially recognized in the British House of Commons debate of July 1899, the name "Nigeria" has continued to apply to that artificial creation which has been called a "geographical expression" by a leading Southern politician (Awolowo 1947:32). The final seal of agglomeration was placed, in 1914, with the now famous, or infamous, Amalgamation of the Protectorates. Even this amalgamation decree has also been referred to by a Northern politician as "the Mistake of 1914" (Sardauna of Sokoto, quoted in Okpaku 1972:56). It was truly a mistake for, in the words of Margery Perham, British "rule was imposed like a great steel grid over the amorphous cellular tissue of tribal Africa and the hundreds of independent and often hostile communities" (Coleman 1958: 45). More recently, Noser Igiehon has described the system of government bequeathed by the colonial regime as "a *damnosa heredita* on the people of Nigeria. Such was its general unsuitability that some people have gone so far as to say that it was a deliberate prescription for disaster" (Igiehon 1975:23).

In imposing this grid of British rule and the parliamentary regimen on Nigeria, the colonial rulers did not take into consideration the peculiarities of the peoples, nor of the local situations. Being "the system they themselves practised and knew best," it was considered by the colonizers to be "the best form of any government for any civilized community" (24). As Zik (Dr. Nnamdi Azikiwe, died in May 1996) saw the situation, "it is a declared policy of Britain that no colony can be considered ready for self government until it has made parliamentary democracy a political reality" (24). It is the same policy that Ali Mazrui was criticizing when he observed that "the capacity for self-government" was synonymous with the "capacity for Anglo-Saxon liberalism. And the right to such government rested on that liberal capacity and not on national distinctiveness" (24).

Because of this utter disregard for "national distinctiveness," the conglomeration and imposition of an unmodified grid resulted in a tension which was, at once, both primordial and "nationalistic." Primordialism accounted for the interethnic/inter-sectional animosities, rivalries, and conflicts among the different cultural sections. According to Clifford Geertz, "primordial attachments" constitute:

> the assumed "givens". . . of social existence: immediate contiguity and kin connection mainly, but beyond them the givenness that stems from being born into a particular religious community, speaking a particular language, and following particular social practices. These congruities of blood, speech, custom, and so on, are seen to have an ineffable, and at times overpowering, coerciveness in and of themselves. One is bound to one's kinsman, one's neighbour, one's fellow believer, *ipso facto*; as the result not merely of personal affection, practical necessity, common interest, or incurred obligation, but at least in great part by virtue of some unaccountable absolute import attributed to the very tie itself. (Post & Vickers (1973:11, quoting from Geertz 1963.)

The ties of primordialism are indeed metaphysical.

Nationalism, on the other hand, was that movement which, occasionally appearing to have transcended and drowned all primordial differences, sought to dismantle the colonial structure and win self-determination and freedom for Nigeria, while at the same time providing a transethnic bond that would act as a potent integrative force in prospectively independent Nigeria. But this was largely utopic because the forces of primordialism ensured that protonationalism and nationalism remained incongruent (Hobsbawn 1990:77); ensured also that the disarticulation among the cultural sections, the nation-state, and the political system would continue to mark and plague Nigeria, as well as impede her political evolution. Post and Vickers got it right when they remarked that:

> The core of the problem of the relationship between nationalism and cultural sectionalism seems to lie in the structural relationship of both with the political system. Nationalism takes it

as axiomatic that nation and the political system will be coterminous, or . . . that every nation will have its own state. The nationalist movement as a political force in Nigeria was a short-lived phenomenon, whittled away in the early 1950s by the primordial demands of cultural sections which influenced both the masses and all but a few of the elite. The process of mobilization in the crucial decades—roughly 1920-1950—was diffused (or refracted) in such a way as to produce a feeling of identity with section, rather than with a Nigerian nation. (19)

Even with the incorporation of the cultural sections into the Nigerian polity, albeit differentially, and even with social mobilization, "Nigerians" did not, indeed, become "one." This is because the entrenchment and virtual politicization of ethnicity resulted in the "endurance of several critical cleavages in society that one might have expected to disappear under the impact of rapid social mobilization and modernization" (Divine 1980:214). These cleavages are an obstacle to political solidarity because the continuing disarticulation of—in fact, violent disjuncture between—the interests of the major players at the biographical-diachronic axis, and the systemic needs of the country made it impossible for a truly national culture to be created and imposed at the institutional/modular-state axis. In other words, the creation of a coherent and cohesive national meaning conflicted seriously with the disparate and divergent desires for hegemonic and counter-hegemonic cultural/political positionalities. So there has continued an intensification of primordialism, as well as an aggravation of its centrifugalities. To quote Post and Vickers again:

In fact, as we have seen, in Nigeria people were mobilized and became aware that they were living in a system which bound together many ethnic groups, but at the same time did not have their commitment to their groups "eroded," and did not "break away" from their old setting. Rather their primordial loyalties were intensified . . . by their realization that their section was now in competition with others within a common (colonial) political system. (21)

8

In the light of this fact, one can even surmise that, but for the insensitive economic expediency of colonialist Britain, most of the problems plaguing Nigeria and impeding her cultural integration and evolvement of national consciousness might not have arisen. And what is now being referred to pejoratively as ethnicity, primordialism, or cultural sectionalism might, indeed, have become positive enablers of national cohesion—that is, if the "pagan and Mohamedan tribes" had been left alone, administered as separate nation-states, or brought together as a confederation of relatively autonomous "states" held together by common interests, cooperation, equality, and mutual respect. For, as I had earlier indicated, the major cultural sections were, indeed, nationalities in their own rights prior to colonization and amalgamation. But because of other (largely self-serving) considerations (rather than common sense, logic, or the interests of the "natives"), imperialist Britain did otherwise. If we overlook, for one moment, their many and intractable internal problems, do not Albanian, Latvian, Romanian, Czech and Slovak republics exist, more or less viably, as nation-states? But in the racist eyes of colonialist Britain, the Igbo (13 to 15 million) and the Yoruba (15 to 17 million), as well as all the other cultural sections, were merely "tribes" which needed to be lumped together, however incongruously, to form a larger and more viable market and cheap source of raw materials for Britain (Post & Vickers 1973:19).

This insensitivity to the human, cultural, and political peculiarities and needs of the constituent cultural sections of the newly created polity also accounts for the monstrous size of the North relative to the rest of the country. This imbalance has continued to have far-reaching political consequences. And it was not a result of an oversight on the part of the creators of that country: with them, nothing happened that was not carefully, painstakingly, and meticulously calculated and planned. The lopsided political/structural arrangement served, at once, three British interests: Britain was assured a continued monopoly of a large market for her goods, and a huge, almost inexhaustible source of raw materials for her industries; the "conservative" North with its disproportionate size and population, and hence disproportionate voting/electoral strength, was assured virtual, if not perpetual, political dominance of the country, which meant that Britain could sleep, assured that the slavish relationship of her ex-colony would continue long after "independence;" and the structural imbalance was a guarantee of political imbalance and instability, lack of development and progress, and continued reliance and dependence of Nigeria on Britain. This worked out well for Britain, for when "independence" was eventually granted after protracted foot-dragging by the North, it was to the same reactionary Northern Region that the leadership of the country was, as it were, entrusted. As Chinua Achebe puts it:

> The British who had done precious little to create a spirit of nationality in Nigeria during the fifty years they were in control, made certain on the eve of their departure that power went to that conservative element in the country which had played no part in the struggle for independence. This would ensure Nigeria's obedience even unto freedom. As a first sign of this the British High Commissioner took up residence next door to the Prime Minister, who of course was a British Knight. (*Morning Yet on Creation Day*:82)

In the Northern Region itself, unlike the other Regions, a white Governor had remained behind, after "independence," to groom his indigenous Northern successor-vassal. The result of all this was that, with such subservient, even servile, leadership of the quisling political elite, independence was not worth more than the paper on which the deed was written. And those few "nationalists" who were ready to lay down their lives in the cause of freedom and national self-determination saw themselves outmaneuvered, and their dreams for the country thwarted, by the departing colonial rulers. Nigeria continued thus in a state of servile inebriation, a state exacerbated by primordial divisiveness and brazen plunder of the country's wealth, staggering inexorably towards the inevitable national calamity of 1966–1970.

As everyone saw, Nigeria could not be saved by the self-aggrandizing comprador politicians, and the Army struck to put an end to the death-dance of the country. Everyone, it would appear, welcomed this intervention of the military, for there was widespread jubilation which seemed at the time to transcend all primordialism. One had the sense that this coup had suddenly infused in Nigerians, for the first time, a sense of unity, cohesion, and solidarity. Okigbo articulated this feeling of the many when in his poem, "Path of Thunder," he sang:

> Fanfare of drums, wooden bell: iron chapter;
> And our dividing airs are gathered home.
> This day belongs to a miracle of thunder;
> Iron has carried the forum
> With token gestures. Thunder has spoken. (*Labyrinths*:63)

But it would not be long before disillusionment set in. For soon there began to circulate rumors that the military coup was actually an ethnic putsch by the Igbo bent on dominating the whole country. Otherwise, it was asked, why were all but two of the coup plotters Igbo? Why were none of the victims Igbo? As if these native/local doubts and rumblings were not enough, the British intensified their "advisory" role, which they never really ceased playing, and "authenticated" the ethnic interpretation of the coup. As Professor Okwudiba Nnoli puts it:

> The picture of the January coup became increasingly distorted as a result of the capitalist, imperialist, and neocolonialist propaganda championed by the B.B.C. and the British High Commissioner in Nigeria [with the result that] perceptions and images [of the coup as an Igbo plot and of the Igbo as a group] became increasingly negative, and hostility toward the Ibos (sic) by the Northerners became possible. Unscrupulous politicians urged on by British imperialism seized the opportunity to show their pent-up hatred of Ibos [sic] (Quoted in Okpaku 1972:121)

This "infallible" interpretation of the coup by the British, whose love, sincerity, and benevolence the Northern elite, civilian or military, had no reason to doubt or suspect, became the official Northern story. Consequently, all confusion, all doubt, all uncertainty, all reflection and calculation, all vacillation ceased: the January 1966 coup was a plot by the Igbo whose singular purpose was to wrench from the Northern cultural section its divine right of political dominance and rulership of Nigeria. And, as if the primordial cup of vengeance

11

needed a shove to spill over, came that ill-fated musical performance, earlier mentioned, which, by apparently "celebrating" the Northern calamity, vindicated the British ethnocentric interpretation. The smoldering fire needed no more fodder to feed it.

This metaphor of fire is not gratuitous; is, indeed, doubly appropriate for the fire erupted, literally, everywhere the Igbo resided in northern Nigeria; it also performed, for the Muslim Northerners, the purificatory function of exterminating "infidel" elements who had defiled the sacred North. The furious onslaught on the Igbo living among them by the Hausa-Fulani Muslims was, if I may appropriate the words of Mary Douglas (1966), meant to "cancel out the pollution" (136) which the musical performance had apparently both participated in and celebrated. Words are indeed a potent force. For like the divisive and intemperate utterances of the now discredited politicians, the lyrics to which I referred earlier as representing commonplace animal vocalizations, like all discourse, can and in this case did "trigger off cataclysms" (4).

In a culture founded upon and circumscribed by fatalism and blind obedience to religious/spiritual authority, sacrilegious utterances—in this case, musical lyrics composed by an infidel—represent a double anomaly and threat to the systemic order, and must be rooted out, as pollution, if the social order is not to be allowed to disintegrate into "formlessness" (38-40). For again, according to Douglas, "ritual pollution . . . arises from the interplay of form and surrounding formlessness. Pollution dangers strike when form has been attacked" (104). Thus the only recourse open to the "bereaved," "aggrieved," and faithful Muslims, whose cultural/religious/political order had been desecrated, was violence aimed at the very heart of what they perceived to be formlessness or disorder or impurity: the stranger Igbo in their midst.

What followed was a series of slaughters which were performed, everywhere, in accordance with strict prescriptions of ritual. First, there would be a gathering of the faithful in the city (*birnin*), construed as a sacred site from where, after the logistics had been planned, they marched, as one man, to the strangers' quarters (*sabon gari*), construed as sites of defilement, where the infidels were descended upon, beaten, mauled and mangled, dragged to the outskirts of the city/town, and slaughtered. Of course, many were killed inside their homes, in churches, and in other places of doubtful refuge. But essentially, the ritual pattern, usually associated with cleansing, was meticulously observed, and was replicated in different towns in all subsequent eruptions of carnage.

Even when the Northern counter-coup of July 1966 took place, the killings which followed meticulously observed the same ritual pattern. The July coup was, thus, not aimed at restoring order to Nigeria, as such, but was part of an orchestrated ritual of blood whose double purpose was to revenge the January coup which had been read as an Igbo-ethnic coup; and to restore to the Northern cultural section its "God-given" political leadership of Nigeria. The only difference this time was that the celebrants in the ritual had at their disposal the whole country's armory. As a result, all preceding eruptions were mere prologue to this main event. As St. Jorre describes it:

> [A] terrible new cataclysm (erupted) in the North which made all the year's preceding violence look like a barrack-room brawl. Ever since the July coup, persecution of the Ibos [sic] in the North had gone on with varying degrees of intensity. On 19th September a band of Northern soldiers from the now infamous 4th Battalion . . . drove down to Makurdi and Gboko . . . and started killing Ibos [sic] . . . . On 29th September soldiers from the 5th Battalion in Kano tore Ibo [sic] refugees off a B.O.A.C. aircraft and shot them. Troops and mobs raced through the *sabon gari* (strangers' quarters) of all the major towns in the North, killing, looting and burning. . . . As in the May troubles, students, civil servants and local politicians led demonstrations and helped to get the mobs out on to the streets. Once again the killings were organized. . . . (St. Jorre 1972:84)

The organizational control of the hatchet-men was simple enough, for the masses as well as the elite had long been used to blind obedience and it would be unthinkable for any faithful to question or disobey the orders of the Sarkin Musulmi or Commander of the Faithful. As has been observed, "the pan-tribal unity which Islam created also tended to rally everyone behind the religious leaders" (Okpaku 1972:33). Therefore, given the force of primordialism, and the blinding power of religion, especially in its fanatical manifestation, the fury of the onslaughts was both deep-seated and irrational: the killing of the Igbo was seen as a religious duty, an ethnic

13

cleansing which assumed all the characteristics of ritual extirpation.

The ritual pattern can also be illustrated with the fate, during the July coup, of the then Head of State and Supreme Commander of the Armed Forces. An Igbo, his murder was a precise enactment of ritual cleansing, and followed the same dramaturgic pattern which the zealots had already established, elements of which I have indicated with italics in the quotation below, whereby an arrest or overpowering was followed by beating/flogging or flagellation; the victims were then taken/dragged to beyond the borders of the town/sacred site, where they were literally *killed ritually*:

> Major Danjuma . . . took some of his men upstairs, confronted and questioned the Supreme Commander, saluted him and *ordered his arrest*. The General was led downstairs to join the others. The three captives . . . were now *stripped and their hands tied behind their backs with wire*. They were *flogged, tortured* and then put into separate police vans. . . . [the convoy *drove off out of town*]. The captives were ordered out and *led along a footpath off the right side of the road*. These Northern officers and men *beat and tortured the captives* so badly that their bodies were swollen and *bleeding profusely*. . . . The Supreme Commander and the Governor, who were almost dead by now, were separately *finished off* by a few rounds of machine gun fire. (St. Jorre 1972:68; my italics)

Another bizarre illustration of the ritual nature of the ethnic killings involved another Igbo officer who was literally crucified: "others performed ritual killings, the most terrible being that of an Ibo [sic] Captain, caught at airport, who was tied to an iron cross, whipped to the point of death and thrown into a guardroom to die" (80).

It is important to note that in all these convulsive and agonizing misadventures in nation-building, which culminated in the deluge of fratricidal and genocidal blood, the official systemic axis was not only involved, but was actively so, with massive (though sometimes clandestine) assistance from the most powerful of imperialist nations, namely Britain and the United States, whose envoys in Lagos always "hovered in the wings and occasionally came on stage to give their advice" to the Northern junta (71). This "meddlesomeness" evolved into active military participation on the side of the Federal government when the crisis escalated into the Nigeria-Biafra War. It would appear that it was in the interests of imperialism that the Biafran/Igbo anti-imperialist effrontery be stopped. The result was that when people of wisdom saw and advised a confederal arrangement as the most sensible and pragmatic way to end both the bloodshed and primordial politics in Nigeria, "the British and American envoys strongly urged Gowon (then military dictator, following the July coup) not to break up the Federation" (72). Nigeria, it must be remembered, was still the largest single market for the West in Black Africa, and the integrity of this market must not be jeopardized by the assertion of the right to life and to self-determination by the over-enterprising Igbo/Biafrans. Thus it was that after thirty long months of blood and carnage, the Biafran assertion of the right of the Eastern cultural section to separate and sovereign existence was stopped. Nigeria returned to the *status quo ante bellum* a most important "Britain's sphere of influence" (179), and a precarious and unstable polity whose defining characteristic remains primordialism and cultural sectionalism.

If we conceptualize the tortuous journey of Nigeria-in-search-of-nationhood in terms of rites of passage, we can see that it is the resilience and persistence of primordialism and ethnic consciousness which has prevented the country from ever advancing beyond the second, "transition" stage in the tripartite cycle. Arrested in the limen or threshold, the country has refused cultural, social, political, even economic "incorporation" or "re-aggregation" (Turner 1982:24).

In appropriating the concept of liminality for the nation-state, Nigeria, I am aware of the positive and active connotations of the concept with regard to an individual person undergoing the rite of passage. The individual comes out at the end of the ritual a transformed and reformed, an integrated and reincorporated member, equipped to assume adult roles in society. Unfortunately, with respect to Nigeria, primordial thinking and attachment, ethnicity "objectively threatens all and subjectively halts humanistic, 'modern' progressivism in mid-stride" (16). Caught in "limbo existence" the Nigerian "social order may seem to have been turned upside down" (27). Consequently, that formulation which sees liminality as "the settings in which new models, symbols, paradigms, etc. arise—as the seed bed of cultural (and political) creativity in fact" (28) cannot be applied to the country. For even as recently as 1993, the rumblings, threats, and counter-threats, grave portents pregnant with the possibility of another primordial drama of blood, have only just been forcibly muffled by the staged return to power of the military, this time in the person of General Sanni Abacha who would appear, contrary to interpretations and reinterpretations, to have simply succeeded General Babangida, also from the Northern cultural section.

The panoramic discussion has taken us back to the status quo in which the concept of nation, with regard to Nigeria, remains, not only not yet "imagined," but an oneiric imaginary. For did Abacha not, with a sweep of the bayonet, and with great contempt for Nigerians and the whole civilized world, sweep away all vestiges of democratic institutions in Nigeria, thus returning the country to a 1954-like situation, with a "promise" of possible constitutional rearrangements? One cannot help seeing the astuteness in Robert Collis' observation that "Nigeria . . . (is) really not a nation either racially or geographically, but a conglomeration of ethnic groups" (Collis 1970:4).

At this juncture, I wish to attempt an extended reiteration of the saliencies of the discussion so far, not only because such a recapitulation will emphasize the deep roots of ethnicity in the perennial "dilemma of nationhood" (Okpaku 1972), but, more importantly, because it will foreground the radical vindication, by the tumultuous events leading up to the present impasse, of the sad prophecy of Christopher Okigbo's poetry regarding the nation. To do this, I will construct a tripartite periodization: the first period, 1914 to 1960, which locates the genesis of the dilemma of nationhood; the second, 1960 to 1970, during which the clouds gathered and the storm overtook the country; and the third period, 1970 to 1996, in which the country—its leaders and people having learnt nothing from its checkered history, from the crucible of the Nigeria-Biafra War, and from the many fitful steps and false starts—still flounders.

II. THE UNSTABLE TRIPOD: 1914–1960

The period 1914–1960 represents the momentous genesis of an amorphous and unwieldy political amalgam which, though it has served the economic and political interests of a megalomaniacal British empire at the zenith of its global brigandage, has been and continues to be only a source of constant discomfiture and bafflement and friction to the inhabitants of that "artificial creation," Nigeria. The creation has been widely and rightly called artificial because "the union has been so sudden and has covered such widely differing groups of peoples that not only the British who created it, but the inhabitants themselves have often doubted whether it could survive as a political entity" (Crowder 1962: 20). To everyone's surprise, Nigeria has tottered precariously through eighty years of strifes, conflicts, riots and thuggery, coups and extended military dictatorships, short-lived *interregna* of civilian and hardly democratic administrations, chronic political instability and economic stagnation, and even a genocidal blood-bath. It would appear that the peoples of Nigeria, having been forced to occupy a single polity for so long, find it almost impossible to contemplate separate existences. So they have remained in that state of paradoxical unity which can be described, in terms of a sad but jocular injunction, in popular parlance, to "get away closer."

For, in spite of what Crowder calls "their wider cultural affiliations" (21), the inhabitants of Nigeria have yet to devise a single cultural icon of cohesion, nor yet a common tongue, with which to transact amicable and frictionless trans-sectional communication, and with which, as a possible single community or collectivity, to articulate with the modular-state axis. But what, indeed, is the need for such collective articulation when the State is conceivable only in terms of a distant no-man's cake to be scrambled by all comers, whose only dependable assurances of well-being and long-term security remain the cultural sections, the clans, and the kinship groups. This reliability of the "social security" coming from the cultural sections accounts, in part, for the resilience and viability of ethnicity in Nigeria, and for the refusal of the birth of a nation.

Again, how can these peoples function as formidable interlocutors with the "distant" State when, between them, the inhabitants of Nigeria have and speak several hundred dialects of two hundred and one languages—languages belonging to such different families and sub-families as Niger-Congo, Kwa, Cross-River, Adamawa, Central Branch (Semi-Bantu), and Hamitic! (Crowder 1962:21-23)? Such a diversity, disparity, and mutual unintelligibility have created what I have called linguistic cacophony in Nigeria. And until that market place of tongues is quieted, or an icon of coherence and solidarity for the people is created, it seems to me that it is still a very long way and time before any meaningful "gathering of the tribes" can take place.

But it was in the interest of colonial suzerainty to maintain the prevalent mutual unintelligibility: as long as the different cultural sections could not and—because of the suspicion inherent in non-communication—would not talk to and with one another, the task of overall political control and domination was made easier. For that reason, every effort was made to keep the sections distinct and separate from one another, especially the North from the South. The consequence of this policy of "divide and rule" becomes more apparent when we consider the unwieldy structure of the tripod which the title of this section has already characterized as "unstable."

The mutual suspicion among East, West, and North was exacerbated by Lord Lugard's smothering and paternalistic dotage on the North. For, since he considered the Fulanis as "born rulers" whose "wonderful intelligence" he was "anxious to utilize" in his experimentation with Sir Goldie's concept of Indirect Rule (Crowder 1962:196), he went out of his way to preserve the distinction between North and South (East and West). Even when such seasoned colonial administrators as E.D. Morel advocated a more rational division of the country into four large, but more equitable, provinces, Lugard saw that as a threat to the envisaged, eventual permanent political rulership of Nigeria by the North. This lopsided cartography has continued to compound Nigeria's political problems. Indeed, as Crowder rightly says, Lugard's regional policy "only exacerbated the growing differences between the two regions (North and South)" (215). But nothing took place by accident under the administration of this crafty imperial official, who was so capable that in his hands a mere concept, a mere idea of Sir Goldie's, that of Indirect Rule, became "transformed into a complete theory of administration" (196).

Moreover, it was in the Empire's great interest, in the long run, to ensure, even after eventual devolution of sovereignty on the peoples of Nigeria, the continued friendship, gratitude, and dependence of the leadership of that country. This could only be done if the leadership of the country was permanently secured for that section of the country whose people, in Lugard's eyes, were innocent and unspoiled by the pernicious influences of modernism and Westernism; whose people remained the object of his lasting dotage. Consequently, while missionaries were making deep inroads into the South, dispensing the twin "gifts" of Christianity and Western education, often with the direct military assistance of the colonial State, these same missionaries were deliberately, firmly, and officially "excluded from the Moslem areas of the North by Lugard's agreement with the Sultan of Sokoto that he would not interfere with Moslem religion" (209). Indeed, as Elizabeth Isichei puts it, "the British in the North came to see themselves not as agents of any form of 'development,' but as the defenders of a feudal structure which must be protected from change" (Isichei 1983:381). One consequence of the unequal educational and other "developments" was the reluctance of the North, later, to demand, with the rest of the country, self-government for its region in 1956.

Lugardism, or Lugard's application of the system of Indirect Rule, was so successful, and effective in enforcing total allegiance and ensuring complete control in the North, that it was exported to the South where traditional governmental systems were more amorphous and less centralized, and where it consequently met with varying degrees of opposition, failure, and chaos. But as implemented in the North, the system of Indirect Rule or:

> Native Administration . . . had been based on the authority of the Native Chiefs. The policy of the Government was that these Chiefs should govern their people, not as independent but as dependent Rulers. The orders of Government are not

conveyed to the people through them, but emanate from them in accordance, where necessary, with instructions received through the Resident. While they themselves are controlled by Government in matters of policy and of importance, their people are controlled in accordance with that policy by themselves. A political Officer would consider it as irregular to issue direct orders to an individual native, or even to a village head, as a General commanding a division would to a private soldier, except through his commanding officers. The courts administer native law, and are presided over by Native Judges. . . . Their punishments do not conform to the Criminal Code, but, on the other hand, native law must not be in opposition to the Ordinances of Government, which are operative everywhere, and the courts . . . are under the close supervision of the District Staff. Their rules of evidence and their procedure are not based on British standards, but their sentences, if manifestly faulty, are subject to revision. Their prisoners are confined in their own gaols, which are under the supervision of the British Staff. The taxes are raised in the name of the native ruler and by his agents, but he surrenders the fixed proportion to Government, and the expenditure of the portion assigned to the Native Administration, from which fixed salaries to all native officials are paid, is subject to the advice of the Resident, and the ultimate control of the Governor. The attitude of the Resident is that of a watchful adviser not of an interfering ruler, but he is ever jealous of the rights of the peasantry, and of any injustice to them. (Crowder 1962:217-18)

The foregoing is the definition of Indirect Rule as articulated by Lugard himself in his *Amalgamation Report* of 1919. Even though the application of the system in the South met with resistance, it eventually got forcibly entrenched through series of bloody "pacifications," ruthless suppression of opposition, and the arbitrary appointment and installation of "Warrant Chiefs" in places where there had been no Chiefs. For without the control of all the resources which the subtle system ensured, the economic benefit of the whole imperial adventure could not be maximized. Of course, everyone knows that "Britain's overriding interest in Nigeria (as in other forcible possessions) was economic" (Crowder

1962:206).

Part of the understanding behind the whole colonial enterprise was that, not only was wealth to be siphoned from the colonies to the metropoles, but that the colonies would not depend on London financially; they should be self-supporting. But that was not the case with Northern Nigeria. Since the South was not only self-sufficient, but could support the North, it was considered both prudent and expedient to merge the two groups of possessions. Thus, "the immediate reason for the decision to amalgamate the two Nigerias was economic expediency" (213). As Crowder goes on to explain:

> The Northern Protectorate was running a severe deficit, which was being met by a subsidy from the Southern Protectorate, and an Imperial Grant-in-Aid from Britain of about three hundred thousand pounds (Sterling) a year. This conflicted with the age-old colonial policy that each territory should be self-subsisting. Apart from the fact that it seemed logical to amalgamate the territories, the one land-locked and the other with a long seaboard, it was felt that the prosperous Southern Protectorate could subsidize its northern neighbour until such a time as it became self-supporting. Furthermore, there was the pressing need to co-ordinate railway policy, which at the time was practically non-existent. The Southern track had been started in 1901 and reached the River Niger in the Northern Protectorate at Jebba in 1909. It was to continue to Minna, where a Northern line was being constructed to reach Kano. At the same time, Sir Percy Girouard, the Governor, was intent on extending the Northern line to Baro on the Niger, where goods would be shipped down to the sea on barges. By 1912, then, there were two competing systems, the Minna-Baro-Niger system rivalling the Minna-Jebba-Lagos system. . . . Ironically Girouard's railway had been built with Southern revenues. Since a new line was envisaged from Port Harcourt through Enugu to the North it was essential that there be more effective co-ordination of railway policy and this could best be ensured through amalgamation. (213)

Just as economic expediency had forced the amalgamation of the Protectorates, so "Western economic forces have contributed to the unity of the arbitrary block that is modern Nigeria (as) the various ethnic groups comprised within its frontiers have necessarily become more dependent on each other as the economy has expanded" (207-08). This assessment was made in the days immediately following "Independence," which explains its overt optimism, whereas the reality ever since has been that of constant ethnic strife and rivalry. But what makes the optimistic assessment suspect is that long before Self-Rule was granted to Nigeria, Lugard himself had insisted, even after the Amalgamation, on keeping the administrations of the North and South separate, fully convinced that "his Amalgamation merely lumped together groups of mutually incompatible peoples" (225). And Lugard was not alone in his pragmatic realism. For much later, in 1922, Sir Hugh Clifford, who as Governor of Nigeria was to author that Constitution which provided for the election of African members of the Legislative Council, had these choice words on the very notion of "a Nigerian nation":

> Assuming . . . that the impossible were feasible—that this collection of self contained and mutually independent Native States, separated from one another, as many of them are, by great distances, by differences of history and traditions, and by ethnological, racial, tribal, political, social and religious barriers, were incapable of being welded into a single homogeneous nation. (228)

But, in spite of these permanent "ethnological barriers" among the mutually incompatible peoples, there began to arise "a certain number of Africans" who would "identify themselves not with their old tribal allegiances, but with the new political entity known as Nigeria" (225). As would be expected, this phase of supra-ethnic thinking was very short-lived. But while it lasted, it brought together a "new class of Africans:"

> ... clerks, teachers, traders, parsons, doctors and lawyers who could no longer think in purely tribal terms [actually because] by and large [they] were excluded from office in the native administration, so that they tended to look towards the central administration for an outlet for their natural desire to have

some say in their own affairs. (226-27)

Two points need, however, to be underlined here. First, these early champions of supra-ethnicity, these militants of Nigerian nationalism, were non-Nigerians, whose primary focus was on Africa as a whole and not on the fragments and agglomerations created by European colonialism. For example, Edward Blyden was from the West Indies; J.P. Jackson was a Liberian; and even Herbert Macaulay, that revered father of all Nigerian nationalism, was a member of the family of Bishop Ajayi Crowther, "that most famous of all freed slaves" (226). Second, these early nationalists, as they were called, fought more for personal aggrandizement and individual participation in the political process, than for the dismantling of the colonial structure as such. In fact, as K.O. Dike (1957) put it in his *A Hundred Years of British Rule in Nigeria, 1857–1957*: "After amalgamation in 1914, what the nationalist fought was the exclusiveness and racial basis of the Crown Colony system of government. At the beginning, the fight was not so much for self-government, but for a measure of participation in the existing government" (quoted in Crowder 1962:226).

Thus personal interest rather than the common and collective good of the entity called Nigeria was the major stimulus "to early nationalist activity" (234). Even when the militancy of this foundational nationalist movement had become "dissipated in the tangle of Lagos [local and ethnic] politics" (237), and needed the revitalizing spirit of a new crop of educated Nigerians in the late 1930s, these latter, first and foremost, prided themselves on their qualification and intellectual ability to compete with, and possibly oust and displace, the members of the "closed aristocracy of Lagos politics" (237). Like their forerunners', their own appeal was narrow, and also ethnic.

It was only with the return from the United States of America in 1937 of Dr. Nnamdi Azikiwe (Zik), and his entry into, and leadership of, the Nigerian Youth Movement that the organization became radically transformed from a parochial movement to something approximating the national. And his *West African Pilot* became the articulate and militant organ for "nationalist" activism. But this pan-Nigerian activism was to be short-lived because internal rivalry and sectional dissension prevented the NYM from consolidating its stature and accelerating its new-found momentum.

What happened was that Ernest Ikoli of the *Daily Service* had been put forward by the NYM for a Legislative Council seat, but Zik openly and vigorously favored and supported Samuel Akinsanya, an Ijebu-Yoruba, for the same seat. This open conflict was too much for the unity and cohesion of NYM, and the eventual departure of Zik with his Eastern followers left that organization effectively Yoruba. It must be pointed out, however, that even as the tension and conflict were personal and sectional, it was Zik's support for Akinsanya which exposed the latent fissures in the very structure of the NYM. Zik himself was to remain a strong believer in the possibilities of "one, united Nigeria." But, as Crowder puts it, "unfortunately for the future of Nigerian nationalism [the Ikoli-Zik rift] introduced an element of tribalism that had been largely subdued until then" (240-41).

It was at this time that Sir John MacPherson, coming after Richards, threw open for country-wide debate a new constitutional arrangement for Nigeria. But the tares had already been sown which polarized the country into three antagonistic, daggers-drawn, ethnic camps: the Ibo State Union metamorphosed into the National Council of Nigeria and the Cameroons; the Egbe Omo Oduduwa became the (Yoruba) Action Group; and the Bauchi Improvement Association was transformed into the Northern People's Congress. From their genesis these Unions/Parties drew their followings mainly from their ethnic-regional bases, for people joined them, not because their programs, plans, or even (that unutterable word!) ideologies were progressive, radical, or nationalistic, but because they "are our own parties," led by "one of our own sons." Given this widespread ethnic motivation, it surprised no one that "the three years during which the new constitution was negotiated was dominated by tribal nationalism with the NPC taking the part of the North, the Egbe Omo Oduduwa, which with elements of the old NYM became the Action Group, taking the part of the West, and the NCNC, whilst it outwardly presented its pan-Nigerian aims, taking the part of the East" (248).

Already, even before a constitution had been adopted, even before self-government, the conception of Nigeria as loot or booty had begun with the three Regions acting as inveterate predators bent on appropriating the largest share. Thus, while the Constitutional Drafting Committee recommended that the composition of the Federal House should be "twenty-two from the East and West respectively and thirty from the North," the North was adamant in its insistence on having a representation equal to those of the east and West combined because "its population was greater than that of both combined" (249-50). But the haggling for sectional aggrandizement did not end with this demand for "proportional" representation. The North also wanted revenues and grants to "be made on a *per capita* basis" (250), and would not hear of any changes in the Regional boundaries which had been established in 1914 by the British rulers. When, therefore, Sir Louis Chick submitted his Revenue Allocation Report, it was obvious that he had followed his instructions to the letter: one of his terms of reference had been to base such allocations on "the need, on the one hand, to provide the Federal Government and Regional Governments with an adequate measure of fiscal autonomy within their own sphere of government" (255). Chick's proposals laid the foundation for Regional separateness, autonomy, and exclusivity. And as the *West Africa* magazine editorialized, "the endorsement of the Chick report means economically as well as politically there will be three Nigerias" (quoted in Crowder 1962:256).

It was to this quarrelsome and haggling Trinity, this composite and unstable tripod called Nigeria, that "independence" was granted in 1960. Given the protracted reluctance of the North to "go along" with the East and West, it was one of the inexplicable historical miracles wrought by imperial Britain that "independence" was granted, indeed, to "one" Nigeria, and not piecemeal to the Regions. But the political-structural arrangement in place at independence, and continuing since, marks for us the permanent importance of fragile compromises, and of ethnic strife and balancing, as a feature of Nigerian political-social equation.

III. CAKE, CLOUDS, AND BULLETS: 1960–1970

So, what the magazine *West Africa* had characterized as "three Nigerias" was granted independence in 1960. But before then, the 1954 Constitution had actually laid the foundation for the unstable tripod. It had also marked the "end of nationalist struggle with Britain" (Crowder 1962:258). For, between 1954 and 1960, the political elite was preoccupied with learning the rudiments of Westminster-style parliamentarism, with closing deals and counter-deals aimed at self- and sectional aggrandizement, and, in short, with getting ready to step into the royal shoes of the soon-departing British colonial officials. As Chinua Achebe, in his novel *A Man of the People*, explains the frenetic scramble just prior to "independence" proper:

> A man who has just come in from the rain and dried his body and put on dry clothes is more reluctant to go out again than another who has been indoors all the time. The trouble with our new nation . . . was that none of us had been indoors long enough to be able to say "To hell with it." We had all been in the rain together until yesterday. Then a handful of us— the smart and the lucky and hardly ever the best—had scrambled for the one shelter our former rulers left, and had taken it over and barricaded themselves in. And from within they sought to persuade the rest through numerous loudspeakers, that the first phase of the struggle had been won and that the next phase—the extension of our house—was even more important and called for new and original tactics; it required that all argument should cease and the whole people speak with one voice and that any more dissent and argument outside the door of the shelter would subvert and bring down the whole house. (Achebe 1966:37)

The problem was that the argument and bickering continued, not outside, but inside "the door of the shelter." For, in spite of the deals and compromises cut inside the shelter which appeared to transcend ethnic and sectional lines, the embers of primordialism were still very much a-flicker. The pattern of victories in the 1959 general elections is illustrative. Even though the NCNC won twenty-two seats in the West, which was a clear majority, it did so, not because the generality of the Yoruba were impressed by its nationalistic program, but because the bickering minority ethnic groups, now restive under the harsh taxation policy of the Action Group, saw in the NCNC an alternative to what they considered an oppressive political instrument of the hegemonic Yoruba. And even though the NEPU had become a powerful articulator of the interests of the minority ethnic groups in the North, it could not win any seats in the North controlled by the Hausa-Fulani groups. Thus, it was clear that although the three major political parties won comfortable (if not landslide) victories in their "home" regions, yet none of them was national enough to assume clear majority rule in the Federal House in Lagos. For, even though NPC had won the most seats in the Federal House, because NCNC had won majority votes in both East and West, it won, thereby, the trump right to choose six federal ministers. This curious dilemma forced a marriage of convenience on the two major political (ethnic) combatants, NPC/NCNC, who now formed a coalition government, leaving the Action Group with UNIP (formerly NIP) to constitute a formidable and discomfiting, but also fractious, Opposition.

So once again convenience and expediency, not ideological congruence and affinity, nor yet "national" interest as such, forced another "national" compromise among cultural sections which were/are yet to learn to see eye to eye. For it is my view, given the perspective of decades of observation of the political scene, that this compromise neither demonstrated the possibility of national unity, as Crowder believes (1962:259), nor showed the leaders as unselfish and altruistic statesmen. The compromise merely postponed the days of reckoning.

It is in the same light that I see the "truce" called earlier in 1956 by the leaders of the three parties on the eve of the visit of the Queen (Elizabeth II) of a fast fading Empire. The truce remained what it was, a truce, and, in spite of "the enthusiasm and devotion that the visit has aroused," there is no basis for endowing that visit with the mystical ability "to symbolize the unity for which Nigeria was striving" (259). The Imperial Sun which never set was fast becoming senescent, and the Queen, visiting Nigeria on the verge of its independence, wanted to demonstrate the legendary goodwill of the Queen-Mother-Ruler to her "loyal" subjects who, sadly, were now on the precipice of self-rule for which they might not have been adequately prepared. She also wanted to ensure that, even after "independence," the economic-political ties between Subject and subjects remained umbilical and strong. (A Defence Pact would be discussed, and violently protested not long after this visit.) Whether the Nigerian masses trooped out enthusiastically and spontaneously to behold a miracle and curiosity in the person of a queen and woman who ruled over half the world, the British Empire, or whether the comprador bureaucrats, assisted by the police, merely herded the masses, together with heavily starched school children, to the ceremonial squares, the instantaneous "unity" was only carnivalesque, and it was wrong for *West Africa* to editorialize that as "'devotion . . . beyond expectation'" (259). Have subjugated masses everywhere not been known to be sheepish and devoted even to their slaughterers and colonizers and enslavers? It would, of course, not also occur to *West Africa* that the truce itself, among the warring but impatient political leaders, might have been mere expediency and temporization aimed at avoiding anything that could upset the timetable for "National Independence."

It is in the light of this pragmatism that one can read the sudden *volte-face* of the Sardauna of Sokoto, leader of NPC and of all Nigerian Muslims, who, just before the 1957 Conference, shocked the world with his announcement that the North, would, after all, also want self-government in 1959 (Crowder 1962:263). This was after the North had persistently rationalized its protracted vacillation and refusal to "be rushed into self-government, on the grounds that Northern cadres were not ready to take over the region's administration" (262). It is in the same light that one can also read that compromise which resulted in the selection of the Deputy President of NPC, Alhaji Tafawa Balewa, as the first Nigerian Prime Minister, charged with the formation of a "national" government. For the same man, Balewa, had been a very vocal advocate of "Northern separatism" (262). But conversion, spiritual or political, has a way of transforming or even occluding reality, which accounts for why, of Balewa, Crowder says that "by 1957 he had become as convinced as anyone else of the necessity of national cooperation . . .—and as a member of a small tribe, he could in a way, symbolize Nigeria as a whole and not one faction of it" (262).

But Balewa's political conversion did not stop his own people "of a small tribe" from demanding liberation from Hausa-Fulani domination. Forming the United Middle Belt Congress, these people, whom "the cavalry of Usman Dan Fodio had never conquered" (263), now wanted a Middle Belt State of their own. Since ethnic waters run deep and infectious in Nigeria, the same demands for minority self-determination were made in the West, where the Edo-speaking ethnic group wanted a Midwest State, and in the East, where the movement for the creation of the COR State (Calabar-Ogoja-Rivers State) would acquire virulence and would not abate until 1967, when both Rivers and Cross-River States were created by Yakubu Gowon in order to break the backbone of Biafra's own demand for self-determination. The important thing, however, is that, as Crowder rightly points out, "in all these cases the movements were inspired by fear of the dominant group, and by *ethnic chauvinism*" (264; emphasis mine).

Even though the Sir Henry Willinck Minorities Commission had recognized the reality of this ethnic fear, it did not recommend the creation of ethnic-minority states. But, importantly, it made significant Human Rights provisions which, it was hoped, would alleviate these fears and guarantee the accommodation of the interests of ethnic minorities by ethnicities-in-dominance. The most important of these provisions was the"nationalization" of the Police Force contrary to the demands of the North (NPC) and the West (AG) for Regional Police Forces. Opposed only by NCNC, such a potent tool as a regional police force in the hands of dominant ethnic groups would have meant the virtual liquidation of ethnic minorities. In addition, the provisions of the Willinck Report made it impossible for any of the three major, ethno-political parties to dominate the others without courting support from outside its home region, and, in effect, from minority ethnic groups in the other regions.

Indeed, I consider as highly plausible, Peter Ekeh's structural analysis of Nigeria's crises, which attributes the continued existence of Nigeria as a unit to the centripetal force of ethnic minorities. In his view, the three major ethnicities—Igbo, Hausa-Fulani, and Yoruba—would long have gone their separate ways but for the reluctance of minority groups who dreaded the possibility of further marginalization, if not annihilation, in the threatened "countries" where they would be denied the benefits of oversight and checks on dominance by the other majority ethnic groups. According to Ekeh:

> Secession became a household word in Nigeria as early as 1954, when the majority Yoruba in western Nigeria openly hinted about the possibility of secession, and indeed pressed for a secession clause in the constitution of Nigeria. No concept has appealed more to majority Nigerians, as a bargaining weapon, than that of secession—and no concept has been more dreaded by minority and marginal Nigerians than this notion of secession. (Okpaku, 1972:100)

On the question of state creation itself, the commission felt that ethnic fears, though real, were being exaggerated, and could be better addressed within existing geo-political configurations. Still, it is important to note that, in spite of the prevailing atmosphere of compromises, the North was ready and threatened to pull down the whole political structure and, hopefully, delay indefinitely the independence process if the other parties insisted on the plebiscite for Kabba and Ilorin provinces as recommended by the Willinck Commission. It would appear that, for the dominant ethnic groups, hegemonic control over and domination of ethnic minorities within their regions were more important sectional considerations than "national" independence.

This independence, which, for the sundry, meant, in reality, only the replacement of visible bureaucrats of the lighter complexion with more darkly complected indigenous ones, was indeed "granted" to Nigeria in October 1960. Nigeria was celebrated throughout the Western world as the showpiece of parliamentary democracy. Even though the Prime Minister's Palace in Lagos was only a telephone call away from Number 10 Downing Street in London and a mere drive away from the British High Commission in Lagos, and even though scores of white-skinned technical and administrative "experts" stayed behind to ensure the "smooth sailing" of the new ship of State—a similar situation in Senegal is expertly castigated by Sembene Ousmane in his film *Xala*—it was said that this peaceful transition from colonialism to democratic self-rule was a vindication of the imperial enterprise, for otherwise, how could Nigerians have managed, in spite of all the odds, especially ethnic ones, to govern themselves after the manner of good old English parliamentarians, after so short a preparatory period?

There was joy, of course, almost ebullition, everywhere, as Nigerians joined the British composer of the Nigerian National Anthem to sing:

Nigeria, we hail thee
Our own dear *native land*
Though tribe and tongue may differ
In *brotherhood* we stand. (my emphasis)

But the sentiments expressed in this stanza were as patronizing as they were insincere and alien; they might have been an expression of the desire of a well-meaning Briton, but they remained wishful. (One does not wish to go into any analysis of the verse, only to emphasize the imperial anthropologism of "native land" and "tribe," and the metaphysical wish expressed by the incongruous collocation of different "tribe and tongue" and "brotherhood.")

But the joy and wishful sentiments were only as short-lived as the parliamentary showpiece itself. The experiment in "parliamentary democracy lasted just over five years, from October 1960 to January 1966" (Isichei 1983:468) because it could not withstand the combined forces of ethnicity and personal aggrandizement. This crux of my argument has been so succinctly articulated in Elizabeth Isichei's analysis, that I wish to quote part of it:

The parliamentary experiment was wrecked by two related factors: the politics of ethnicity and the theory of winner-take-all. Some have written savagely about the materialism and corruption of the First Republic, but its origins were various and complex. Apart from those who, like the Sardauna (of Sokoto) belonged to a hereditary aristocracy, most politicians had made a desperate and successful struggle to escape from rural poverty. The frantic accumulation of wealth was meant to build a wall between themselves and poverty, between their children and poverty. And, like their predecessors, the Warrant Chiefs . . . they were expected to be generous . . . to relations, fellow townsmen and constituents. A successful man had to be seen to be successful —to wield power, to display wealth, to spend it freely—or his constituents would begin to wonder if he was really successful at all. (Isichei 1983:468)

So, a complex combination of poverty, moral and material turpitude, hunger, greed, nepotism, ostentation, and ethnic mentality produced the strange personality, a clownish phenomenon, that came to be known world-wide as the Nigerian politician. Materialism and the monomaniacal pursuit of material pomp were pushed to such absurdity that they became unrecognizable even to the materially obsessed Western world, which saw the Nigerian politician as a person who was capable of selling even his own country for the material benefit of the self and cultural section. In a similar but no less perfidious way, the Nigerian politicians ingeniously sold their political "beliefs" and allegiances to hegemonic parties on the promise of cash, lucrative appointment to boards of corporations, or token social amenities and development for their ethnic constituencies. This capricious oscillation of allegiances for the sake of wealth and position and power came to assume a peculiarly Nigerian lineament, and became widely known—and accepted—as Carpet Crossing.

This phenomenon also found expression beyond the individual political players. Parties and splinter-parties sought and consummated often short-lived alliances of convenience with strange ethno-political bedfellows for the benefit of their parties and ethnicities. Thus, for the 1964 general elections, there were such curious amalgams as the United Progressive Grand Alliance (UPGA) which temporarily brought together blood enemies NCNC and the Action Group together with the Northern minority opposition party, the UMBC; and the Nigerian National Alliance (NNA) composed of NPC, NNDP (Akintola's faction of AG), the Midwest Democratic Front, the Niger Delta Congress, and the Dynamic Party (led by Professor Chike Obi, the famous Igbo mathematician).

As fragile as these alliances were, their precarious brevity was already ensured by a few antecedents. Among these were the belated conversion of Awolowo to "Democratic Socialism" which brought to a head the disagreement between him and the more conservative Akintola; the miscarried national census of 1962, repeated in 1963, when rival hegemonic parties accused one another, not simply of inflating census figures, but of counting dead, unborn, and non-existent persons—as well as livestock—in order to assure for their respective regions numerical superiority and, consequent upon that, other developmental and representational advantages; the use of thugs to intimidate and maim or kill political opponents during electioneering campaigns; the over-inflation of election figures, whereby numbers of votes often were in excess of the total populations of the constituencies; the treason trial and subsequent imprisonment of Awolowo, Tarka, and other oppositional voices; and the partial boycott of the 1964 general elections by UPGA. These factors created conditions so conducive to full-blown national upheaval. This was, however, headed off by the appointment by the NNA of many NCNC ministers in the "national" government. But this assuagement was too little too late, for already the air had become thick with the smell of smoke and blood. The scandalous election malfeasance in Akintola's Western Region, with all the accompanying bribery, intimidation, thuggery, looting, arson, murder, mayhem, and blatant inflation of election results, was thus only a last ignition which set in motion the conflagration of the already prepared tinders.

This Western election took place in October 1965, and the whole country felt the heat from the fires. But apparently, since the crisis was taking place in the West, among the Yoruba, it did not matter to the rest of the country. And amidst all advice to the contrary the Prime Minister, unconcerned, proceeded to lavishly and ceremoniously host the Commonwealth Nations' Conference. In the early hours of January 15, 1966, the military struck and brought down the edifice of the insensitive showpiece of Western parliamentarism, ending with it the unbridled jamboree and profligacy of the politicians. A radical putsch, this Nigeria's first military coup was intended as a pan-Nigerian, trans-ethnic project whose purpose was fully articulated by its leader, Major Chukwuma Kaduna Nzeogwu:

Our enemies are the political profiteers, swindlers, the men in high and low places that seek bribes and demand 10 per cent. . . . [t]hose that seek to keep the country permanently divided so that they can remain in office as Ministers and VIP's of waste, the tribalists, the nepotists. . . . rotten and corrupt ministers, political parties, trade unions, and the whole apparatus of the Federal System. We wanted to gun down all the big wig in our way. . . . We could not afford to let them live if this was to work. (Isichei 1983:471-72)

So this coup had aimed at the real threats to Nigerian unity, progress, and development: the twin bane of ethnicity and corruption. But given that politics in Nigeria has always been ethnicized, and that Nigerians have never, in the larger "national" interest, stopped to question and examine their ethnic world-view, it surprised no one that this coup, which received countrywide acclamation and inspired general euphoria, was soon to be interpreted as a Southern, indeed, an Igbo coup. Were the leader, Nzeogwu, and five of the seven plotters of the coup not Igbo? Were not all the victims of the coup non-Igbo? Was the new Head of State and Government, the inheritor of the coup, not Igbo? And was the trial of the plotters not being delayed because they were Igbo? These misgivings and questionings were, therefore, only exacerbated by the BBC which "authoritatively" explained the coup as part of an Igbo master-plot. And the reliance of the new leader on economic and political advisers from the South was sure sign that the BBC was right, the reliance by the Head of State on Hausa body guards, and his appointment of Lt. Colonel Gowon, a Northerner, being construed only as a ruse of nationalism. For was his Unification Decree which sought to impose a unitary system of government on the country not the final facilitation of the plan for Igbo irredentism and domination of Nigeria?

To the formulators of these rhetorical questions, the answer was obvious. And in May 1966, the same month the Decree was published, there erupted a succession of riots, arson, looting, murder, and the general vendetta against the Igbo which I had delineated in "Introit." Two months after, in July 1966, a successful counter-coup was executed. Whether logic or necessity would have dictated a second Igbo coup, one cannot be sure, but the planners of the July coup said that they had struck to preempt that rumored second Igbo coup. Whatever their reason, the coup was bloody, thorough, and systematically executed. All the plotters were Northerners, and all the victims Southerners, including the Head of State, Ironsi, and his able and loyal hero-host, Colonel Fajuyi, the then Governor of the Western Group of Provinces. (In an attempt to minimize the import of ethnicity, the former regions had been abolished under the Unification Decree, and replaced by "Groups of Provinces.")

Rather than bring to an end the ethnic violence that had begun in May 1966, rather than quell the turmoil, this coup validated and sanctioned it, added more fuel to the fires, and infused more ruthlessness, virulence, and systematicity to subsequent massacres. The killings and destruction were so well planned, organized, orchestrated, and executed, and their targets so unmistakably identified that, in spite of the refusal of decent commentators on the Nigerian crisis to accept or apply the word, what took place now, and culminated in the thirty-month war, was pure and simple genocide or, in euphemistic terms, ethnic cleansing. Only the outrage that is taking place now in Bosnia Herzegovina can begin, very imperfectly, to exemplify the unfolding of this darkest page in the history of Nigeria.

The exodus of the surviving Igbo from Northern and other parts of Nigeria was massive and unprecedented, about two million Igbo returning as refugees fleeing from their "own dear native land" to the East. Whether Britain would have been happier with her ex-colony, Nigeria, cleansed of a whole ethnicity, the upstart and unslavish Igbo, or not, it made sure that the World Body, the United Nations, ignored the refugee problem. Did one not have to cross a national border to qualify as refugee? Surely, the Igbo had not crossed a national border, and should be left at the mercy of the Hausa-Fulani ruled Nigeria. The Igbo problem was Nigeria's internal problem which it should solve as it saw fit, without the interference of friendly nations. One is, of course, reminded of the relatively smaller-scale problems involving the Arabs, and the Sudanese Christians. Their problems were immediately and massively confronted and contained by the United Nations High

Commissioner for Refugees (UNHCR), a Body set up in Geneva in 1951 for the "protection of refugees—victims of persecution in search of asylum" (Nwankwo & Ifejika 1970:5). One is also reminded of the Kurds and Iraqis of Southern Iraq: these have not been abandoned to their fates in the hands of Iraqi leadership.

As if the pogrom and the forced eastward exodus of the Igbo, who now constituted a colossal administrative and financial challenge to the Government of the Eastern Group of Provinces, were not enough, Yakubu Gowon, now *de facto* Head of Government in Lagos, issued a decree, his own version of the Unification Decree, in May 1967, which created a twelve-State structure for Nigeria. It must be remembered that the Unification Decree of May 1966 was the ostensible cause of the riots, slaughters, and counter-coup of that year. It must also be remembered that immediately after the counter-coup, Gowon had in a radio broadcast announced to the world how it had pleased the Almighty to restore to the North the leadership of Nigeria. In that broadcast, he had also declared the intention of the North to secede from Nigeria. Following a reprimand or advice from the British advisors, Gowon had quickly recanted this Northern intention. The creation of a twelve-State structure was, therefore, a diametrical reversal of the secessionist intention of the North, as well as a reversion to the "unificatory" policy of General Ironsi. Ostensibly, the creation of States was supposed to begin to address the long-standing fears of ethnic minorities within the larger polity, Nigeria: the minority ethnic groups now had their own States! But actually, it was only a strategy meant to break the backbone of the intransigent East because, without the manpower, resources, and revenue and without the loyalty and solidarity of the two new States (Cross-River and Rivers) now carved out from the East, Enugu was expected to buckle under the immense new problems created by the return of two million Igbo, and capitulate to Lagos which had effectively abdicated its Federal responsibilities both to the East and to the fleeing Federal civil servants. As a final act in this drama of abdications and repudiations of responsibility, Gowon/Lagos reneged on the Aburi Accord. The meeting in Aburi, Ghana, of Nigerian leaders, had only recently approved a confederal structure for Nigeria.

With the provision for a confederation now cast aside, the

only assurance of security for the Igbo lay in their ability to remain in peace and safety within the borders of a sovereign State of their own. The Igbo people demanded this from the Government in Enugu, and on May 30, 1967, the Declaration of the Independent Republic of Biafra, a sovereign state coterminous with the former Eastern Nigeria, gave them that assurance, and they got ready to defend its sovereignty, as well as the lives of its citizens. Underestimating the resolve of the new Republic, and meaning to crush the "rebellion" in a matter of days, Gowon launched against Biafra what he called Police Action. This police action, whose motto was "To Keep Nigeria One," quickly turned into a large-scale war that lasted thirty long months.

This fratricidal agony—and the genocide—eventually ended, not because of the superior military might and savagery of the Nigerian military with all the assistance and collusion of Western countries and multinational corporations, but because by January 1970 most Biafrans had become disenchanted. Biafra which started off as a repudiation and negation of Nigeria and Nigerianism, had become infested with all the plagues and maladies of Nigeria; born as an antithesis of all the negativities of Nigerianism, Biafra was now suffering, like Nigeria, from "moral decay, decay in military leadership, [and] transferred loyalty . . . from the nation to the self" (Nwankwo 1972:56). Biafrans were fed up with leaders who would not accept the socialist provisions of the Ahiara Declaration; who fought among themselves over ownerships of corporations and mineral wealth even as the war was still being fought by ill-fed, ill-clothed soldiers; who appropriated for their personal use large sums of money donated to the Biafran cause by well-meaning friends of groaning humanity in Europe and America. It was therefore with an audible, sadly disappointed sigh of relief that Biafrans greeted the announcement on January 15, 1970, by the remnant of the Biafran leadership, of an unconditional surrender to Lagos.

IV. FALTERING STEPS; FRAGMENTS AFTER THE DELUGE: 1970-1996

The war thus came to an end in January 1970; the Igbo had been badly beaten and broken, but they had not been annihilated as an ethnicity, and they are now back in Nigeria. But this capitulation of Biafra did not represent the victory of nationalism over primordialism. For the duration of the war, Biafranism was a powerful negation of Nigerianism, including its ethno-politics, and the very idea of the Nigerian nation. The sad truth is that Nigeria has remained "no more than a counterfeit reproduction of, and by, its former conqueror . . . , having neither a discrete history nor logic that would convince . . . the citizens of its legitimacy or authenticity" (Miyoshi 1993:730). In fact, the war itself was the culmination of the continual battle between "the will to fragmentation" and "the will to totalization" (730). The success of the Federal forces would appear to have secured the triumph of the latter "will." But the contrary remains true, for even the oxymoronic proclamation, at the end of the war, of "No Victor, No Vanquished," and the inauguration of the magnanimous Three R's program (Reconciliation, Rehabilitation, Reconstruction) belied the reality. The war had a definite victor and an acknowledged vanquished; the deliberate official economic and other developmental neglect of the former Biafran territories of Imo and Anambra States left no one in doubt as to the actual, *post-bellum* statuses of the former combatants.

As if to drive the point home, in January 1970, soon after the surrender of Biafra, the Biafran currency was voided and made illegal tender, even inside the former Biafra. This completely beggared most Biafrans. Since there was no meaningful "rehabilitation" of former Biafrans, the Indigenization Decree—which transferred the ownership of certain foreign businesses to Nigerians in 1972—was a calculated attempt to permanently exclude Biafrans from the economic mainstream, while the promulgation of the Abandoned Properties Decree further dispossessed Biafrans. This decree, which transferred ownership of real estate and other properties outside of Igboland from their Biafran owners to other Nigerians, (thus making it "illegal" for Biafrans to own property in other parts of Nigeria), made real a mockery of the whole concept of nationality and citizenship. Since what used to be Biafra comprised mainly Igboland, it is clear that the exclusionary and repressive economic policies of post-war Nigeria represented a legitimization, by decree, of ethnic politics, half a century after the Amalgamation of the Protectorates. Happening under the dictatorship of General Yakubu Gowon, whose characteristic equivocation has already been marked, it is no surprise that this legitimization of ethnic exclusion and reprisal should proceed at the same time as he was enunciating an acclaimed program of social justice and egalitarianism devoid of "oppression based on class, social status, and ethnic group or state" (Isichei 1983:474), for which he was soon to be given honorary doctoral degrees in such disciplines as Social Engineering and Law by Nigerian universities.

As a "Social Engineer," Gowon was eminently qualified to analyze the Nigerian situation under his dictatorship. Indeed, he made one very apt characterization of Nigeria in the 1970s as that of "want in the midst of plenty" (474). For, even though Nigeria became extremely wealthy as a result of unprecedented revenues from oil, the wind of this affluence did not blow in the direction of the masses. Instead, they knew the pangs of extreme shortages, of inflation, and of real poverty, especially keenly in former Biafra, while Gowon was widely quoted in the world press as saying "that money was no longer a problem in Nigerian development—that the constraints came from lack of executive and managerial skills" (475). Indeed, Gowon left a legacy of stupendous mismanagement and misappropriation, the most unpardonable in the history of Nigeria: within a few short years, Nigeria plunged from mind-boggling wealth to near-bankruptcy. And "all over the country there were allegations of graft, misuse of public funds. . . . There were complaints of ostentatious living, flagrant abuse of office and deprivation of people's rights and property, perversion of time-honoured procedures and norms . . . nepotism and favouritism . . . all of which gave the impression that the states were being run as private estates" (475).

This statement, attributed to General Murtala Muhammed, was the latter's rationalization of his intervention which brought to an abrupt end the nine years of General Gowon's scandalous carnival. For Gowon had become a classic comprador ruler whose wasteful clowning and ostentatious displays drew the acclaim of his Metropolitan masters, while his people languished in hunger, disenchantment, and discontent (475). The fawning of this comprador ruler, indeed, earned him an honorary doctorate from Cambridge University, but when, after his overthrow, he wanted to enroll there for a Bachelor's degree, he was refused admission! Gowon reminds one of the descendants of the *Askaris*, the quisling political and economic elite whose dead weights straddle the African continent. It is one of such ancestors, a zombie who is so grotesquely delineated in Ayi Kwei Armah's *Two Thousand Seasons* (1973):

> We have been handed down a vision of a slave man roaming the desert sand—a perfect image of our hallowed chiefs today. Language he had not, not ours, and not his own. It had been voided out of him, his tongue cut out from his mouth. He pointed to the gaping cavity. Thinking he still had a soul, even mutilated, we imagined he was after sympathy. We were mistaken—he was pointing to the hole with pride. They who had destroyed his tongue, they had put pieces of brass in there to separate the lower from the upper jaw. The slave thought the brass a gift. Its presence made sweet to him the absence of his tongue. He communicated his haughty pride to us, indicating in the sand with precise remembrance when he had achieved each piece of brass, what amazing things he had been made to do in order to be given them.
>
> Hau! It is not only rife among the fatted chiefs, this idiocy of the destroyed. Among ourselves we have seen beings thus voided of their souls, sent deep into earth on their mission of destruction, injected with the white people's urge to devastation, sending what they take across the sea to the white destroyers' homes. (10-11)

So, Murtala Muhammed intervened to save Nigerians from the clutches of this clown. Unfortunately his rule was so brief that one cannot adequately and fairly assess him. It is true that, between July 1975 and February 1976 when Murtala was in power, he had begun a drastic program of cleansing of the filthy Nigerian stable; had renounced the vast blood-wealth he had amassed as

Commander during the war; had created seven more States; had announced plans to demobilize the unwieldy and unproductive Nigerian military; and had struck a radical and uncompromising posture against both Apartheid South Africa and the Multinational Oligopolies. But, in spite of his wide popularity, it would be wrong to attribute this popularity to the transcendence of "ethnic divisions in Nigerian consciousness" (Isichei 1983:475). If "Southerners, and Igbos" were among those who welcomed the arrival on the scene of Murtala, it was not because "social problems had replaced ethnic divisions" (475); and certainly not because the Igbo had forgotten the principal and decisive role played by Murtala in the war of Igbo destruction. The Igbo are yet to be found guilty of ethnic/cultural amnesia. On the contrary, to the pragmatic Igbo, the whole idea of identity is tied up with ethnic memory. *Echezona* (Don't Ever Forget) and *Afamefuna* (May My Name/Lineage Never Be Lost) are very important Igbo patronymns. This collective remembering is facilitated by the possession, by the Igbo, of great sense and wisdom. In fact, this whole notion of collective wisdom and ethnic memory is the subject of the 1993 Ahiajoku Lecture by Professor Emmanuel Obiechina, titled, "*Nchetaka*: The Story, Memory, and Continuity of Igbo Culture." The Ahiajoku, deriving from the Igbo festival homage to Yam, that "male" Igbo staple, is an annual celebration of pan-Igbo intellectual-cultural achievements; it is also a demonstration of the Igbo resolve never to forget the past as they envision, and march into, the future. In Obiechina's words, "Memory is the key to a people's relationship to their past, their heritage and their sense of identity. They remember in the present those things which in the past lent significance and continuing value to their existence, singly and collectively" (Obiechina 1994:13).

This brief digression on Igbo cultural remembering has been necessary not only to address the implication of ethnic amnesia contained in the passage from Isichei, but also to more sharply focus the issue in relation to Nigeria as a whole. For, an Igbo proverb believes that a people who do not know/remember when the rains overtook them cannot know/remember when/where they dried their bodies. It is another way of saying that a people who have no past may likely not have a future. The trouble with

Nigeria is that its peoples have no common past or history, before 1914, to sustain or validate their dream of community. What Miyoshi says, writing about a different situation, can, with very slight modification, very well apply to Nigeria:

> earlier, while struggling against the oppressors, self-definition [as Nigerians] was not difficult to obtain: opposition articulated their identity. Once the Europeans were gone, however, the residents of [Nigeria] were thrown back on their old disrupted site that had in precolonial days operated on a logic and history altogether different. Retroversion to nativism might have been an option, but [Nigeria] was fraught with inequalities and contradictions among various religions, tribes, regions, classes, genders, and ethnicities that had been thrown together. . . . The golden age of a nation-state's memory proved to be neither just, nor even available, but a utopian dream often turned into a bloody nightmare. (Miyoshi 1993:730)

That transformation of "a utopian dream" into "a bloody nightmare" was precisely what happened in Nigeria during 1966–1970; and the period 1970–1993 represents faltering and tentative, but as yet unsuccessful, steps towards the healing of the deep wounds. It was said that General Murtala Muhammed made or intended to make bold efforts in this direction. His transformation/conversion from a blood-thirsty war commander to a peace-seeking, trans-ethnic, national "leader," it was announced, consisted in (among other things) his renunciation of the vast wealth he had amassed during the war. But an abortive military coup of February 1976 prove fatal to him and his "nationalist" and pan-African program.

Because that coup was unsuccessful, Murtala was succeeded by his second-in-command, General Obasanjo, a Yoruba, whose regime was characterized by extreme haste to hand power over to those whose birthright it was to rule Nigeria, the Hausa-Fulani House, that is. I had tried to convey this sense of hurry of an uncomfortable ruler in my poem "Ulysses' Bastard":

> It little profits that a tumid General
> Unmatched by a paragon
> Among these hungry States

I mete and enforce unprintable laws
Unto a rough and rude race
That drink and fuck and know not me
I have tasted of frothing power,
have enacted Shows at Bar Beach, not a few,
have traveled among Kings and enforced rulers
who have embraced me with plastic warmth
and shown white-washed teeth of friendliness
Indeed, I have become a Name,
have carved a symbol of idiocy
Oh my counselors, prepare for me
a Book to ensure my escape
for I must depart these corridors
make room for youthful old blood
for those versed in the art
of wrangling and battering of souls. . . .
(Okafor 1981:39)

It is interesting to note that while his discomfiture as a Southerner/Yoruba was responsible for his haste to relinquish power as Head of State, it still left General Obasanjo enough time to promulgate the Land Use Decree, which made it possible for him to acquire vast tracts of land which, with his "savings" and "bank loans," he was able to transform into the largest individually owned agricultural business in the whole of West Africa. He was now ready to hand over power to the newly elected political elite, with Shehu Shagari, a Fulani, as President.

Two important developments marked this new civilian arrangement. First, the adoption of the American presidential system was an ostensible "break with the Westminster tradition" (Isichei 1983:477), but it was also an indication of the accentuated profligacy of the Nigerian political leadership. For the presidential system is a far more expensive alternative which requires a lot of political and intellectual sophistication, but which also gave the functionaries unprecedented executive powers which they deployed to drain the country's treasury dry. Second, the five registered political parties were very recognizable transmogrifications and reconfigurations of the older ethnic-based political parties. Thus, the NCNC mutated into NPP, which soon split into NPP and

GNPP (Nigerian Peoples' Party and the Great Nigerian Peoples' Party), "over the question of whether Alhaji Waziri Ibrahim (a Northerner) should be both presidential candidate and party chairman" (477). The Action Group resurrected into UPN (United Party of Nigeria), led by its former founder and leader, Awolowo. The NPC reappeared, new and improved, as the NPN (National Party of Nigeria). The fifth party, PRP (Peoples' Redemption Party), was an innovation in Nigerian politics, for its radical social program attracted intellectuals and political activists across ethnic lines. Still, its leader and presidential candidate had to be a Northerner, Aminu Kano. Because the Nigerian electorate needed first to be weaned off the ethnic nipple before they could embrace a trans-ethnic political anomaly, when the breathing ghosts of the old ethnic-based parties won landslide victories in their respective home States, the PRP won only one State (Kano) —which, coincidentally, was also the home of its leader.

With the clear victory of NPN both in the States and at the Federal level, and with the inauguration of Shehu Shagari as the new President of Nigeria, not only was the familiar "pattern of politics in Nigeria" repeated, but the cycle was completed and spun into dizzy motion again. As Peter Ekeh puts it, "The general pattern of politics in Nigeria came to be that the majority Nigerians' primordialism was sublimated in their attachment to their regions of origin, while the federal center represented now a civil center and now a primordial center—depending on who exercised power" (Okpaku, 1972:99).

The election of Shagari, thus, saw once again, the assumption of political ascendancy by the Hausa-Fulani ethnic section. Even though the Cabinet was as "broad-based" as a Nigerian Cabinet could ever be, and even though the Vice-President was Igbo, the non-majority members of the Cabinet were assigned relatively unimportant portfolios, while the strategic and, in the Nigerian spirit, "lucrative" ones went to the true party and ethnic loyalists. With characteristic speed, these functionaries pursued the aggrandizement of self and section through unbridled despoliation of the treasury. The result of this megalomania and misrule was that in less than four years of this civilian/democratic inter-regnum, many of the ministers and party functionaries had become richer than some States, and publicly celebrated the fact in metropolitan capitals, especially London, where their loot had been safely deposited in coded bank accounts. Meanwhile the people starved, helpless.

It came as no surprise to anybody, therefore, when Generals Buhari and Idiagbon struck and ousted the cavaliers, one early morning in December 1983, three months into the second term of the civilian administration. These two men nearly succeeded in restoring sanity to Nigeria, but their uncompromising insistence on order, discipline, probity, and accountability was too much for the elite, now bloated with the spoils of the country. Moreover, because Idiagbon, though a Moslem, was Yoruba, he was seen as incapable of truly representing the interests of the Hausa-Fulani "Royal" House.

Thus, on 27 August, 1985, General Babangida, capitalizing on the absence from the country of Buhari and Idiagbon, who were on an Islamic pilgrimage to Mecca, struck and ended the brief reign of discipline and order in Nigeria. His regime, which I have termed "Maradonnism," after the fast-paced, dribbling, slippery, elusive, evasive, and cunning soccer star, was a protracted reign of terror, intimidation, unaccountability, and brazen self-enrichment and mass bribery. This regime was also characterized by a combination of Machiavellian ruthlessness and equivocation, and Nigerians were too slow in realizing that Babangida was the cleverest con-artist/politician/dictator ever to wield power in Nigeria. His rule, like the AIDS virus, operated insidiously to destroy the immune system of the country whose members became so debilitated morally that they could not say No to his institutionalization of corruption nor to his ethnic politics. But then, he had behind him the Hausa-Fulani power-brokers.

So it was with great reluctance, after much resistance and wheeling and dealing, that Babangida agreed to a democratic election in June 1993. But even before all the votes had been counted, because leading politicians from the North had promised chaos if they were not "given" the presidency which, in their eyes "belonged" to them since the South had all the economic power, and because the victory appeared clearly to be going the way of a Southerner/Yoruba, M.K.O. Abiola, Babangida quickly annulled the fairest ever elections held in Nigeria, and appointed a Transition Administration which, in spite of appearances to the contrary, was designed to be only a stop-gap. Sonekan, a Yoruba, was merely put there to hold the fort, as interim "President," until, at the opportune moment, another Northerner would assume power. This "opportune" moment came on 17 November, 1993, when Sonekan suddenly "resigned" and General Sanni Abacha, a Kanuri from the North, came to center stage, and in blatant contempt for the people of Nigeria, and, indeed, of the whole world, swept away all vestiges of democratic institutions in Nigeria, while promising that "Nigeria will some day get a democratic government. But for now the country will be run as a police State" (Abacha, 18 November 1993, Broadcast).

While Abacha's suggestion of a Constitutional Conference appears to have taken Nigeria back to the 1954 constitutional uncertainties, his political maneuvers, aimed at neutralizing all possible opposition to his regime, as well as destroying remnants of Babangida's legacy, are interesting for they have made more visible the deep-seated contradictions and cleavages in the cultural-political structure of Nigeria. His dismissal from the Army of the son of a Northern Emir, who used to be the "eyes and ears" of the Hausa-Fulani Emirate in the military, must have upset the Northern power base, while his appointment of functionaries mainly from the minority ethnic groups from the North and West, thus sidelining the dominant ethnic groups, must have alienated, or at least, aroused, political sensibilities. But Abacha's strategies represent a realignment of forces and a revelation of the urgency of the need for Nigerians to find answers to the perennial national question. This urgency is loudly articulated by Roland Ainabe in his article, "The Futility of Forced Unity," which appeared in the December 29, 1993, issue of *National Concord*, where he says:

> We want to talk about the corporate entity called Nigeria as it is today. We want to talk about and consider confederation as an option to the present political arrangement. These are the issues we picture when we talk about constitutional conference or whatever. And we have to talk about them. If this is not confronted now, it [sic] shall in the future. One way or the other, it will get to be addressed, so, for the avoidance of bloodshed, Nigerians must sit together now in a constitutional conference and agree on [the] terms of governance of their

country. (7)

As everyone knows, Nigeria is not a nation, not even a stable "nation-state," but a fragile anti-structure so deliberately and cunningly contrived by the British to ensure the permanent instability of that structure, as well as its eternal political control by the Feudal forces of the North. As Ainabe so bluntly puts it in the earlier quoted article:

> Nigeria is a collection of several nations living in the present geographical expression not by free consent, but by the whim of one Lord Lugard who, as colonial and slave master in the year 1914, amalgamated the northern and southern protectorates. We, under bondage, could do nothing about it. That was then. We are no longer under bondage. We are a free people today, despite the fact that gun-totting military men who have again usurped the collective will of our people have taken over the atrocities of our past colonial lords. (7)

As long as these forces continue to be in charge, so long will the fortunes of Nigeria continue to be determined and controlled by forces of her former colonizer. So, Abacha's intervention might well prove a blessing in disguise; that is, if it forces Nigerians to define the structure of co-existence and of responsibilities. It is clear to me that Nigerians have a clear choice only among three structural options: 1) because the thirty states are so small and economically unviable, their option for autonomy and sovereignty would appear to be the least desirable; 2) because of the insurmountable barriers of primordialism which often militate against decent and sophisticated negotiation, diplomacy, and compromises in the interest of the constituent states, the option for a confederation seems impracticable; 3) since it is clear that the British trick has led the country nowhere, having benefited only the feudal ally of imperialism, it would appear that the only option left is for clearly articulated principles of federalism, where coexistence is understood to be on the basis of equality; where duties and responsibilities are unambiguously assigned and assumed by the states and the center, concurrently and residually, very much like in the United States of America which is also a multi-ethnic, multilingual, multi-cultural, and multi-religious Federation. According to Edward Said in *Culture and Imperialism* (1993), "Despite its extraordinary cultural diversity, the United States is, and will surely remain, a coherent nation. . . . Much of the polemical divisiveness and polarized debate . . . is there of course, but it does not . . . portend a dissolution of the republic" (xxvi). Nigeria can surely borrow a page from the United States. Perhaps, then, the ideological pillars of nationhood can begin to be constructed; only then can the soul of nation begin to be formed and the nation begin to be built; only then can the fragments begin to be gathered. But until that is done, the country continues to falter.

CHAPTER II

THE NIGERIAN/AFRICAN WRITERS AND THEIR MILIEUX

The pluralization here of *milieux* is studied and deliberate because, as the discussion so far must have made clear, the Nigerian writers, like their other African counterparts, are caught in the vise of antagonistic loyalties and, at the same time, operate in unstable and shifting historico-political conjunctures. Their biographical, diachronic axes intersect with ever-evolving systemic, syntagmatic axes which are at once ethnic, regional, and statal. That they manage to keep their wits about them is tribute to the resilience of their creative powers.

It is in order to point out here that, in the discussion that follows, if the pronominalization tends to be masculine, it is so, not because women writers are devalorized or excluded, nor even because they are subsumed under the patriarchal "He/His." It is clear to anyone who has studied the Nigerian/African scene that women have always been positively catalytic agents of history, never lagging behind their menfolk, and often playing vanguard roles. That importance is also clearly marked in literature. Yet, I am aware of the continued neglect, even "exclusion of women from theory and research practice" (Ogundipe-Leslie & Boyce-Davies 1994:1). It is not my intention to proliferate that "exclusion." Indeed, I would respond to that question reiterated by Ogundipe-Leslie and Boyce Davies and originally posed by Warren Azvedo in *The Traditional Artist in African Societies*—

[A]re women actually less involved in artistic activities and, if so, how is this to be explained with regard to societies ... in which women frequently perform leading roles in the political, economic, and ritual spheres of action?

by declaring that, far from being "less involved," women have been both prolific and important as creative writers and critics. Still, it must be remembered that before 1970, but for the lone voices of Grace Ogot (Kenya) and Flora Nwapa (Nigeria), writing by women was a rarity.

In all of human history, writers and artists have occupied an ambiguous and precarious position in society. Depending on time and place, this position has ever oscillated between envy and chastisement or benign neglect, between elitism and bohemianism, between populism and social irresponsibility, and between activism and sensuous narcissism. Because discussions of the relation between art/literature and society and/or the position and role of the artist/writer in his/her society usually cite Plato's exemplary discourse on that subject, and because no radical critical-epistemological rupture has actually been made with Plato's philosophical position—which does legitimate that indissoluble marriage of the "Useful" and the "Delightful" which has continued to mark African Art and Literature—I believe that a brief discussion of Plato's position is here in order.

The popular view of Plato—by no means absent in academic circles—is that of a notorious philistine who banished poets from his ideal Republic. This erroneous view continues to be widely disseminated by critics who, failing to adopt a totalizing view of Plato's callistics, have continued to foreground the deprecatory sections of the *Republic*. In order to arrive at a more sanguine or balanced picture, we need to take cognizance not only of the articulations of Plato's critical position scattered throughout his writings, but also of his own rhetorical *praxis*; for a writer who profusely and competently deploys such artistic conventions of invention and embellishment as myths, fables, figures, and personification for purposes of illustration, reification, emphasis, digression/suspense, and delight as well as edification, cannot, in any wise, be described as philistine or adversary of art. Plato is, in his own right, an accomplished artist who happens to be fanatical about the moral responsibility of the artist.

The *Republic* encapsulates Plato's denunciation and deprecation of the mimetic arts and has to that extent generated the greatest controversy, and created the sharp division between the apologists who would, with Plato, banish the poets, and the lovers of art whose "righteous" indignation that document continues to elicit. Plato does not quarrel with art *qua* art but with what artists have *done with* art, with the *purpose* art has been made to serve; Plato's denunciations are dictated largely by ethical considerations.

But it is not as if Plato had had the last word. In seventeenth century England, for instance, the English Puritans who were then in power, through devious manipulations of parliament, flagellated and ostracized dramatists and jesters (artists), whom they nominated as "the caterpillars of a commonwealth," an unmitigated nuisance who did a moral disservice to England (Sampson 1973: 286). These overzealous and self-appointed guardians of state morality overreached themselves and, in the process, wreaked an ever-greater disservice to the country. Their philistinism and vandalism remain unprecedented and unsurpassed for, in the end, they destroyed playhouses and theaters which, they had no doubt, harbored all perversities and abominations. The result of these "godly" outrages was a yawning hiatus in the history of English drama.

During the Victorian period in England, that great age of paradoxes and hypocrisy, that age when the morally unassailable and enlightened British empire subjugated most of the world and brought it under the covering wings of its civilization, the importance of a work of art was in direct proportion to its moral content. The artist's first duty was supposed to be to his society. That duty was *to communicate,* and the substance of his message was necessarily of social and, therefore, moral significance. Those artists who dwelt in the elitist towers of isolation, obscurity, sensuous introspection and social irresponsibility were denigrated and despised for their works, naturally, were lacking in immediate practical utility. It is an interesting coincidence, given African social-utility-functional conception of art (Udechukwu 1971), that the collision of cultures took place during this period which marked the height of European imperialist expansion, and that, through colonial conquest and colonial education, the aesthetic moralism of the exogenous cultural products found fertile soil, indeed receptive bedfellow, in the indigenous functional-communalistic-moral aestheticism. When the colonized began to write in the new graphological system, it is no surprise that their writings were characterized by high seriousness and didacticism.

From this Western doctrine of moral aesthetics which valorized the social and moral significance of works of art, often with complete disregard for the hedonistic element, the evaluative pointer swung again to the opposite end of the scale. The writer's first duty was declared to be to himself/herself; thus he/she could comfortably dispense with or, at least, ignore society. And by laws of reciprocal relations, such a writer was in turn considered not indispensable to society. Society tended to ignore the lunatic, the anarchist, the iconoclast, the social misfit, the ex-centric. The writer, on his/her part, sought rather to cultivate refined tastes and whimsical sensibilities, while the satisfaction of the reading needs of the uncultured many was left to "journalists and commercial artists" (Tindall 1956:4).

As a result, his/her writing tended to become privatist, arcane, obscure, and difficult. It also became characterized by a disdain for society and for social issues. This was the Art for Art's Sake Movement which preached the autonomy of art and of the practitioner of art; which rejected all didactic aim in art; and which refused to subject art to the "polluting" rigors of ethico-social judgment. To writers belonging to this "Decadent Movement" in literature, "art is so independent of common morality that it becomes immoral; so superior to nature that it becomes unnatural; so remote from subject matter that it becomes substanceless" (Romanus Egudu 1972; see also later discussion of Mazrui's critique of Okigbo). In this esoteric preoccupation with solipsism the artist had left society behind and, glowing with self-conceit in his/her Palace of Art, was supposedly unaffected by, and did not affect, society. S/he had become an exile in his/her own society which, in turn, precipitated his/her exile.

This situation continued into the twentieth century where the artist was said to remain "exiled, broken, spoken against, mistrusted, and thwarted" (Ezra Pound, "Rest," in *Selected Poems* :100). Nor has there been an attenuation in the philistinism and crass materialism of the "rank-scented many" who are depicted as despising art as much as they abhor the lack of material comfort. Thus in another of Pound's poems, "The Lake Isle," we come across this prayer:

O God, O Venus, O Mercury, patron of thieves,
Lend me a little tobacco shop
Or install me in any profession
Save this damned profession of writing
Where one needs one's brains all the time.

These enemies of art are also the ignorant but modish class who, denigrating the arts which they hardly understand, would still present a façade of cultural respectability and distinction by flaunting half-understood references to artists and philosophers, like the women in T.S. Eliot's "Love Song of Alfred J. Prufrock" who "come and go/Talking of Michelangelo."

In my reading of literary history, which I have attempted to abbreviate here, it is obvious to me that a recurrent pattern operates, whereby artists/writers have in all ages, been required to justify their existence as *zoon politikon* by proving the practical utility of their work. The choice for the artists has always been between connection with the social and perdition. It is salutary to note in this connection that Okigbo's flirtation with European Decadence was very short-lived for he quickly recognized that his art must be psycho-culturally grounded if it must have any relevance and significance.

The privileging of the social functionality of art is nowhere more marked than in Africa, where the artist is first and foremost a social animal, an integral member of the *communitas* on behalf of whom s/he functions as "a central social intelligence" (Bradbury 1972:112). Thus the position and role of the artist in Africa have been always already defined, understood, and accepted. Between the traditional artist and his/her audience, between art and society, between practical utility and pure aestheticism, the dividing line was very thin and tenuous (Achebe, *Morning Yet On Creation* Day 22). The artist and the consumers of his/her art were one; his/her art belonged to all, and was a function of society. The artist was an integrated member of the culturally homogeneous collectivity. S/he thus belonged to, and was part of the society which, in turn, though always jealously guarding its supremacy over the individual members, recognized his/her merits and often rewarded him/her materially and socially. The artist, in carrying out his/her function of imaginative creation saw himself/herself as performing an essentially social function. We shall see later that, in spite of the criticism of Okigbo and even of his own earlier assertions to the contrary, that is of his belief in the elitist esotericism of poetry, Okigbo's mature assumption of the role of oracle and poet of destiny links him directly to this long communalistic tradition of art in Africa.

Because of this social, communalistic conception of art, it was considered the first function of art to express and celebrate the "continuity and perennity" of the community and to symbolize the unity and cohesiveness of the group. This art at once elucidated in myriad ways the basic notions of virtue and morality, executed functions of religious and practical utility, and stunned by its sheer aesthetic appeal (Udechukwu 1971). But in all, this art emanated from and was an artistic expression and capsulation of the mores and experiences of society. The artist himself/herself was regarded as the producer, guardian, and disseminator of the lores and myths of society; the guardian of social justice; and the upholder of truth. S/he was in many respects like Walter Benjamin's storyteller who had "ventured into the depths of . . . nature" (*Illuminations* 1969:107):

> Seen in this way, the storyteller joins the ranks of the teachers and sages. He has counsel—not for a few situations . . . but for many, like the sage. For it is granted to him to reach back to a whole life-time. . . . His gift is the ability to relate his life; his distinction, to be able to tell his entire life. The story-teller: he is the man who could let the wick of his life be consumed completely by the gentle flame of his story. This is the basis of the incomparable aura about the storyteller. . . .

The storyteller is the figure in which the righteous man encounters himself. (108-109)

Without overly anticipating our own argument, one may just observe that Okigbo's life and his story of that life, as well as his story of the society of his birth and death, are so intertwined that by the time he had lived the oracle dry, the wick of his life had become, in Benjamin's words, consumed by the flame of his story: the strands of his story tell of the vanishing and imminent approach of the star of his life and of his country in a doomed or eternal cycle of repetition.

But how do we explain the privileged insight, as well as the burden of the artist? From antiquity, artists have always been associated with the divine in its creative aspect. Because s/he created only when possessed of the "divine afflatus," the poet/artist has been regarded as seer, prophet, or *vates*. Himself a poet, P. B. Shelley had called artists "the unacknowledged legislators of the world". The artist is not very unlike the Ewe poet who today still sees himself as the carrier of divine messages. As Kofi Awoonor explains it:

> Among the Ewes we had, have still, what you call Hadzi voodoo, which was the God of Songs. A man sang because he had a god of songs; it was created for him by the shrine, by the household god, around whom he has his being and moved. And he had to perform certain ceremonies, he had to erect a little shrine for his God of Songs. And if a day came and he had to perform and he went and poured libations and the divination told him not to sing that day he had to agree, because his God of Songs was not in any mood . . . to sing.
> . . . in a performance when they were singing they could, as it were, be translated into somebody else. They became not-part-of-this world; they became the god himself who had descended into and through them. And they went through a frenzied period of identification with that god. . . . Then they went back among the living.
> . . . And when the god descends upon them in public, everybody knows that it is not they who are singing, it is their Hadzi voodoo who is right there with them by their side. And he is

telling them to say the sort of things that they are saying.
. . . He may be responsible for their producing new songs.
In fact I remember I did a poem some years ago called "My
God of Songs Was Ill": "I had to cross a river with my God
of Songs because he was ill. And when I went to this shrine
they said I should come in with my backside; because of my
God of Songs being ill I could not sing any more. I just
couldn't sing until there was this rapport between myself and
my god. It is only then that I can sing." That is a paraphrase
of "My God of Songs Was Ill." (Pieterse & Duerden,
1972:47-49)

Of course, we are talking about inspiration, the creative process,
even divine possession. This passage has been quoted at length
not because it echoes a deep-seated and dimly felt exoticism and
spiritism, or because it reminds us of the ancients' discourse on the
metaphysical realms about substantial forms and shadows and the
Divine. No, Kofi Awoonor is not only very much alive, he is a very
highly educated and accomplished poet, novelist, and scholar from
Ghana, who has served as his country's Ambassador and as
Professor of Comparative Literature in top North American and
other universities, and knows what he is talking about. I have quoted him at length mainly because, as we shall soon see, his elaboration of the divine intervention in creativity resonates with
Okigbo's views on the matter of poetry as craft and art. In traditional, as in contemporary African/Nigerian, society, cultural pro-
duction/labor is a ritual which the artists perform on behalf of their
community, and in which the fingers of the ancestors are present.
Only a misunderstanding of this deep connection between the
aesthetic and the social can account for the suggestion by Ali
Mazrui, for instance, that Okigbo committed high aesthetic treason by putting his society above his art (Mazrui 1971).

It is their solidarity with and integration within their social
milieux, which give validity to the acute and heightened vision, sensibility, and oracular clarity of the artists. Hence, there is no dis-
puting the fact that they see more and farther than the average
member of the community. Given their sensitivity, they also feel
more than the rest. It is no surprise, therefore, that they tend to

be spiritual and cultural carriers of the burdens of their societies. Because I believe that they are specially equipped to perform these specialized functions for society, I wholeheartedly subscribe to the view of them as the guardians of justice, disciples of truth, and barometers of our moral climate (Egudu 1972); as the "calibrated anemometer" and "sensitive points of society" (Bradbury 1972:112); and as a central social intelligence and conscience, "as the record of the mores and experience of [their] society *and* as the voice of vision in [their] own time" (Soyinka, Wastberg, 1967:21). In fact, this paragraph can have no better conclusion than these words by Malcolm Bradbury: "[The artist's] role can be priestly" especially as "there grew up . . . with the breakdown in the church's claim to contest for spirituality and truth, the belief that this was literature's function—a writer could, by the practice of his art, become the timeless and unlocalized mind, the universal man" (Bradbury 1972:109).

It is this release of spirit, this unbounded and unlocalized attachment to spirituality and to truth which connects the traditional artist to his contemporary counterpart. Both were not only just committed but were fully integrated social beings who saw their art as both performing a social-cultural function, and fulfilling a social need; both were at peace with the fellow members of their communities; and both were in harmony with the environment.

It is this integration and this harmony, together with the legitimating support of the community which, more than anything, adumbrate the social-political and cultural utility of art during the colonial period. Under this harsh imposition, the artist became the visible and vocal articulator of the desires and dreams, the wishes and aspiration, the pain and anguish, and the protest and agitation of the colonized. All literature produced during this period which Ngugi has usefully periodized as "the fifties whose sentiments—Tell Freedom—were largely in harmony with the general sentiments for independence" (Ngugi 1993:108), can be said to be protest literature, for the artist, far from glorying in masturbatory aestheticism, used his art for definitely suasive ends. His was commitment in the truest political-social sense of the word. For commitment is neither attachment or allegiance to, nor glorification of the Establishment, this time the imperial-colonial; true com-

mitment is to the base, the quadrangle of oppressed and disen-
franchised victims of colonialism; true commitment in literature is
to human values, not to selfish and sectarian interests, not to the
consolidation and entrenchment, but to the embarrassment and
dismantling of the inhuman status quo (Pieterse & Munro 1969:
ix-xii, 109 ff.).

Thus conceiving literature as "a weapon in the struggle that
man wages against evil" (Sartre 1949:233), the colonial artist
used his art to articulate the largely muffled but universal suffering
of imperialized peoples, and to try to undermine the colonial
regime. It is this silent groaning of the colonized people which
Armattoe captures so well in "The Lonely Soul" where the weeping woman attains a typological stature:

> I met an old woman
> Talking by herself
> Down a lonely road.
> Talking to herself,
> Down a country road.
> Child, you cannot know
> Why folks talk alone.
> If the road be long
> And travelers none,
> A man talks to himself
> If showers of sorrow
> Fall down like arrows
> The lone wayfarer
> May talk by himself.
>
> So an old woman
> On lone country roads,
> Laughing all the time,
> May babble to herself
> To keep the tears away.
> Woman, you are sad!
> 'Tis the same with me.
> (Nwoga, 1967:9)

We must remember that the protagonist of this poem lived in the
remote recesses far removed from the metropoles of civilization

where talking to or laughing by oneself in the streets, or even danc-
ing in public to the noise of boom-blasters or to the music in one's
head, constituted a normality protected under the Right of Self-
Expression and Free Speech. In this woman's "uncivilized" world,
such expression/display in public would indicate psychiatric
marginality, and if she lived under any Rights at all, they were
Rights that imposed upon and exacted, not ones that allowed and
guaranteed. Her anguish was, therefore, real, while her hysteria
was symptomatic of the general condition produced by colonialism.

The colonial artists thus vocalized the generalized pain that
was in the hearts of the colonized, and for which no sign of ame-
lioration loomed in the foreseeable future. Yet, the recognition of
their helplessness in the face of the technologically superior military might of the colonial yoke did not deter them. They kept on
complaining; they kept on waiting for the hour of fulfillment when
the regime of oppression of man by man would come to an end.
It is this inertia of spirit which Osadebay articulates in his poem
"Who Buys My Thoughts":

> Who buys my thoughts
> Buys not a cup of honey
> That sweetens every taste;
> He buys the throb,
> Of Young Africa's soul,
> The soul of teeming millions,
> Hungry, naked, sick,
> *Yearning, pleading, waiting.*
>
> Who buys my thoughts
> Buys not some false pretence
> Of oracles or tin gods;
> He buys the thoughts
> *Projected by the mass*
> *Of restless youths who are born*
> *Into deep and clashing cultures,*
> *Sorting , questioning, watching.*

Who buys my thoughts
Buys the *spirit of the age*
The unquenching *fire that smoulders*
And smoulders
In every living heart
That's true and noble or suffering;
It *burns all over the earth,*
Destroying, chastening, cleansing.
(Nwoga 1967:15-16; *my italics*)

The inertia suggested by the poem is neither complacency, acqui-
escence, nor capitulation. For, in time, the ineffectual "pleading"
will give way to a conflagration that will not only "wreak and
wrack" the colonial tutelage but will also chasten and cleanse the
colonizer and the colonized alike.

But the people did not merely complain, and question, and
watch. Ngugi talks of a strong popular culture of resistance to
colonialism:

This is a patriotic national tradition developing in resistance
and opposition to imperialist-sanctioned African culture.
Under colonialism this was a culture which through songs,
dances, poetry, drama, spoke of and reflected people's real
needs as they struggled against appalling working conditions
. . . or which sang their hopes as they took up arms against
colonial exploitation and political oppression.

. . . During the colonial period the practitioners of this culture were often jailed, maimed, or even killed. Their songs,
dances, and even their sculpture were often banned. . . . writers and poets were jailed without trial or else killed.

. . . patriotic cultures . . . reflected people's total opposition to the continued plunder of their labour and wealth by
imperialism and its local black allies. Artists and writers
belonging to this tradition have been jailed, maimed and
killed. (Ngugi 1993:44-45)

Given this asphyxiating climate, which can only be described as
traumatic emergency, it would be unrealistic to expect aesthetical-
ly finished or polished great works of art from Colonial writers. In

fact, such great works of art would have indicated a disconnection between the artists and the milieux; would, indeed, have been discrepant with the perceived role of art in the African Society. The art of this period was not great art in that Decadent sense, for it was written for the moment and milieu, written for that "intersubjectivity, the living absolute, the dialectical underside of history [which] gives birth in pain to events that historians will label later on" (Sartre 1949:234). The literature of this period was written not to reflect its reality passively or to chronicle events after they had taken place with the writer withdrawing to the position of "chronicler or post-mortem surgeon" (Soyinka, in Wastberg 1967:21); the literature of this period was written with a strong desire to change the colonial system. This desire for change is what Sartre considers the essence of real transcendence in literature:

> Insofar as literature . . . is a creation and an act of surpassing, it will present man as *creative action*. It will go along with him in his efforts to pass beyond his present alienation toward a better situation.
>
> [The writers] have been led by circumstances to bring to light the relationship between *being* and *doing* in the perspective of [their] historical situation. *Is one what one does?* . . . *what* should one do . . .? What are the relationships between ends and means in a society based on [colonial] violence?
>
> The words deriving from such preoccupations can not aim first to please. They irritate and disturb. They offer themselves as tasks to be discharged. They urge the reader on to quests without conclusions . . . . The fruits of torments and questions, they can not be enjoyment for the reader, but rather questions and torments. . . . They will give not a world "to see" but to change. (Sartre 1949: 236-37)

The literature of the colonial period was truly the "fruits of torments," the creative tears forced by the oppressive milieu which the writers wanted to change. Because such literature was the articulation of the age it was not alienated. For alienation in literature results when that literature is still groping towards a clear sense of its identity and function, and panders to the whims of temporal, even imperializing, authority, or to a sectarian ideology. The literature of this period was truly a literature of *praxis*, of production, of change. According to Sartre, "*praxis* [is] action in history and on history" (239) and the literature of *praxis* reveals its *being* and *doing*, which *doing* begins by a declaration of a determined stand against "those who want to possess the world, but with those who want to change it" (238).

But no temporal authority wants to see its position undermined or its image tarnished. The neurotic reaction of the colonizers to the subversive activities of these "nationalist," anticolonial writers can be better apprehended if we consider for a moment the fevered and trembling nostalgia with which Britain clings to—and clutches at—her last colonial possession, Hong Kong, whose imminent cession to Mainland China is a painful recapitulation of the scandalous beads of Britain's imperial history. Having learnt from the history of her loss of direct control of colonies never to relinquish a lucrative territory without having sown the seeds of instability, conflict, and continued post-independence dependency, Britain now hopes, by creating in Hong Kong a "democratic" culture, which it had assiduously denied the colony all these years it had controlled and exploited it, to create permanent political instability and rupture between China and Hong Kong after 1997. The machinations of Governor Patten thus constitute an enactment of the final act in that long historical drama of "Divide and Conquer and Rule" or failing which, to "Destabilize and Cut and Run." The Patten Package is actually an incendiary of potentially cataclysmic explosiveness. But that is not what is being told the world even though one suspects that, given the British history of mischief in its colonial possessions, both Patten and London understand the ramified implications of the democratization of Hong Kong. Hence, one is not unmindful of the frightening irony of Patten's rationalization of his Hong Kong policy as "lifting the burden of the nineteenth century with some dignity and decency and without the bloodshed that has accompanied decolonization in other parts of the world involving other colonial powers" ("ABC, Good Morning America." Patten's interview with Charles Gibson, February 22, 1994).

So one is not surprised at all that the audacious and outspoken African/Nigerian writers fell afoul of the colonial regime. As the sensitive spots of their societies, the writers expressed the people's dissatisfaction with the high-handed imposition. Many of them tasted the joys of incarceration, if they were not shot by the colonial police, for their "seditious" activities. But they came out resilient and more determined and undeterred. Those temporizers, the selfish self-seekers as Okigbo would characterize them, who acquiesced to the *status quo*, and those who actively or clandestinely allied with the oppressor were the equal target for the shafts of these writers. These comprador elite included the Warrant Puppet Chief created by the Colonial Administration in regions that had been famous, historically, for their republicanism; the reactionary Emirs whose oppression and exploitation of the masses under them now received the legitimization of a higher, though foreign and imposed, temporal adjudication; the soft-pedaling nobility, newly emerging travesty of the bourgeoisie class; and prostituting intelligentsia. All these whose prototype had been delineated in the earlier quoted portrait of Koranche in Ayi Kwei Armah's *Two Thousand Seasons* (see Chapter One) are the butt of R. E. G. Armattoe's "Servant-Kings":

> Leave them alone,
> Leave them to be
> Men lost to shame,
> To honour lost!
> Servant kinglets,
> Riding to war
> Against their own,
> Watched by their foes
> Who urge them on,
> And laugh at them!
> Leave them alone,
> Men lost to shame,
> To honour lost.
> (Nwoga, 1967:12)

The colonial writer was, thus, like the traditional artist, the articulator of the mores and values of society. Like him too, he saw his duty as primarily social and public, even communal. This reading enables me to feel uncomfortable with Soyinka's assertion that "in pre-colonial days there was no real collaboration between the creative mind and the political; there was hardly the practical, fruitful acknowledgement of the existence of the one by the other" (Wastberg 1967:18). Even though I recognize the thrust of Soyinka's argument, it is my understanding that in precolonial days there was no dichotomy between the aesthetic/creative and the political, nor between the artistic and the social. But, unlike the traditional artist, the colonial artist's desire for radical psycho-political transformation brought him into collision with the regime whose aims were clearly discrepant with the writer's. Jean-Paul Sartre's remarks seem to me to apply to the situation here. According to him,

> if society sees itself and, in particular, sees itself as seen, there is, by virtue of this very fact, a contesting of the established values of the regime. The writer presents it with its image; he calls upon it to assume it or to change itself . . . thus, the writer gives the society (regime) a guilty conscience; he is thereby in a state of perpetual antagonisms towards the conservative forces which are maintaining . . . (Sartre 1949:60)

the oppressive colonial system which he sought to upset. This was the unenviable lot of the colonial writer.

In the end, the agitation and resistance, the protest and confrontation paid off and the people regained their "freedom." Or did they? For the political independence and freedom which these writers demanded was "granted" to African societies not before the colonial circus-masters had completed the major task of denigration and deculturation of African peoples. It would appear that these people were sadly spared the happy fate of the Algerians who escaped "all the degrading and infantilizing structures that habitually infest relations between the colonized and the colonizer" (Fanon, [1969] 1988:102). Thus the colonizers did not find it difficult to recruit and groom a tame and subservient, even servile group of local politicians who would succeed them and ensure the continuity of the master-servant, center-periphery, relations; in short, successors who would be content with their perquisites, and inebriated with their powers as the leaders of independent African countries even though the real power-players were now in the metropoles. As Ruth First put it in *The Barrel of a Gun* (1970), the colonial lords aimed at "breaking the back of African resistance and grooming a tame and emasculated generation of politicians for the independence era" (46). In Nigeria they did not have to go to that trouble, for they had long identified a natural aristocracy, those born with the sterling genetic qualities of rulership. An alliance with this group meant a simple reciprocal political equation: create and support a screwed-up geo-political structure which would perpetuate the political rulership of the country by one cultural section; in return rest assured of the eternal friendship of a dependent former colony. With this kind of arrangement the whole notion of independence was, *ab initio,* travestied and compromised.

And it did not help matters that when independence was finally "granted" by the "grandly giving hand" of empire (Said 1993:22), Africans had already come dangerously to the precipice of lost identity, servility, and cultural shame. But how would the writers even begin to assume their role as teachers and help their people regain that faith in themselves which they had all but completely lost over the years of cultural-psychological, economic-political subjugation and domination and exploitation (cf. Achebe 1989:40-46); how would they do that when right there on the continent there arose sharp ideological cleavages. Some groups, very much like Booker T. Washington whose book, *Up From Slavery,* had "argued that slavery had actually been quite beneficial to black people" (Ngugi 1993:43), "believe that the bitterness and humiliations of the (colonial) experience which virtually enslaved them nevertheless delivered benefits—liberal ideas, national self-consciousness, and technological goods—that over time seem to have made imperialism much less unpleasant" (Said 1993:18). The other polarity is constituted by people who, very much like the colonial "agitator," have taken time and trouble to reflect "on colonialism the better to understand the difficulties of the present in newly independent states" (18). The double jeopardy for such writers is that they are at once castigated "by many Western intellectuals as retrospective Jeremiahs [for] denouncing the evils of a past colonialism, *and* . . . treated by their (own) governments . . . as agents of outside powers who deserved imprisonment or exile" (18).

But in spite of Soyinka's disappointment with African writers on the whole, Africa still boasts of a handful of writers, including himself, Chinua Achebe, and Okigbo who is the subject of this study, who still function as the "sensitive spots" and "conscience of society." These few writers have continued the traditional role of the artist in Africa, and thus produced works which, for reason of their total commitment to the freedom of the people, have been characterized by overt or implicit didacticism and political criticism.

Beginning with the cultural crusade launched by Chinua Achebe with *Things Fall Apart* (1958), Africans needed to be told that the myth of a historyless past, of savagery and barbaric darkness, was a convenient confabulation of the Western imperialists who, in the first place, conveniently forgetting and actively suppressing the African and Semitic roots of Greek/Western civilization (Said 1993:15-16), saw the whole world through a white, superiorist periscope: Sartre talks about "the proud serenity and that tranquil certainty, common to all white Aryans, that the world is white and that they own it" (Sartre 1949:80); and, in the second, needed the salvific fiction to rationalize their incursion into, and expropriation and domination of, large portions of the world. As Edward Said explains it, there was, over and above, sheer economic and profit motive,

> a commitment in constant circulation and recirculation, which on the one hand, allowed decent men and women to accept the notion that distant territories and their native peoples *should* be subjugated, and on the other, replenished metropolitan energies so that these decent people could think of the *imperium* as a protracted, almost metaphysical obligation to rule subordinate, inferior, or less advanced peoples. (Said 1993:10)

Africans needed to be shown that, since no people can be said to be without a past, a history, or a culture, that discourse of civilizational imperialism was merely one of many Darwinistic absurdities (cf. Moore, 1969[b]:3-4). Africans also needed to be shown that, although the white rulers had been replaced by Africans, it made no difference, for the only change that took place was the replacement of the helmet, boots, and suits with flowing gowns (*baba riga*), and trace quantities of melanin with surplus melanin. Beyond those superficial, merely skin-deep changes, the people merely substituted one slaver with another who, himself, continued to slave for his predecessor. In short, Africans needed to be told that the battle for freedom, far from being won and over, was only just beginning: They needed to be shown, in the words of Edward Said, that:

> The nations of contemporary Asia, Latin America, and Africa are politically independent but in many ways are as dominated and dependent as they were when ruled directly by European powers. . . ; that the idea of *total* independence was a nationalist fiction designed mainly for . . . the "nationalist bourgeoisie," who . . . ran the countries with a callous, exploitative tyranny reminiscent of the departed masters. (Said 1993:19).

This awareness that independence has not changed anything is dramatically articulated by the pathetic West Indian slave in George Lamming's "The West Indian People": "When I woke up after the drunken joy of finding myself free, the hard reality that stared me in the face was that nothing had changed either for me or my friends who had been in chains with me (Salkey 1973:8). Like this man before the manacles, many an African had, before colonialism, known freedom. But "independence" had not brought back to him his freedom. He continued to drudge, under the supervision this time, of a Chief Nanga or a Koomson (the lampooned anti-heroes of Achebe's *A Man of the People* and Ayi Kwei Armah's *The Beautyful Ones Are Not Yet Born,* respectively), for the old master who, though departed, still operated the remote control and garnered the profits of the ex-"empire of business" (Said 1993:23). As the Igbo would put it, the old master still held the yam and held the knife.

Relaxing thus in comfort, like absentee landlords, the colonial countries had no cause for worry for those they had groomed in the "master's image" proved very loyal indeed, and saw their first duty as protecting the interests and the flickering embers of the empire, and of course, like all "representatives of foreign concerns," drawing their lucrative commissions in terms of fat ministerial salaries and security of tenure of their regimes. So one understands why these local politicians, the comprador elite, not only rushed in to fill the positions vacated by the departing imported oligarchy and share the loot, but inherited the master's notion of "divine right to rule and prosper" (First 1970:65), while the people went largely unfed. Even those who acceded to power after mouthing "nationalistic," soap-box oratory and vacuous promises of progress and full stomachs, treated the poverty and misery of their countries with execrable frivolity. To that breed of politicians, it was neither discrepant with "nationalist" aspirations and integrity, nor anomalous to sign Defence and Friendship Pacts with the former colonial rulers of their countries; nor did they conceive of the gross inhumanity and reckless insensitivity of opening up their territories as dumping sites for radioactive wastes from civilized Western countries who had enough sense and decency not to expose their own people to the hazards of such wastes. These politicians did not consider also that leasing their territories as bases to the Western military powers made a mockery of the flaunted policy of non-alignment. And it did not occur to these overzealous leaders of newly "independent" countries that the Association called the British Commonwealth of Nations not only clearly recognized and respected a certain statal hierarchy whereby Britain was the 'head' member, Canada, Australia, and New Zealand the senior/special members, and the rest, depending on their size and wealth, oscillating between visibility and polite silence, but was a structural negation of the idea of independence, a glamorized euphemism for (a reluctantly dying but continuing) empire. The new leaders who truly were "natives," not in the proper sense of the word, of being born in a place, but in the Eurocentric and touristic sense of backwardness and inferiority, could not see the anomaly in the whole post-"independence" arrangement. Yet, it was clear enough to arouse the indignation of the writers whose consternation is capsulized in Freddie Thompson's lamentation in Kofi Awoonor's novel *This Earth, My Brother* (1972): "I am being sold into slavery a second time! . . . By the Gods of Africa I am being sold again. . . . And ye Gods of Africa, I am being sold into slavery a second time" (164).

Given this measureless chasm between the dreams and promises of independence and the grim reality of life in "independent" African countries, the situation surely stood in dire need of change. Again it was the burden of the "voices of the collectivity," the writers and the artists, to champion the cause of change. As Achebe articulated it, "I have a deep-seated need to alter things within that situation [because] our world stands in just as much need of change today as it ever did in the past" (1975:14-15). Indeed. But the trouble was that the only people who wielded the actual wherewithal to give or to withhold were the politicians whose presentist preoccupation with self-aggrandizement blinded them to the need for change. As a matter of fact, they all attended the enactment of Wole Soyinka's *A Dance of the Forests* which was produced as part of Nigeria's "Independence" celebrations. They all toasted the independence of their country, their glorious ancestry, and the artistic achievement of Wole Soyinka. But the play which unfolded before their very eyes was the most savage indictment of the present social order which was, like the past, steeped in injustice, savagery, barbarity, inhumanity, and, like the past, boasted nothing glorious to celebrate. They failed to see the order they represented as only a sad point in the doomed cycle of repetition.

It is not surprising, given this intellectual deficit of the new leaders, that the writers were generally tolerated, even respected and, except in a few African countries like Ghana and Malawi, left free to do their job. This job included a nativistic interpretation and reinterpretation of Africa's past, legitimating Africa's culture and history, analyzing the causes of the cultural dilemma of contemporary fluid (schizophrenic?) society, castigating the political gluttons and comprador elite, and exposing the ills of society: in effect educating the people and holding the mirror full of pocks and warts up to society. Whether the writers succeeded or not remains, to this day, an open-ended, unanswerable question. What is clear is that society continued to do "the death-dance . . . in a banquet hall of its imaginings, proclaiming its salvation with trumpets" (Awoonor 1972:117).

In this atmosphere of trumpeting festivities and delirious inebriation, in an atmosphere of massive displacement of national priorities, of national circus performances by the political elite, and of international jamborees and junketing by them and their equally quisling, comprador-entrepreneurs whose billion-dollar business empires merely distributed to the populace goods and trifles, "shiny things" (Armah's *Two Thousand Seasons*) produced by and imported from metropolitan firms; in this condition of national hysteria, everyone knew that Africa was ripe for the shaking. African countries had paid little or no heed to the voice of warning of their writers and thus succeeded in driving the engine of national, even continental, progress along the sharp and precipitous incline "from complexity to simplicity, from the civilized to the primitive" (Muir 1965:155). African post-independence politics, in effect, tended to redirect man away from the course of moral uplift, social regeneration, and spiritual development, away from sanity and integrity, and African writers were unable to arrest the drift. Almost providentially and, in fact, as prognosticated in Chinua Achebe's *A Man of the People* (1966), the military struck.

But the jubilation that greeted the arrival of the soldiers on the political scene, the euphoria at the prospect of cessation of a national death-dance, was almost immediately negated by the accompanying disillusionment. For, instead of striving to initiate, and possibly achieve, the long-awaited psycho-political and moral transformation; instead of burying once and for all the bane of ethnicity and primordial divisiveness which had bedeviled life and politics in Nigeria, as in all Africa; instead of trying to clean up the ethico-social order and rescue the unregenerate citizenry thwarted by the now overthrown political system; instead of settling down to severing the bonds of tutelage and (ex-)colonial dependency; instead of working selflessly to bring about those changes for which they ousted renegade politicians, the soldiers soon settled down, not only to enjoy the loot and power from the corridors of which they had apparently been long excluded, but also, and more unforgivably, to exacerbate the embers of divisive sectionalism. The situation could be likened to that in William Blake's "The Grey Monk" where:

> The hand of vengeance sought the bed
> To which the purple tyrant fled.
> The iron hand crush'd the tyrant's head

(And usurp'd the tyrant's throne and bed)
And became a tyrant in his stead.
(Blake, in Keynes 1974:419)

Where the politicians had been megalomaniacal, corrupt, and tyrannous, their military successors, aided by the might of the barrel of a gun, outdid them a hundred-fold. People began to doubt if the military really could, or even wanted to, change anything; if they even saw anything fundamentally wrong with the structure and character of society. For a quick succession of military coups in Nigeria, for instance, only widened the politico-cultural cleavages, restored and made permanent the exercise of cultural-political hegemony by the Northern cultural section, and made the political-military culture in Nigeria a periodic rite of relays whereby the baton was simply handed over by one group of Northern officers to another in a cycle of plunder and brazen aggrandizement of the self and section. As for the need to break the political-economic structure of dependence, that issue could arise for contemplation, discussion, and possible implementation, only by an enlightened political (even if military) leadership. Where the leadership was besotted and hardly literate or politically aware, or where it saw as its first duty the consolidation and perpetuation and reproduction of the hegemonic *status quo,* one should not expect political miracles. Indeed, the only time Nigeria was blessed with such a possibility in the person of Murtala Mohamed, the world painted him radical and, in a *coup* that was rumored to have been funded from sources far removed from Nigeria, snuffed him off the scene only six months after he had threatened nationalization of resources in Nigeria, and total decolonization of the rest of Africa. Such miracles are not repeatable, and this short "episode" in Nigerian history remains consigned to the realm of subjunctive speculation: "he could have, only if . . . ; he might not have . . . ; had it not been for . . . ."

If, generally, the soldiers saw no need for a true revolution, or were unable to champion it, or even tried to resist the forces of radical change, how would that change ever be achieved? The sensitive spots of society, the writers have been giving a pitiless and critical and unsentimental look at their societies in their works.

And here I must note that in the tortured and tortuous history of Nigeria, in which the military have colluded with reactionary forces to uphold and legitimize injustice and inequality, the writers have generally been aligned against the forces of reaction, and it will not be an overstatement to say that Soyinka spoke for all true, sensitive writers when he asserted that the time had come for them to have "the courage to determine what alone can be salvaged from the recurrent cycle of human stupidity" (Wastberg, ed., 1967:20).

Unfortunately, this is easier said than practiced. For, even though one hesitates to accuse the military leaderships of sophistication and cultural literacy, they are aware of the ultimate superiority of the pen over the bullet, aware of the power of art to move inert and despondent populaces against regimes of oppression. So whether or not the rulers read and understand the works of these writers, they have not made life easier for them than it was for their colonial predecessors. Writers have been detained not infrequently without charge or trial, imprisoned without due process, forced into involuntary exile, or compelled into linguistic duplicity whereby their works, couched in unintelligible idiom, are meant to ensure their safety and freedom from detection and detention by the "cartel of organized robbery and murder," as Soyinka would describe the 'military politicians' (*Season of Anomy* 1973:102). Soyinka knows, first-hand, what he is talking about: he has been detained and imprisoned, providentially escaping death in the "Crypt" (cf. *A Shuttle in the Crypt* [1972], and *The Man Died* [1972]), for upholding the truth; his books, particularly *The Man Died,* have been impounded and banned; and he has known the pleasures of exile. For writers, living under insensitive and intolerant regimes—civilian or military—can be as asphyxiating as living in intense war situations, as in Biafra; for in both situations the writers are denied both the physical and the emotional convenience of exercising their creativity (Achebe 1975).

Yet writers traditionally are supposed to have the privilege of attacking and criticizing society, to hold up as in a mirror society's image, as it is seen and as it should see itself, "warts and all", of exposing the foibles of its members, including their leaders; indeed, of freely acting as the gadfly providentially sent to keep society and its members on moral tip-toe. But in Africa the writers cringe under the bayonets of "mind-butchers" who dread truth as the bat fears daylight. In Soyinka's words, "in new societies which begin the seductive experiments in authoritarianism, it has become a familiar experience to watch society crush the writer under a load of guilt for his daring to express a sensibility and an outlook apart from, and independent of, the mass direction" (Wastberg 1967:15).

Soyinka's castigation applies to every known country on the African continent, but even more so to Nigeria where that "experiment in authoritarianism" has been so particularly seductive that in all the years of its "independence" from Britain, Nigeria has known only two eruptions of civilian administration, properly two interruptions (1960-1965 & 1979-1983) of otherwise continuous military totalitarianism. It has been said that if literature is to continue "to be a true criticism of life and a revelation of its essential nature, it had to express the horror of such a world. . . . the poets would have to immerse themselves in the destructive element" (Pinto 1972:142). And as Michael Thorpe puts it in his elegy to Christopher Okigbo:

Poets must go on describing the sickness
though the patient keeps looking away
(Achebe & Okafor 1978:22)

Given that the concatenation of political-social conjunctures under which Nigerian writers have so far operated can only be defined as regressive and asphyxiating, the wonder is that they have largely retained their clarity of vision, have not given up, even when it is clear to everyone that the patient in Nigeria does not just look away, but is, in fact, the "sower of death." Moreover, the writers in Nigeria have *largely* escaped the lure of primordialism and, when the leaders, civilian and military alike, have colluded to keep the primal embers of division alive, have "*generally* directed [their creative] energies to enshrining victory, to re-affirming [their] identification with the aspirations of nationalism and the stabilization of society" (Soyinka, in Wastberg 1967:16). In this respect, given the exigent experiences of the Nigerian nation-state, of the stark political reality which, even as we write, is a very pregnant issue whose outcome no one can prognosticate; and given that, to date, the writers have failed, collectively, to produce a body of *fictions of nation* which the people may refer to as the articulation of their nationness, it seems to me that the nationalist aspirations of the writers can only be described as utopic and idealistic. In the end, perhaps, it is that idealism that we need, the politicians and the soldiers having failed, to bring to an end the present debasement of human life and human values; to inaugurate a spiritual, moral, and psycho-political transformation of society; to transcend the primordial walls of cultural sectionalism; and, indeed, to avert what Soyinka calls "the very collapse of humanity" (Wastberg 1967:16).

I should not, on account of the optimism of the foregoing paragraph, be accused of having myself lost sight of the reality of the Nigerian society. I am fully aware that literature never exists in a psycho-cultural vacuum; indeed, literary practices everywhere mediate and are mediated by the social *milieux* and formations. Ruth Finnegan, in writing about oral literature in Africa, observes that "in Africa, as elsewhere, literature is practised in a society. It is obvious that any analysis of African literature must take account of the social and historical context . . ." (1970:48). I agree completely with her, but would go further to assert the overdetermination, in the Nigerian instance, of the historical-cultural-political conjuncture. For this peculiar conjuncture has resulted in the production of *Literatures,* which, far from belonging to and elucidating a simple national-literary tradition, are, on account of ethnicity and the insidiousness of the divergent interests of the different cultural sections, deeply rooted in the primordial-ethnic soils of these sections. Nigerian writers, being usually "true sons and daughters of the soil" carry in their bodies and in their texts the marks of the sickness—ethnicity—which has continued to blight the African society, and for which the Nigerian society is symptomatically paradigmatic. It is true that these marks and pocks have not blistered into festering sores; it is also true that the writers have not usually, like the political/military elite, made a career of their primordial affiliations; but it is also true that these pocks and warts are evident in their works. It is for the reason of the visibility of these ethnic markers that it has not been easy to describe the *corpus* of Literatures issuing from Nigeria, especially before the Nigeria-Biafra War, as constituting a National Literature.

In the same way that Nigerians have continued to hold dearly and firmly to their ethnic-cultural roots, the writers, particularly those of the "founding" generation, not only sank their creative probosces deeply into, and dealt with, matters of immediate psycho-cultural relevance to, their cultural-ethnic *milieux*, but also all looked beyond the artificial boundaries of the nation-state to that larger "community" of Africans and the Black race. According to Bruce King, to whose present view I subscribe, "the generation of writers who appeared at independence—Soyinka, Achebe, Okigbo, Clark, Okara, etc.—at first thought of themselves in non-national terms. Their identification was more tribal and African than national" (1986:45). I disagree with Bruce King, however, with respect to Okigbo, whose trajectory constituted a different order: he began as a *world*, universal—not ethnic—poet, even questioning the concept of African Literature, and seeing no affinity between "African" and "Negro" Literatures (cf. his 1963 interview with Dennis Duerden, in Nwoga 1984:224). After flirting with Graeco-Romanism, Modernism, Cubism, and other Western Avant-gardist isms, he came back to the Nigerian cultural-political *milieu*, at which time his poetry became suffused with imagery from the Nigerian cultural landscapes and motivated by nationalism and love for the people. This mature phase of his poetry encompassed cultural crusade, anti-colonialism, postcolonial politics, and social-political criticism, which culminated in the prophecy and disillusionment of *Path of Thunder.* As we shall be elaborating soon, Okigbo never saw himself or his poetry in ethnicist terms. But Bruce King is right to the extent that the fitful process of nation-building cannot even be said to have taken off in Nigeria.

The Western powers at the Berlin Conference of 1884 *made* what they thought were nation-states following the European model; it is now left to the inhabitants of these "nation-states," after their several, long, tortuous, and conflicted historical experiences, to *build* their polities into nations. Nigerians are still in the process of "building," still engaged in "'birth pains—that near-fatal euphemism for death throes" (Soyinka, in Wastberg 1967:17)—of a nation; and it is my contention that the Biafra-Nigeria War, in spite of the stupendous dissipation of resources and senseless waste of human lives, while it did not finally result

in the creation and inculcation of the consciousness of nation—
"One Nation, One People, One Destiny"—did at least sow the
seeds. There have been seasons of blight and uncertainty, and the
seeds have taken rather long to germinate and grow. But there are
signs that they are beginning to break the ground/soil. So while,
given the story of Nigeria, the founding fathers of Literatures from
Nigeria have neither had, nor created, any common icon of nation
which would stamp their work with a "national cultural identity"
(King 1986:44), it is the hope, utopian and metaphysical, that the
post-war generations of Nigerian writers would succeed where
their predecessors had failed. If the blood of Okigbo and that of a
million others could thus join to fertilize the *milieux* of the Nigerian
writers, then that exercise of genocidal carnage would have been
worth it. The Nigerian writer, then a contributor to the *corpus* of
Nigerian National Literature, would proudly assume his role as
"recorder, . . . analyzer . . . [and] visionary recreator" (Anyidoho
1986:23).

CHAPTER III

ETHNICITY AND CACOPHONY: THE DILEMMA OF TONGUES

The last chapter ended on a note of almost utopian optimism. For one might be asked for signs of the miracle suggested in the closing sentences of the last paragraph with regard to the reality of Nigeria, both as a polity and as a site for cultural productions. What follows will neither produce such a sign, nor even constitute a justification of the said optimism. For so far, literature from Nigeria has not lived up to the so-called "responsibility of literature, and of other cultural forms, to be the production and mediation of a sense of national identity" (Lloyd 1987:xi). David Lloyd is indeed concerned here primarily with Irish literature, but what he says becomes important *by default*, in the sense that it does *not* apply in the Nigerian situation. According to him:

> the goal of creating a politically *unifying* concept of Irish identity demands the virtual reconstruction of Irish literature as it were *ab origine*, forcing a development that would theoretically have been the normal course of a national literature uninterrupted by colonial power. In such a literature all Irishmen could trace a common origin in the very commonalty of the history of their difference. (3)

In Nigeria, such dreaming of commonalty has continued to be elusive, rendered almost impossible because the very construction or constitution of the identity of nation was doomed *ab initio* by the structural craftsmanship of the colonial political engineers who made sure that difference rather than commonalty would continue to define the corporate political existence of Nigeria and its cultural articulations. Even though one knows that the metropole, London, still exerts influence by remote control, direct colonial domination in Nigeria ended more than thirty years ago, and one should not spend the rest of eternity bemoaning that historic encounter. Generations of thinking women and men, including the writers, have flourished, who have had, and still have, the opportunity to embark upon unselfish introspection, social analyses, and a course of treatment of Nigeria's bane. But not much has been done generally in that direction. Thus it is ironic that what Lloyd says, in discussing Matthew Arnold's ethnocentric and imperializing theorization, applies so aptly to Nigeria, again by reason of its negation in practice:

> each writer's work, to a greater or lesser degree, prefigures the ultimate unity or synthesis of ethnic types in the production of which his works participate both as evidence and as influence. The aesthetic work, exactly to the extent that it is a product of "imaginative reason," represents in itself a unity that is prior to it while at the same time, by drawing together disparate ethnic characteristics, prefigures the future self-reflexive realization of that unity. (12)

No one seriously talks about "unity" or the "synthesis of ethnic types" in Nigeria. I must make it clear, as I continue, that since my affiliation and loyalty is with "the quadrangle" (this refers to *the people*, "you and me," "the rest of us," in Okigbo's geometric characterology), my castigation is, consequently, of the comprador elite, the new-fangled bourgeoisie, the counterfeit, opportunistic, and self-serving intellectuals, and the political charlatans and *rulers* (never *leaders*) who have continued to misdirect the course of affairs in Nigeria. The quadrangle has always gotten along, and even in the cacophonous linguistic situations in Nigeria, has either learnt the languages of the others or created a *lingua franca* of harmonious coexistence and intercommunication. But the people have always been exploited by the wielders of economic and political powers who exacerbate ethnic rivalry and tension by always appealing to primordial, cultural, and linguistic differences. Thus, the dilemma that is the subject of this section is a problem, not of the people as such, but that is sustained by the elite and intellectuals who, apparently, stand to benefit from the preservation of the cacophonous *status quo.*

So, while scholars and intellectuals elsewhere, like David Lloyd from Ireland, are interested in finding ways of resolving socio-political and cultural disarticulations in their societies, what we have in Nigeria can be best exemplified by the bickering exchange that took place not too long ago on the pages of *Okike* (1982), [*okike* = divine creation; creativity], a journal dedicated to creativity and scholarship in Africa, and edited (then) by Chinua Achebe, the father of African Literature, between two accomplished Nigerian writers, critics, and university professors. The one, Emeka Okeke-Ezigbo, an Igbo, and the other, Femi Osofisan, a Yoruba, both understand the multifarious problems of Nigeria, including the language problem which is partly the subject of Okeke-Ezigbo's article, "The Role of the Nigerian Writer in a Carthaginian Society" (*Okike* XXI:28-37), which the editors saw fit to submit to Osofisan for a critique that would be printed alongside the article in the same number of the journal. While it is my conviction that, sitting face-to-face and parleying, these two critics would agree on most of the points and counter-points of their respective articles, the trouble with Nigeria is such that even where, in matters of vital importance, like that of language, it is possible to come to an understanding and agreement, acrimonious debates which resolve nothing are the preferred route. Thus Osofisan's comment, "Enter the Cartheginian Critic . . .?" (*Okike* XXI:38-40), begins with a quick disclaimer of any "kinship," intellectual or otherwise, with Okeke-Ezigbo: "Okeke-Ezigbo's . . . tone is bold and acerbic. The editor must have thought of me spontaneously as a kindred spirit. It is promptly to refute this implied kinship that I have agreed to write this commentary" (38). Osofisan then goes on to respond, almost line by line, to Okeke-Ezigbo's essay. My concern here is not whether one is right and the other wrong; my concern is that they do not and *would not* arrive at a consensus or agreement, which is both very possible and desirable if their intentions were to contribute to the task of solving Nigeria's linguistic dilemma and of nation/community building in the bedeviled and distracted state of Nigeria.

In a country of "about 250 languages" (Barbag-Stoll 1983:102), and their one thousand and one dialects, if one jettisoned the colonial and neocolonial language, which made possible in the first place the exchange between these two scholars, what would they have in its place? There have been cries for the recuperation, development, and creative deployment of indigenous languages. But it seems to me that such cries are meant primarily to call attention to the criers, and not necessarily to the issue, because no serious-minded person really believes that that would facilitate inter-ethnic communication among the many language and dialect groups. And no one has addressed the prospects of the epistemological nightmare and curricular disaster that will attend that linguistic free-for-all. If the miraculous happened—a rare dream in Nigeria—and everyone acquired literacy and competence in their indigenous languages, and writers sprouted overnight who created in these languages, would the proliferation of such Literatures not require translations to get to the larger audiences, yet? Would that miracle then be enabling the cohesion of the cultural-linguistic sections or driving them further apart? Whose interests are actually being served by these nativistic surges of linguistic sub-nationalisms? The peoples who want to get along or the misrulers and opportunists as well as their masters who profit from the cleavages? In the end are we helping to build a nation or finally to quicken the explosion of the dry and ready oil-bean pod of state? Okeke-Ezigbo's suggested adoption of *Pidgin* is dismissed swiftly and even derided, whereas it might well be that that linguistic salad-bowl is what holds the secret of Nigeria's corporate being. But the trouble with Nigeria is that while everyone knows the solution to Nigeria's bane, everyone is busy, like the cowardly proverbial urchin, trying to capture the rats, even shrews, fleeing from our conflagrating homesteads instead of helping first to put the fires out. Finally, regarding the contentious exchange between our exemplary scholars, one only needs to say that we have had enough of the divisiveness, and that vituperative name-calling and *ad-hominem* discursive bellicosity hardly belong in cultural criticism.

But this exchange, which took place in 1982, is important for pointing to the peculiar resilience and recalcitrance of problems in Nigeria. Some time ago, I had actually hoped, wishfully it has turned out, to have had the last word on, thus ending the fractious debate over, the language question. I had then written, among other things:

Since some have argued that a writer cannot sincerely and meaningfully be engaged in cultural nativism who writes in an alien language, we wish, first of all to dismiss the language question and, hopefully, to end the debate that has been going on around it.

The argument has been raging for years around this question with undiminished vigour and rancour. The protraction of the debate raises a fundamental question as to the very sincerity and seriousness of the contestants' intentions. For, I believe, they all realize the futility of the exercise and are merely flaunting facile erudition. This is because all the points adduced for and against the use of a "colonial" language ignore a basic issue, which is the socio-historical inevitability of such usage. And the condescending advice to writers in a country like Nigeria where there are about two hundred languages—not dialects—to write in their different languages if they mean to address their countrymen, sounds puerile, to say the least. The point is that that historical "accident" which produced diffident Africans, which produced cultural apes, which produced politicians who are content to be agents of Westminster or Paris, which made it imperative for African countries to use English or French or Portuguese as their official languages, also created that situation which has compelled African writers to use the same languages (that colonized them in addressing their audience). Whether the writers have their ears cocked to the West or have their eyes on the bigger slice of the gains of the publishing trade accruing from their mastery of the language of Prospero is beside the point. Like Caliban, they have been given the language of the master and they have learnt to curse in it as well. Until those factors are changed which colluded to bequeath to Caliban a strange tongue, all arguments are a futile exercise in semantics and we can comfortably dispense with Obi Wali's prophecy of a dead end of African literature until African "writers and their Western midwives accept the fact that any true African literature must be written in African languages." (Okafor 1980:45-46)

It was actually Obi Wali (murdered in 1993) who started off the debate with his controversial presentation at a 1962 African Writers' Conference titled "The Dead End of African Literature," later published in *Transition* 1:10 (1963). Incidentally, Obi Wali taught me Introduction to Literature at the University of Nigeria, Nsukka, and it is interesting that during that one-year-long, 9-credit course, not only was no mention ever made of the literatures produced in indigenous Nigerian languages but, apart from J. P. Clark's *Song of a Goat* (a play), and Ngugi's *Weep Not, Child*, not much was talked about or taught that *was* African literature. Instead we forayed among English, European (in English translation), and American literatures, relishing such texts as *The Great Gatsby, Room at the Top*, and *The Wild Duck*, while imbibing a sturdy dose of English metaphysical poetry.

Yet the controversy he inaugurated has not only continued unabated, but has recently polarized into the Achebe and Ngugi polemical schools or camps: on the one side are those who, like Ngugi, see "African languages and traditions as expressive of the collective essence of a pristine traditional community" and insist that true African independence requires a literature of one's own in one's own language (Appiah 1991:157). It does not occur to these followers of Wali, apostles of essentialism, that they might, in fact, through a curious political/ideological irony, be preaching the same relegation, marginalization, and eventually silence, through inferiorization and secondarization, of African cultural productions, which imperialism once arranged, and which have in no wise abated. For we all know that even now "the usual attitude of Commonwealth-Literature scholars towards *Third World verbal art in vernacular languages* has been one, not merely of benign neglect, but rather of blissful, complacent ignorance" (Davis & Maes-Jelinek, 1990:95; my emphasis). Notice that even in this large-hearted critique of the negligent attitude and unconcern of scholars, such cultural productions in indigenous languages do not get called "Literature"; they belong in that undignified category of "verbal art." One is not surprised by that relegation of *Third World* "verbal arts" to the dust-bin of inconsequence, which has nothing to do with the quantity or literary/aesthetic quality of such vernacular labors. The truth is that "no one will learn the language of a people without any economic or political power" (95). And economic and political disenfranchisement remains the fate of the laboring peoples of the *Third World*.

On the other side of the polemical divide, are those who are persuaded by the "fatalistic logic" which enables Achebe to see the use of the imperial language (or is it still that?) as a matter of prophetic inevitability, but which is amenable, at the same time, to creative manipulation which purges the language of its Eurocentric *Sprachgeist*. Since Achebe, in his own creative practice, has shown this to be possible, his position becomes an eloquent and effective contestation of the supremacist and imperialist concept of *Sprachgeist* which assigns essentialistic attributes and spirit to a place and people whose language thus possesses a magic of meaning-making which no other people can access.

It is this belief in the mystique of *Sprachgeist* which enables Thomas Davis to write, in his article on "Our National Language," that:

> The language, which grows up with a people, is conformed to their organs, descriptive of their climate, constitution, and manners, mingled inseparably with their history and their soil, fitted beyond any other language to express their prevalent thoughts in the most natural and efficient way.
>
> To impose another language on such a people is to send their history adrift among the accidents of translation—'tis to tear their identity from all places—'tis to substitute arbitrary signs for picturesque and suggestive names—'tis to cut off the entail of feeling, and separate the people from their forefathers by a deep gulf—'tis to corrupt their very organs, and abridge their power of expression. (Lloyd 1987:66-67)

These are the effects which colonialism and colonial education, and with them the imposition of the English language, were supposed to have had on all colonized peoples. In Nigeria it wasn't quite deleteriously the case. For English, had it succeeded in displacing indigenous languages would, indeed, have given the people an alternative tongue with which to transact inter-ethnic communicative acts and thus, if not completely, eliminated, the consequences of multi-ethnicity and linguistic cacophony. But it did not quite do that, so that among the quadrangle, the indigenous languages, as well as the incipient *lingua franca*, are very much alive and well, while among the elite, including the writers, it is a case of serious bilingualism which cannot be simplistically addressed by the Ngugian either/or facility. In real-life, including linguistic, situations, the "barbaric simple-mindedness" of such either/or residue of Western philosophical tradition, which always bifurcates the world into a hierarchized evaluative binarity that recognizes only two terms: inside/outside, indigenous/alien, western/traditional, black/white, is not always sustainable. In fact, as Achebe sees it, "I see no situation in which I will be presented with a Draconian choice . . . between English and Igbo. For me no either/or; I insist on both" (Achebe 1989:61).

Moreover, one begins really to wonder, with Achebe, why English should continue to be called a colonial or imperial language. Does that language still belong to any one country, imperial or not? And with all the creative mutation and indigenization it has undergone in such resourceful places as Nigeria, can it still qualify as a non-African language? And so Achebe dilates on the question of language thus:

> . . . there has been an impassioned controversy about an African literature in non-African languages. But what is a *non-African* language? English and French certainly. But what about Arabic? What about Swahili even? Is it then a question of how long the language has been present on African soil? If so, how many years should constitute *effective occupation*? For me it is again a pragmatic matter. A language spoken by Africans on African soil, a language in which Africans write, justifies itself. (Achebe 1989:93)

So, for Achebe and the pragmatists, not only will English continue to be used, but they "intend to do unheard of things with it" (74). It is my belief that these "unheard of things" are the *recipe* for the long-elusive linguistic-ethnic harmony in Nigeria. For with the evolution of a *lingua franca* devoid of any derogating socio-economic class implications, Nigerians of all "tribes and tongues" will have been given a common tongue with which they can begin the song of unity and community-building.

But these unheard-of things have not yet been given full chance. For the circus performers and academic/intellectual gladiators are still on stage, unexhausted by a fractious debate that has now gone on without reprieve for thirty odd years. Thus special issues of *Research in African Literatures* were devoted completely to the old question of language (RAL XXI [1990]). But the remarkable thing about the continuing debate is that it designates our predilection for cyclicity and circularity, which are no longer restricted to the movement of the seasons and the reckoning of time in African societies, but extend to the general direction of affairs, be they economic, political, or academic-cultural. This may, perhaps, very well account for the perpetual state of stagnation, lack of development and progress, and continuing dependency of Africa. For it is clear from reading the entries in *RAL* (1990) that none of them represents an advance on the points and counterpoints enunciated at the 1962 conference; they have simply restated, reformulated, disputed, contested, and not progressed beyond, those well-worn suggestions, first put forward in Kampala, Uganda.

In his contribution to the debate, Biodun Jeyifo (*RAL* XXI, 1 [Spring 1990]:33-48) gives a useful, though hardly novel, definition of culturalism as the sharing of an ethnic identity and a common "native" language between writer and reader who both live in the same culture and are "rooted in its customs, mores and codes" (38). It is not clear, however, how such a "rooted" writer can still connect the "freedom of artistic expression, experimentation, and innovation with a commitment to the task of constructing a socialist democracy in the conditions of underdevelopment" (43). It seems to me that this requirement of the writer must take cognizance of the multiplicity of cultures and native languages in Nigeria, and of the dilemma of many writers who, at best, are only bilingual (in English and their own particular native languages) and, at worst, have lost their native tongues in a colonial/neo-colonial condition, appropriately designated glottophagia, and must thus sing their anguish in the tongue which, in the first place, had colonized them.

If the writer is the sensitive point of the society; if s/he is the calibrated anemometer of that society; if the writer is indeed his/her society's teacher, who intends to show it where the rains began to beat it and where it dried itself, how can s/he afford not to communicate to the generality of that society? How can s/he write in a *lingua* or, in fact, a *cultic lingo*, which is inaccessible to the majority of the members of that society?

Chinua Achebe, who espouses this fundamental pedagogic and didactic role for the writer, has himself blazed the trail by writing in a style whose surface clarity cloaks the profundity and complexity of thought, and which some have called "translation" (Okeke-Ezigbo 1984), but which happens to be accessible and comprehensible to anyone averagely competent in the English language. And he is definitely not engaged in translation, even though his writings embody the Igbo world view, and even though the palimpsest is clearly Igbo (Zabus 1991). Achebe's creative use, his deployment of the potent forces of the English language let loose in his milieu by the careless colonizers, is only an intimation of the "unheard of things." Unfortunately, while he has had a following, Achebe's footsteps have not generally been followed by many important writers whose texts, like those of Wole Soyinka and Kalu Uka, remain linguistic acrobatics and teasers incapable of speaking to the many.

The need remains urgent, therefore, for a body of literature that can function as the center of articulation or cohesion or commonalty of the various cultural-linguistic sections. Such a literature cannot lack for those ingredients from the cultural *doxa* or repertoire of the various ethnicities which will make it not only meaningfully relevant, but importantly accessible, to them. Because these cultural sections are still largely *oral*, the task for the writers, as Abiola Irele summarizes it, is actively "to write an oral culture" (*RAL* XXI 1:61). Irele goes on to explain that:

> Within the very form of expression of the modern African writer, the tensions and ambiguities that mark the African writer's situation are reproduced. The question that presents

itself to the African writer then becomes how to create a formal harmony between expression and the objective reference
of the expression. Formulated differently, the problem of the
African writer employing a European language is: *how to
write an oral culture.* (61)

Irele's position is important for my argument because it goes
beyond diagnosis to a prescription or a solution. The futility of
beating the suspiring horses of native languages is recognized and
a case is being made for a creative practice which, by utilizing
material from the *fauna* and *flora* of local languages and culture
in a creative deployment of the domesticated English Language,
will both transcend the ethno-linguistic divide, and make English
a homely tongue. According to Irele:

> The fact of a direct progression from the oral literature is
> important here, since it is a question not merely of drawing
> upon material from the oral tradition, but essentially of re-pre-
> senting such material through the medium of print in order
> to give wider currency as well as new expressions to forms
> that are already structured within the languages themselves.
> This practice does not preclude a modification of the tradi-
> tional forms within the new modes; indeed, such modification
> is inevitable . . . (given) the assimilation of modes and con-
> ventions of the Western literary culture. (57)

If Irele's position sounds both sensible and practicable, it still does
not command the reasoned consideration of some critics, whose
argumentation must continue *ad nauseam.* Whereas Irele has
clearly identified the problem, "the situation of dual competence
in an African and a European language [as] indicative of a fundamental issue of modern African expression raised by the situation
of diaglossia" (57), a situation I have chosen to describe as
cacophonous polyglossia, there are still many who would keep at
that dead horse of language. Thus Mlana in the same issue of
RAL is indignant:

> How can an African writer today address the African masses
> without using their African languages? We are all aware that,

even though our countries have maintained English, French, or Portuguese as national languages for over twenty years, these are not the languages of the people. The majority of all African countries' populations still communicate in the indigenous languages which are their mother-tongues. The writer, in a way, seems to have no choice but to write in these languages. Writers who use languages foreign to their audiences also place themselves outside the community and operate as outsiders, as people who can reach their audiences only through translation. (10)

That is the point. The problems of Nigeria happen to be more intractable and complex than those of some other countries. And where no institution in Nigeria can be called truly national because languages and ethnicities continue to pull the country from/in two hundred different directions, the need for unity and cohesion is more urgent, and we cannot afford the luxury of the examples of places like England, for example, where, after centuries of confusion, the Wessex dialect achieved ascendancy over the other dialects as the carrier of culture and means of national communication. Moreover, we are not talking of dialects but languages in Nigeria where, were I to write my poetry in Igbo for instance, I would be making sense only to those who have literacy and competence in that language. And were Soyinka to write his plays and poetry in Yoruba, he would make sense to me only after they had been translated into Igbo or English. And it makes no sense to suggest that people learn each others' languages, for one is hardly aware of any polyglot anywhere in the world who has demonstrated competence in two hundred languages, as there are in Nigeria. This fact does not deter Mlana who dismisses the problem as he goes on:

> Writing in the mother tongue for the African writer may require not only writing in the writer's mother-tongue but also in the mother-tongues of one's audience [what a task!]. There are many cases where writers are actually fluent in other African languages but refrain from using them on the grounds of political or ethnic prejudice. In situations where the writer is not competent in the audience's languages, the question of translation from the writer's mother-tongue to other African languages becomes important. . . . It is high

time we emphasized the need for translations into the different languages of our linguistically diverse audiences. (13)

The whole ponderous impracticability of Mlana's "noble" and
"modest" proposal strengthens the case for that medium of
transethnic, translinguistic, and transdialectal communication which
I have chosen to call Nigerian Language. Indeed, I am happy to be
making this bold suggestion now because, at long last, it would
appear that the most militant advocate of linguistic nativism, Ngugi
wa Thiong'o, has recognized the intractable dilemma confronting
those writers and scholars who would follow in his trail, and especially those who, unlike him, have not achieved or attained the
name and fame which ensure that publishers in every metropole
will, like vultures, scramble to publish any- and everything issuing
from his pen, in whatever language, even in languages yet unfab-
ricated. So, in his "Preface" to the latest collection of his essays
(1993), Ngugi clearly articulates the problem, and I quote:

> There are two [of my essays] that give me special satisfaction:
> "English, a Language for the World?" and "Many Years Walk
> to Freedom: Welcome Home Mandela!" because they are
> translations from the Gikuyu originals. The first piece was part
> of a BBC seminar on English as a possible language for the
> world held on 27 October 1988. The translation was later
> broadcast on the BBC World Service. The English version . .
> . and the Gikuyu original . . . were first published in the 1990
> Fall issue of the Yale Journal of Criticism. The second piece,
> commissioned by EMERGE, . . . was the lead article in their
> March 1990 issue featuring the historic release of Nelson
> Mandela. But whereas the Gikuyu original of the piece on lan-
> guage has been published in the Yale journal, the Gikuyu orig-
> inal of the Mandela piece is still in my drawer among a good
> number of others [why?]. In their different destinies, the two
> pieces illustrate the difficulties in the way of those writing the-
> oretical, philosophical, political and journalistic prose in an
> African language. . . . The Gikuyu language community is for
> instance largely within Kenya. There are no journals or news-
> papers in the language inside or outside Kenya. This is true of
> all the other African languages in Kenya apart from the All-

Kenya national language, Kiswahili. This means that those
who write in African languages are confronted with a dearth
of outlets for publication and therefore platforms for critical
debate among those using the languages. They can only publish in translation or else borrow space from European languages journals and both options are clearly not solutions.
The situation does not help much in the development of con-
ceptual vocabulary in these languages to cope with modern
technology, the sciences and the arts. The growth of writing
in African languages will need a community of scholars and
readers in those very languages, who will bring into the languages the wealth of literature on modern technology, arts and
sciences. For this they need platforms. It is a vicious circle. So
while the two pieces mirror my current involvement in the
struggle to move the centre of our literary engagements from
European languages to a multiplicity of locations in our languages, they also illustrate the frustrations in the way of immediate and successful realisation. . . . (xiii-xiv)

This excerpt speaks for itself and clearly demonstrates Ngugi's
late recognition that the options to "publish in translation or else
borrow space from European languages journals . . . are clearly
not solutions" (xiv). One is, therefore, taken aback to read, a few
pages from the "Preface," that for Ngugi:

> Joseph Conrad had a certain amount of attraction. He was
> Polish, born in a country and a family that had known only
> the pleasures of domination and exile. He learnt English late
> in life and yet he had chosen to write in it, a borrowed lan-
> guage, despite his fluency in his native tongue and in French.
> And what is more he had made it to the great tradition of
> English literature. Was he not already an image of what we
> the new African writers, like the Irish writers before us, Yeats
> and others, could become? (5)

One can only hasten to answer a loud "No" to Ngugi. Conrad can
in no wise be held up as a model for the new African writers. The
suggestion itself is outrageous. Conrad was white, worked in the
service of empire, and wrote (wittingly or no) to perpetuate racist

stereotypes of the *Other*, the savage and sub-human prowlers among beasts in the jungles of the Congo, Africa, of Conrad's racist imagination. More relevantly, however, Conrad's *decision* to write in English was his adult, deliberate *choice*, a luxury that colonialism and colonial education denied many an African who was *forced* to learn English and despise the "native tongue." Conrad was fluent in three languages while most African writers write fluently only in English, even though they also speak their native tongues. Many Africans are making a serious study of their native tongues quite late in life. Conrad made it to "the great tradition of English literature" not because he had written *better novels* than other writers in English whose native tongue like Conrad's is not English; he made it to that tradition because he was white and wrote major contributions to the monuments of imperialism and the Orientalizing/Africanizing Eurocentric tradition. That is why Conrad is taught and studied in the English Departments of Oxford, Cambridge, and London, but not Achebe for instance; that is why Wole Soyinka, winner of the 1986 Nobel Prize for Literature, could be Visiting Professor at Cambridge in the Anthropology Department, but not in the English or Comparative Literature Department. Ngugi's Marxian faith in the goodness of *man* which anchors his unrepentant universalism should be tempered by the knowledge that the *Yale Journal of Criticism* does not go about soliciting papers written in Gikuyu or Swahili or Igbo from just anybody. His call for frenzied cultural productions in *all* languages in Africa seems to me, therefore, to be a prescription for disaster and cultural Babel, a complication and exacerbation of the prevalent cacophony. Being that I myself have been part of the formulation of the text and pretext of Literatures from Nigeria, and an active participant in the cacophonous drama of its linguistic multiplicity, I wish to end this dismissive section on Ngugi by asking a few questions: Were it not better that Nigerians had a common language with which to talk to one another directly rather than many, necessitating translations? Why, for instance, should I write my poetry solely in Igbo? How many Igbo read Igbo? How many non-Igbo would (if they could) read Igbo and my Igbo poetry? If my colonial and neo-colonial education and experiences have produced for/in me a curious and complex cultural and linguistic braid, why should I deny a part of my being by excluding from my poetry influences and matters that are both exotic and indigenous?

It is this strong sense of history—of where and what we have been, of where and what we are, and of where and what we aspire to be—as well as a sense of the serious urgency of the situation which compels me to suggest *Nigerian Language* as a linguistic transcendence of that country's cacophony and ethnicism. Only that literature produced in that language accessible to the people, able to speak to the core of their being, and capable of mobilizing them, as one, to social and political stance, if not action, can assume the role of literature in "the political struggle to achieve self-determination and to constitute a new nationality" and in constructing "a cohesive future by laying bare the havoc wrought by 'civilization' and its agents on traditional Africa, and by restoring to the African the dignity of his past" (Aizenberg 1990:85). Only such a literature will be able to represent the nation as such because in such an imaginative recreation it will be possible to transcend divisive ethnic polarities and boundaries. Only when such a language has been massively adopted and continuously recreated and reinvigorated by the writers and elevated to national—and later international—respectability, can we rejoice at the inauguration of what can be truly called Nigerian Literature. Apparently, my persistent reluctance to designate the Literatures that have so far issued from Nigeria "national" is lent support by the acute observations made by Albert Gerard in his essay on the "Historiography of Black Africa" published in the *African Literature Association Bulletin* 19:3 (Summer 1993). About the general situation in Africa Gerard speaks of:

> Three European languages, Arabic and about fifty African languages, and Afrikaans; three scripts; numerous ethnic groups which are rarely coterminous with the frontiers of the modern nation-state; an enormous geographical surface and a confounding cultural diversity. A domain this vast and this heterogeneous (would hardly be amenable to) our tradition of "national" historiography. (26)

The halting phraseology of this excerpt is reflective and metonymic of the truncation—cultural, linguistic, ethnic—of the situation in Nigeria. And Gerard goes on to explain the cacophony:

> Since decolonialization, the Third World . . . has been divid-
> ed into multiethnic and multilingual nations. . . . The nation-
> al literatures of any of these African countries resemble more
> that of the entire European continent than the national liter-
> ature of France, England, or Spain, if only from the point of
> view of linguistic diversity. (26)

My call for *Nigerian Language* is enabled by the fact that that language already exists and only needs creative and artistic fine-tuning, as well as the abandonment by the writers of the residue of colonial mentality which, because it regards everything that is not "Queen's English" as inferior and derivative (Barbag-Stoll 1983:37), has continued to assign that "dialect" to lowly characters in their works. Once that mentality is jettisoned, and the fact recognized that this language, which is already spoken by millions across ethnic, socio-economic, and even "national" boundaries, can be a vibrant and resourceful and respectable medium of literary production, without the authorizing stamp or nod of Western critical approval, then the journey would have begun towards the imagined community and that national identity capable of subsuming and containing "the formidable heterogeneity of ethnic identities" (30). What I am calling for is neither difficult nor far-fetched; it only demands of the writers to descend from their elitist towers and recognize that as long as we continue to refer to our pots and dishes as fragments, outsiders will continue to collect trash with them; it is time for the "respectable" and renowned writers to join ranks with writers of lesser stature and fame who are already doing the necessary foundational work. As Gerard has also seen it:

> One can observe the emergence of a popular literature all
> over black Africa; this literature caters for a local readership,
> and no longer for a European or Europeanized readership; its
> writers use European languages as they are spoken in Africa,
> creolize them without the slightest scruples. They are, thus,

probably developing the future literary languages of Africa. (1993:30)

On her part, Anna Barbag-Stoll (who devotes a book to the study of the social and linguistic history of Nigerian Pidgin English) talks of the "richness, vivacity and the unlimited resources of word-formation mechanisms of this medium" (1983:101); of its ability to transcend linguistic barriers among Nigerians from different language groups (51); and of "its expressive function as a medium of artistic creativity" (101-18).

My call thus remains insistent because what Gerard observes is not a novel phenomenon. Even before his novel *The Voice* (1964) made him both famous and (to some people) notorious for its radical linguistic experimentation, a similar position had been articulated by Gabriel Okara, during that 1962 African Writers' Conference at which Obi Wali also made his controversial presentation, published in the same issue of *Transition* (IV:10 [September 1963]) as Wali's own lecture. In his "African Speech, English Words," Okara discusses his creative craft which I think is relevant to the present argument because the same technique of calquing or loan-translation or transliteration as well as direct/literal translation is operative in Okara's craft and in the so-called Pidgin. My approach, which calls for resourceful eclecticism, thus recognizes the importance of Okara's contribution which he himself elaborates at length:

> As a writer who believes in the utilisation of African ideas, African philosophy and African folklore and imagery to the fullest extent possible, I am of the opinion the only way to use them effectively is to translate them almost literally from the African language native to the writer into whatever European language he is using as his medium of expression. I have endeavoured in my words to keep as close as possible to the vernacular expressions. For, from a word, a group of words, a sentence and even a name in any African language, one can glean the social norms, attitudes and values of a people.
>
> In order to capture the vivid images of African speech I had to eschew the habit of expressing my thoughts first in English. . . . I had to study each Ijaw expression I used and to discover the probable situation in which it was used in order to

bring out the nearest meaning in English. I found it a fascinating exercise.

. . . Take the expression "he is timid" for example. The equivalent in Ijaw is "he has no chest" or "he has no shadow." Now a person without a chest in the physical sense can only mean a human that does not exist. . . . A person who does not cast a shadow of course does not exist. All this means is that a timid person is not fit to live. Here, perhaps, we are hearing the echoes of the battles in those days when the strong and the brave lived. But is this not true of the world today?

In parting with a friend at night a true Ijaw would say, "May we live to see ourselves tomorrow." . . . On the other hand, how could an Ijaw born and bred in England, France or the United States write, "May we live to see ourselves tomorrow" instead of "Goodnight"? And if he wrote "Goodnight," would he be expressing an Ijaw thought?

Why should I not use the poetic and beautiful "May we live to see ourselves tomorrow" or "May it dawn" (Igbo), instead of "Goodnight"?

. . .

What emerges from the examples I have given is that a writer can use the idioms of his own language in a way that is understandable in English. If he uses their English equivalents, he would not be expressing African ideas and thoughts, but English ones.

Some may regard this way of writing in English as a desecration of the language. This is of course not true. Living languages grow like living things, and English is far from a dead language. There are . . . versions of English. All of them add life and vigour to the language while reflecting their own respective cultures. Why shouldn't there be a Nigerian or West African English which we can use to express our own ideas, thinking and philosophy in our own way? (15-16)

I have quoted this passage extensively in order to mark its present cogency, even though the presentation was made by Okara more than thirty years ago. In fact, in a theoretical redressing, Ashcroft, *et al.* have elegantly described the whole process at work:

The crucial function of language as a medium of power demands that post-colonial writing define itself by seizing the language of the centre and re-placing it in a discourse fully adapted to the colonized place. There are two distinct processes by which it does this. The first, the abrogating or denial of the privilege of "English" involves a rejection of the metropolitan power over the means of communication. The second, the appropriation and reconstitution of the language of the centre, the process of capturing and remoulding the language to new usages, marks a separation from the site of colonial privilege.

Abrogation is a refusal of the categories of the imperial culture, its aesthetic, its illusory standard of normative or "correct" usage, and its assumption of a traditional and fixed meaning "inscribed" in the words. . . .

Appropriation is the process by which the language is taken and made to "bear the burden" of one's own cultural experiences . . . to "convey in a language that is not one's own the spirit that is one's own." [The literature produced in such a language through] the simultaneous processes of abrogation and appropriation . . . is therefore always written out of the tension between the abrogation of the received English which speaks from the centre, and the act of appropriation which brings it under the influence of the vernacular tongue. . . . (1989:38-39)

Even though I eschew Ashcroft et al.'s practice of designating the variants of English used in the ex-colonies in the lower case (*english*), I agree with them that the linguistic experimentation executed by Okara in his novel illustrates "the creative potential of intersecting languages when the syntactic and grammatical rules of one language are overlaid on another" (44). It is the same creative potential that I have seen taking root, especially in post-war Nigerian literary productions, which encourages me to sustain the call for *Nigerian Language*. Moreover, the perennity of the ethno-linguistic rivalry and tensions and the very cloud of political uncertainty and confusion hovering over Nigeria, make the need urgent for a transethnic, transvernacular language of national consciousness and solidarity. This language, "the supreme vehicle of culture" (Okafor 1979:12), together with what Fanon calls "a common life, common experiences and memories, common aims" (1965:175), will produce in time a Nigerian literature, and a Nigerian nation. Already, as is evidenced by its, presently unsystematized, prevalence in literary works produced by Nigerians, this language, so metaphorically rich and nuanced, is capable of adequately embodying indigenous Nigerian experience.

CHAPTER IV

OKIGBO: THE MAN AND THE ARTIST

In the poem, "Among School Children," where W. B. Yeats asks,

> O chestnut-tree, great rooted blossomer,
> Are you the leaf, the blossom or the bole?
> O body swayed to music, O brightening glance,
> How can we know the dancer from the dance?
> (Vesterman 1993:429),

the characteristic fusion of the dancer and the dance represents one of the most famous enunciations on the marriage of Art and Life. Understandably, many critics have often tended to collapse the two domains. Without necessarily subscribing to, or discrediting, (auto)biographical criticism, one wishes to say that one ought to be careful to separate the creator/artist from his/her creations. True, a knowledge of aspects of the life of an artist/poet may elucidate for us certain thematic blind spots and explicate certain associative strands. But in end, the writer should be allowed to exist apart from his/her work. The conjunction of the title of this section is, therefore, a matter only of convenience.

In fact, Okigbo made the point very clearly himself during an interview with Robert Serumaga in 1965:

> if tomorrow night for instance, I happen to write a poem, I write a poem; if I don't happen to write a poem, I don't both-

er. I do other things. Poetry is not an alternative to living. It is only one way of supplementing life and if I can live life in its fullness without writing at all, I don't care to write. I haven't got that type of ambition, which some people may have, of becoming a great writer or something like that. Because that is not an alternative to life itself. (Duerden & Pieterse, 1972:147)

Okigbo's life was thus not consumed with poetry, even though he devoted his time and energy assiduously to it, and even though at times his roles as poet, priest, and prophet became indistinguishable. He lived life, all aspects of it, to the fullest. And, even though the poet's and other people's lives provided some of the raw material which, passing through the poet's creative grill, became transmuted into great poetry, to reduce his poetry to a biographical catechism is to be guilty of the worst form of (non)-critical literalism and naivety. This is why an otherwise brilliant and insightful feminist paper on Okibgo's poetry by Elaine Savory Fido is marred by fantastic extrapolations which have no basis in biographical fact:

In his life, *Okigbo had problems in his relations with women.* He tried to save his marriage by making one last trip to visit his wife at Yola, a trip described in his preface to *Labyrinths* as being "in pursuit of what turned out to be an illusion." Yet women or the concept of the feminine in various forms shape the major images in his poetry. People who were close to Okigbo believe that *the poems are all or almost all based on real relations with women.* Yet the emotional tone of the poem is often agonized, as if *faced with the physical and emotional reality of sexual love Okigbo found great pain* and self-doubt tormented him. Ideals and abstractions are, in that case, a good deal easier. Sunday Anozie has written that Okigbo adored his wife and daughter. But *that surely is too simple a statement.* When the poetry is *closely examined,* there seems to be running through all of its emotional texture a *tension between love and fear,* desire to submit to intensities of emotional and physical love and desire to remain separate, adoration of the mother and *terror of the sexual partner.* Also evidenced is a need to restore the ancient mother-ruled images of *traditional religious cults* and so *rid his culture of colonialism*, countered by a need to be an adult male, independent of needs for softness and protection given by a woman. (Davies & Graves, 1986:227; my italics)

I have already quoted more from Fido's essay than I had wished. But it has been necessary in order to show how wrong-headed the criticism can get when it becomes obsessed with scavenging among poetry for clues to fit new-fangled psychosexual paradigms with which the lives of poets must be procrusteanly matched. Clearly, Fido hardly knows what she is talking about, as I will presently attempt to show: Okigbo had no problems that were peculiar to him or unusual, in his relations with women. If he had any, they were the usual "Woman Troubles." As a young, healthy, and strong man, he liked women, beautiful ones, and had a goodly and worshipful number of them. A sturdy man of courage, he cannot, without offense to his memory, be said to have lived in "terror of the sexual partner" (227), or to have experienced "great pain and self-doubt" when confronted "with the physical and emotional reality of sexual love." Evidently, Fido has left the realm of criticism, but her outlandish assertions cannot be sustained. I lived with the poet for the whole of 1966, until September when we both found ourselves in the Eastern Region of Nigeria (Biafra). Yes, Okigbo made a gallant effort to save his marriage with Safinat Attah whom he loved, a fact recorded appropriately by both Anozie (1972) and myself (Okafor 1981). How Fido finds the uxorial love impossible to imagine is inexplicable. In fact, Okigbo, in my presence, had had not a few long-distance, telephone conversations with his wife, and on one of such occasions had asked if I wanted to speak with her: *she was our wife*. And coming back late one afternoon from the Federal Forestry Research Department, Ibadan, where I worked, I saw my uncle visibly excited and happy: Safi had just left after a visit with him, and I had missed seeing her by only a few minutes. As if more proof of Okigbo's devotion to his wife and daughter were needed, he had dedicated the Heinemann selection of his poetry, *Labyrinths with Path of Thunder*, to them:

For
Safinat and Ibrahimat
mother and child.
("Dedication," *Labyrinths* 1971)

But this love of "mother and child" bespeaks nothing of the "tension between love and fear" which Fido detects in the "emotional texture" of Okigbo's poetry which she had apparently "closely examined." It would appear that Professor Anozie, who became close to Okigbo after their first meeting in 1960, and has since then made the study of Okigbo's poetry one of his serious businesses, had not examined that poetry as closely as Fido, hence his statement of fact, that Okigbo adored his wife and daughter, is dismissed as "too simple a statement." Okigbo loved his wife and daughter, and true to the tradition of his people, also respected his wife. Curiously, a remarkable observation on the "Igbo male attitude to women" made in 1939 by Leith-Ross, which marks this "respect for their women" as a trait of the Igbo, has been quoted approvingly by Fido (224). The love and the respect notwithstanding, the Igbo male does not *fear* women or "women's power." And what an Igbo woman showers on her child is *not* "mother-domination" but mother-love, which creates, not "a fear of woman's power and a desire to dominate women in order to be adult and a man," but a respectful desire for a woman/mate who would be like one's able mother. Obviously, Fido is also doing some exo-cultural interpretations here, unmindful of the fact that psycho-social and other theories, though often touted as "universal," do not always apply in "exotic" cultural formations. This explains why Fido refers to Okigbo's "need to restore the ancient mother-ruled images of traditional religious cults and so rid his culture of colonialism" (224). Obviously, the colonized *Other's* relationship with the Supreme Being can only be explained in terms of a cult; it does not qualify in Fido's view for the *civilized* name of religion. And, even though Okigbo's poetry (except the "Early Poems" *Collected Poems* 1986:3-14; hereinafter referred to as *CP*) was written in independent Nigeria, he is said to be attempting to "rid his culture of colonialism" through a recourse to these "cults." Of course, Okigbo, throughout his poetry, is engaged in a political, cultural, and postcolonial crusade, very serious matters for which he validly appropriated his poetic imagery from diverse areas of life and experience, including "women or the concept of the feminine." But that is a different thing from sexualizing his poetry or reading it through an exclusively sexualized and genitalized periscope: what matters in poetry is not where the images come from but what rhetorical or tropical or political functions they are made to perform in that poetry.

It is the same tendency to overtheorize and overgeneralize about art and life, or to confuse art with life, which in the case of Fido has resulted in the imposition of inapplicable psycho-sexual theory on the poetry of Okigbo, in order to make unbelievable biographical extrapolations, which is behind the fantastications that have marked Ali Mazrui's *The Trial of Christopher Okigbo* in which the greatest charge against the poet is that he was forced, and also chose, to be also a man, a citizen, a member of an historical time and place caught, as it was then, in a very tragic impasse. But unlike Fido's misreading, Ali Mazrui's are different in being so pervasively important and influential. According to Peter Nazareth, even though "Ali Mazrui has never been a good stylist . . . yet his writings have made an impact and have led to highly interesting and controversial discussions" (Nazareth 1973:150). Ali Mazrui's charge, therefore, demands an extended response, especially also as that response will obviate the necessity to discuss again certain aspects of the life and art of Okigbo.

To begin with, then, I wish to present an except from Ngugi's tribute to Nelson Mandela, parts of which speak to us as if the piece had been written with Okigbo in mind, [Okigbo] represents:

> The infinite capacity of the human spirit to resist and to conquer [for Okigbo indeed conquered even in/with his death the forces of butchery and inhumanity]. Hurrah for the spirit of resistance! Do we not for the same reason identify in literature with characters like Prometheus? And in history with people like Paul Robeson, Kwame Nkrumah, Ho Chi Minh, Nat Turner, Toussaint L'Overture, Kenyan freedom fighter Dedan Kimathi . . . ?
>
> All these figures are heroic because they reflect more intensely in their individual souls the souls of their communi-

ty. Their uniqueness is the uniqueness of the historical
moment. They make history as history makes them. They are
the torches that blaze out new paths. (1993:147)

Such was the fate of Okigbo, the true poet and fighter for the people, their poet of destiny, their promethean path-finder, and late-
20th-century Renaissance man who articulated his promethean
role in his own poetry thus:

> The mythmaker accompanies us (*The Egret had*
> *come and gone*)
> Okigbo accompanies us the oracle enkindles us
> the Hornbill is there again (*the Hornbill has had a bath*)
> Okigbo accompanies us the rattles enlighten us (CP:96)

It is precisely to this greatness of the poet that the poems in the
anthology published in his memory speak. And, contrary to what
Mazrui, Theroux, and others think about Okigbo, *Don't Let Him
Die* represents a transethnic, transnational, indeed, truly universal lament for the untimely death of the Star of the People, whose
life and poetry exemplified the transcendence of the pettiness and
constrictions of sectionalism and partisanship: the laments and
elegies and eulogies in the anthology come from all the major
nations or cultural sections of Nigeria, as well as from other
African, European, and North American countries. No parochial
poet or man ever received such broad sympathies and such universal celebration. In the "Preface" to that Memorial Anthology,
Chinua Achebe had said among other things:

> Christopher [Okigbo] . . . had friends, admirers, fans, cronies
> of both sexes, from all ages, all social classes, all professions,
> all ethnic groups, in Nigeria and everywhere. . . . The variety
> of tributes assembled here bears witness to the power of his
> personality, his poetry, his life and death. Some of the con-
> tributors were close friends of his; some only knew him slight-
> ly, and others not at all. Some were his fellow countrymen,
> sundered at the time of his death by a horrendous fratricidal
> conflict and today divided still by its memory, repercussions
> and the hypocrisy it engendered. Some are fellow Africans

who may have heard Okigbo declare at Makerere in one of his impish moods that he wrote his poetry only for poets. And some are from faraway West Indies, U.S.A., Canada, and Great Britain. (Achebe & Okafor, eds.,1978: vii-viii)

Yet, parochialism remains the most scathing charge which Mazrui trumps up against Okigbo. Like Paul Theroux whose superiorist Eurocentrism enables him to confuse a nation/country with a village, thus accusing Okigbo of "characteristically . . . fighting for his village" (*CP*:x), Mazrui accuses Okigbo of confusing art and life, mixing politics with poetry, and of taking up arms against inhumanity—on the side of his "tribesmen"! According to Mazrui, the poet is first and foremost not a social or political being and must under no circumstance sacrifice his poetry and art to the phenomenal and existential; Okigbo should not have participated in the war that threatened the very existence of his people, the Biafrans, with total extinction; he should have stayed back in Nigeria and continued in his ivory tower to sing patriotic paeans to Nigeria even when the outrage threatening humanity was proceeding with vigorous and unrelenting intensity and savagery, and even though he himself had barely escaped with his life from Lagos, and could not return to his house and work in Ibadan, where I was waiting anxiously for him; because Okigbo valued the life of a people over and above sheer aestheticism, his death in defense of that people's right to life was, to Mazrui, an unforgivable loss. But as one most knowledgeable and wise man of letters sees it:

> Thus in a curious novel entitled *The Trial of Christopher Okigbo* Ali Mazrui has a poet tried in the hereafter for throwing away his life on the battlefield like any common tribesman. There is no condemnation of war as such, only of poets getting involved—for "some lives are more sacred than others." In the words of one of the novel's leading characters (an African Perry Mason clearly admired by Mazrui):
> ' a great artist was first of all an individualist, secondly a universalist, and only thirdly a social collectivist.'

> Since these roles and attributes are not known instinctively by the artist in question(otherwise how would Okigbo not know

what was legitimate activity for him?) it stands to reason that he requires some one like Mazrui to tell him (a) the precise moment when he crosses the threshold of mere artist and becomes a great artist and (b) how to juggle with his three marbles of individualism, universalism and social collectivism. (Achebe 1975:53-54)

My first shock at reading Mazrui's *Trial* was the discovery that this neo-New Critical insistence on the radical separation of the political from the aesthetic domain was being articulated by a world-renowned political scientist. How can that suture be achieved, even conceived of, when we all know that the political is the over-determining factor in the very existence of humankind? This escapist insistence on the sanitization of art by critics accounts for what I call their (and some artists') gross social irresponsibility. For in their ostrich-like gambit they hope that by hiding our critical heads in the sand the political problems which beset us will van-ish. Whether we are talking of the battle we wage against inhu-manity and injustice in the guise of racism, imperialism, colonialism, neocolonialism, external or internal domination and repression, foreign or local exploitation and oppression, art/liter-ature remains an indispensable armament and arsenal in that live-die confrontation. The experience of reading *The Trial* was doubly shocking because its erudite author comes from a country in East Africa which has not fully escaped from the clutches of those forces in opposition to which Okigbo gave his life.

The Trial of Christopher Okigbo opens with an enthusias-tic endorsement of the ethos propounded by Miss Bemidi "that politics ought not to be allowed to interfere with aesthetic evalu-ations" (12). She had "argued that political considerations had a host of subtle ways of entering the aesthetic domain . . . which should otherwise remain basically non-political" (12). Since, apart from the name of the nondescript locale, After-Africa remains indistinguishable from Here-and-Now (or Herebefore); since the same orgiastic excesses, concupiscence, and travesty of justice characterize the two places; and since *The Trial*, marred as it is by the unconvincing shuffling of chronology, does not pretend to fictionality, I do not intend to distinguish between Mazrui and his creatures/personae, Bemidi, and Hamishi: they are only three manifestations or voices of a discursive trinity.

Allied to the insistence on the separation of the political from the aesthetic is the penchant for transparent clarity and lucidity of meaning, the absence of which in his poetry constitutes another charge against Okigbo. I intend to address together the two charges: that of the (de-)politicization of art and that of obscurity in poetry.

In the post-interview rendezvous or tryst at his apartment with Miss Bemidi, Hamishi upholds and recommends the obscurity of a Swahili poet, Ali Rajabu, as "evidence of profundity" while denigrating the same quality in Okigbo's "abstract verse." He goes on:

> Of course there is obscurity in these (Rajabu's) lines, but it is a different kind of obscurity from that which we find in Okigbo. Rajabu here is indeed revelling in sophisticated verbal obscurity. Enigmatic expressions, if properly handled, can be evidence of profundity.
>
> In the case of obscure passages from Rajabu, however, there was such a thing as "the *right* meaning" of a given line, and the task of the sophisticated reader was to discover that meaning. It was possible for a reader to be *wrong* about Rajabu. "However, . . . the obscurity of abstract verse of Okigbo's variety is calculated to leave too much to the reader's imagination!" Hamishi picked up a magazine and quoted from Okigbo:

> the only way to go
> through the marble archway
> to the catatonic pingpong
> of the evanescent halo . . .
> "Can there ever be a 'right meaning' to such a passage?"
> (17-18)

Apart from the imputation here of intellectual slothfulness which refuses to make the effort to understand, or to appreciate the "startling new ripples of significance" (*Don't Let Him Die*:ix) of Okigbo's poetry, or to imaginatively apprehend the enthralling mind-picture created by it, the problem with Mazrui's extended sophistry is not that one form of obscurity is inexplicably preferred over another. The problem is the romantic illusion that meaning is something that the poet/writer mystically manufactures and puts there in his/her work, which it is then the happy duty of the sophisticated and diligent reader/interpreter to locate and extract. In this anachronistic adherence to the objective autotelianism of New Criticism, Mazrui fails to consider the possibility of "meaning" or significance being the result of a tripartite "combat" or engagement or transaction between the writer, the text, and the reader (with all his/her baggages, presumptions, pre-suppositions, predilections, and phobias, as well as the over-determinations of text and contexts).

Yet, we do know now that the writer may indeed hold less proprietary rights over "meaning" than the reader or the text itself. In fact, as Roland Barthes puts it, a "text is not a line of words releasing a single 'theological' meaning (the 'message' of the Author-God) but a multidimensional space in which a variety of writings, none of them original, blend and clash. The text is a tissue of quotations drawn from the innumerable centers of culture" (Richter, 1994:224). But Mazrui's position is that which, in New Critical fashion, endows a work with an objective status which in turn determines "its intelligibility and worth." And his "sophisticated reader" is a textual construct, actually the mock-reader who, in the words of Jane Tompkins,

> assumes the value and uniqueness of the literary work of art; it assumes that literary meaning is contained in the words on the page; and it assumes that special training in the critical process is necessary if the student of literature is to grasp the full extent of what the work has to offer. This "concept of the reader . . . is introduced as a way of unlocking further treasures in the text"; of discovering what is already there on the page. (1980:x)

But inasmuch as Mazrui would wish it, that is not the case, cannot be the case in the actual experience of reading. According to Wolfgang Iser, the reader is an active participant in the production of meaning; he is not merely an excavator:

> The literary work is actualized only through a convergence of reader and text, [which means] that the reader must act as co-creator of the work by supplying that portion of it which is not written but only implied. The "concretization" of a text in any particular instance requires that the reader's imagination come into play. Each reader fills in the unwritten portion of the text, its "gaps" or areas of "indeterminacy," in his own way. (xv)

But this undoing of the *aporia* is not "a mere subjective fabrication of the reader's. The range of interpretations that arise as a result of the reader's creative activity" (xv) is evidence rather of the text's "inexhaustibility." Until this creative productivity of the reader is brought to bear on the text, it remains a virtuality. It is the interplay of the text and the reader which thus engenders the literary work. In other words, unlike Mazrui, Iser emphasizes the interactional dimension of meaning-making which is over-determined by the concept of the *gap*. The reader's creative labor consists in filling this gap, in articulating the silence, the non-said, the unwritten part of the text. This activity is almost unlimited for, because the gap "may be filled in different ways," and because "one text is potentially capable of different realisations," the text is inexhaustible (55). This activity, involving a repetitive series of anticipation, retrospection, modification, and advance retrospection, is still, however, circumscribed by the intentions of the text, which endows it with real dynamism, at the same time as it is productive of textual transformation, and the generation of a whole new experience for the reader.

Even though Wolfgang Iser's insights completely demolish Ali Mazrui's Neo—New Critical emphasis on text-bound meaning; even though they facilitate the appreciation of the rich multivalence of the literary work through the foregrounding of the ramifications of intertextuality; and even though they activate the reader, one still needs to go beyond the constraints evident in Iser's position.

In the first place, even though the work remains a potentiality, unrealized without the active and creative participation and input of the reader, in Iser's scheme the author/text is still privileged, still determinant (51). This is because whatever productive role the reader plays, his activity is still circumscribed by what is already explicitly or implicitly in the text. "The reader's activity is only a fulfillment of what is already implicit in the structure of the work" (xv). This concretization is thus only one step away from the fetishization of the text. Moreover, Iser does not make clear how this structure limits the activity of the reader who, alas, in the end enjoys only a simulacrum of parity with, or independence from, the author. In the sense that the work exists in concrete autotely as a repository of meaning which is exfoliated through the reader's "co-authoring" activity, Iser's view is almost essentialistic and empiricist, and accords with his abiding faith in the canon of good/great works. According to Iser, these great/good works valorize indeterminacy and problematize the reader's horizon of expectations, while the bad ones do not engage the reader and are, therefore, not worthy of a place in the canon.

The other problem with Iser's essay is its lack of consideration for the Literary Mode of Production (LMP), generally, nor for the political, specifically. This ideological deficiency which would have delighted Ali Mazrui has, however, been made good in Iser's other project, *The Act of Reading* (1978) which enunciates a political dimension, not unlike literature's function for Althusser, that is, to foreground the contradictions of ideology (Smith 1984).

I have been taken this afar by Mazrui's denial of "meaning" to Okigbo's poetry, not because Okigbo's poetry is devoid of elegant imponderabilities, but because Ali Mazrui's charge has continued to resonate unabated in Okigbo scholarship, serving often as a cloak for intellectual laziness on the part of critics who would not exert the required effort to penetrate the "keyhole chamber" of Okigbo's poetry. In fact, Chinua Achebe, who knows first-hand both the poet and his poetry, as well as the milieu in which he himself lives and has his being, has definitively dismissed this charge of obscurity which, to my mind, is a result of intellectual perfunctoriness on the part of readers/critics. Achebe has said that:

> Critics have often charged [Okigbo] with obscurity. "Occasional inaccessibility" would be a more accurate phrase, for even at his most arcane moments there is never a blocking of vision in his poetry as there often is in some of those of his contemporaries. He always remains as visually clear as

fine crystal glass. . . the "obscurity" in his poetry comes from his "straining among the echoes" to catch his own authentic voice.

There is nothing in Nigerian poetry and little in any poetry I know to surpass the haunting beauty, the mystic resonance and clarity of the final movements of the protagonist's quest in "Distances." And the reader who cares to look will see in all its details the spiritual landscape in which the prodigal, weary of travel, is called at last by the goddess into her cavern. The geometric shapes of his final passageway and the strange phosphorescent inscriptions they bear are all luminously and unforgettably portrayed. (1978:ix)

Only engaged and assiduous scholarship can appreciate that unforgettable luminosity and clarity. But many critics, convinced, *a priori*, of the "obscurity" of Okigbo's poetry, will not make the required effort. Consequently, their criticism has stripped that poetry of much of its social-political relevance and significance, whereas Okigbo's poetic itinerary is a consistent, tortured, and tortuous effort at communication, from the "opacity" of the earlier poems to the final celebratory lucidity, clarity, and directness, exemplified in *Path of Thunder*, which thus represents the climacteric summation of the poetic-prophetic-political-rhetorical trajectory of Okigbo.

Because Political Criticism not only explains, but also valorizes, the place of the political in art, thus providing a more meaningful alternative to Mazrui's New Critical insistence on transparent meaning and the evacuation from the aesthetic domain of the political, I wish to comment briefly on the basic lesson in "Political Criticism" taught us by Terry Eagleton in his *Literary Theory: An Introduction* (Ryan 1989: 200-13).

Eagleton begins with the assumption that because literary criticism, as present practice, has lost its anchorage in socio-cultural relevance and outlived its usefulness, it should be replaced by a resuscitated rhetorical/cultural alternative. This option has the advantage not only of reinscribing literary practice within the larger socio-cultural-political formation, but also (while disposing of anachronistic critical-practices, like Mazrui's) that of distilling and utilizing positive strategies from a plurality of theoretical-critical positions.

111

The proposal is thus clearly not an escape from theory, for it recognizes that no critical position is ever a-theoretical. If anything, it is a strategic syncretism of several theoretical positions which, unlike many of them, acknowledges the indispensability of theory in discourse, and is unashamed in its valorization of socio-political *praxis* and commitment. It asserts that all theories and critical practices, like literary practice itself, are political and interested. It quarrels with other "schools," not because they are political, but because they have been complicit in and instrumental to the perpetuation of the ideological *status-quo*, instead of being agencies of radical social/political transformation. Eagleton illustrates this complicity by reference to "the rise of English" when literature and criticism, in the atmosphere of jingoistic nationalism of the Great War period, ousted the German-centered philological studies and assumed the role of ideological handmaiden of the reactionary and suppressive ruling architects of British imperialism (Eagleton 1983:28-30).

Even the emergence of that most influential man of letters, F. R. Leavis, who "saw the need to address social and political questions" did not change matters, as such, because his journal, *Scrutiny*, which embarked upon a stupendous "moral and cultural crusade" did not have on its agenda the actual radical transformation of society, its belief in the high liberal-humanist meliorist view of literature notwithstanding (33). On the other hand, Leavisian close reading and practical criticism was later to bear fruit in the reification and fetishization of the poem under New Criticism. The New Critic tore the poem both from the intentions of its author and from the social context and was thus able to scrutinize it and comment upon it with "objective disinterest." He was clearly immunized against political commitment, like William Empson whose "Seven Types of Ambiguity" enabled him to maintain an ambiguous and, therefore, uncommitted and safe relationship with the object of his study (48-53). Eagleton further criticizes Saussure whose epoch-making linguistic enterprise he saw as having led to the synchronic studies of literature as lifeless structures dissociable from the social formation, and to the asocial hedonism of Roland Barthes, whose free-floating and free-playing signifiers are unanchored in the social. But while he condemns Deconstruction as a "return of the Old New Critical formalism" (146), Eagleton extols Derrida because he "does" things, assumes a political stance, and thus fulfills a socio-political function as critic. Literature, like its criticism, is part of the social-political context with which, unarguably, it must be engaged (215).

To conclude my attempted repudiation of the unsustainable insistence by Mazrui on the separation of politics from poetry and art (*The Trial*: 12), and of his preoccupation with "right meaning" (18), I wish to excerpt an empowering recent statement by Jay Parini which I consider a brilliant diagnosis of the Neo-New Criticism which Mazrui practices:

> The problem with New Criticism was its pretence to being a-political. As Lionell Trilling wrote in *Beyond Culture* in 1968, "We all want politics not to exist." The supposed purpose of high art was to go beyond politics, to rise above the taint of ideology, to loft us thither into the ozone layer of aesthetic bliss, a place where all ironies, and paradoxical notions of a given test are, at last, harmonized. This approach to literature led to what the critic Mikhail Bakhtin referred to as early as 1926 as "the fetishization" of the text, referring to the tendency to idealize a work of art and desire to remove it from any social context. This attitude was common-place among the New Critics and has lingered in neoconservative circles. (The critic Joseph Epstein, for instance, complained in a recent issue of *The New Criterion* that "the intrusion of politics with culture" is "one of the major motifs" of the last 25 years. (*The Chronicle of Higher Education* [Sept. 9, 1992]:B1)

But Mazrui's anger is not merely with "the intrusion of politics into culture." Okigbo's "high charge" (*The Trial*: 24) is that, having been forced out of Nigeria and his people threatened with extinction, he participated in the war of survival and self-defense. As poet and universalist he should not have embroiled himself, with his people, in the messy and mundane matter of life and death and, in the process, compromising both his art and his life, and "betraying pan-Africanism" (40-41). In the Hereafter of Mazrui's creation, art comes before society (!), thus Okigbo's case concerns the distortion of values. He is to be charged with the offense of "putting society before art in his scale of values" (41). The absurdity of the charge can hardly be over-emphasized for it has been repeatedly maintained that in Africa art has always been at the service of society. Okigbo's poetry was written in service to society; but he went further and put his own life at the service of his smaller, threatened society. But as Mazrui sees it:

> Okigbo gave his life for the concept of Biafra. As it happens that was a mortal concept, transient to his inner being. The art of a great poet, on the other hand, carries the seeds of immortality. No great artist has a right to carry patriotism to the extent of destroying his creative potential. The prosecution is going to suggest that Okigbo had no right to consider himself an Ibo patriot first, and an African artist only second. That was to subordinate the interests of generations of Africans to the need of a collection of Ibos (sic) at an isolated moment in historical time. (41)

Okigbo gave his life not for an abstract concept of Biafra, but for a *de jure* and *de facto* polity whose inhabitants, including Okigbo, were faced with holocaust and "an orgy of genocide," as Albert Hunt saw that war (James Gibbs, 1980:113). Okigbo gave his life in defense of life and of humanity. And if Nigeria at that "moment in historical time" represented death, the negation of life, and the refusal of humanity, Okigbo died for Biafranism which, at that "moment in historical time," stood for the refusal of death and the affirmation of life. Okigbo's was no parochial patriotism, for he would have ascended the cross as easily and as readily had it been any other group or nation of human beings that was faced with extinction: Okigbo's ultimate loyalty was not to ethnicity but to humanity. And it is so insensitive, almost eerily inhuman, for Mazrui to suggest that what was at stake in Nigeria-Biafra was "the need of a collection of Ibos." The Igbo happen to number at least 12 million human souls, and Biafra had a population of about 14 million (cf. Arthur Nwankwo 1972:30), a lot more than several countries, including some East African ones. But, as the Igbo would say, a corpse (i.e., the loss of about 1 million Biafran lives) always looks like a log of wood to a stranger.

It is the same kind of inhuman callousness and insensitivity which strangers like Mazrui exhibit in the face of human calamity that enabled the civilized world to go to sleep and into stupor while millions of Jews were being exterminated in Europe about the end of the first half of this century. It has also made possible the spinelessness, inaction, and empty threats of the *civilized* world in the face of the outrage that has been unfolding in Bosnia-Herzegovina today. Yes, it is the same callous insensitivity which explains the (in)human calculus engaged in by the emissaries of the *civilized* world who converged in Lagos, Nigeria, during the genocidal "Nigerian Civil" war to argue whether the Black counterparts of the Jews— the Jews of Africa/Nigeria, the Igbo—had any right to self-determination; whether the exercise of such a right would jeopardize the sovereign integrity of friendly and *peace-loving* Nigeria; whether it was true that not one million but a mere thirty thousand of them had actually been butchered; whether the sea-land-air blockade was having its anticipated effects on Biafra as rumored; whether Biafran children were truly dying from malnutrition and *kwashiorkor*; whether Biafra could sustain its resistance to the Western-aided Federal Forces; and whether the lucrative viability and security of the vast (Nigerian)markets for the West would be helped or hindered by the prolongation of the war. Such obscene preoccupations are the object of Okafor's ridicule in the poem "Human Calculus":

In the city hall at the center
around the round teakwood table
the factuous world converged
to prove Pythagoras wrong:
how many men might fall
from one stray bullet;
how many houses shatter
from the shell's blast?
The files were handed around
the photographs were scrutinized;
these are wonderful picture,
this is romantic through and through,
consider the marvelous chiaroscuro
of carcasses strewn in green jungle.

They sipped the good spirit
and pulled at their pipes;
they coughed politely
and grinned carefully;
and continuing:
can a headless trunk
join the living
fleeing from the raid of eagles?
did the frenzy claim thirty thousands
or a hundred million?
at the present allowed rate
and the air-tight blockade
can this lunacy outlast this century?
.... Gentlemen I move for adjournment ....
(Okafor 1981:23)

But equally obscene is the whole juridical system in After-Africa,
as well as the judicial process under which Okigbo is to be tried.
The whole set up, even by mundane Here-and-Now standards, is
anomalous and scandalous; it is as if the accused had already been
found guilty even before the trials began. The defense counsel,
called Counsel for Salvation, appointed by the After-Africa
Juridical system, in his amazement protests:

> I? I defend Chris Okigbo? But I hardly know the man! I do not
> understand the charges in spite of what you have said. I do
> not understand the system of trial and defence. I haven't a
> clue what it is all about. Elected to defend Okigbo? By whom?
> (The Trial:44)

It might be argued that one is making overly much of what takes
place within the "autotelic" heterotopia of a "novel." But this is
hardly a novel, nor has it been read as such, in spite of its strategic stylization and thematic fantastication. Thus, one is looking at
the trial (and *The Trial*) as a case of "momentous implications"
(42) in which the author, Mazrui, has evidently taken History quite
seriously. For, like many misguided outsiders and observers of the
Nigerian scene, he has conveniently made interpretations and

unsubstantiated generalizations. Thus when he makes Alobi debate upon the political-economic history of Nigeria, in order to enlighten the newly-appointed Counsel for Salvation, he does so only in order to rationalize the common-place castigation and derogation of the Igbo who, apart from Nnamdi Azikiwe (Zik of Africa), had never run for the highest political office; who, apart from General Ironsi who inherited, for six months, a coup that he did not plan, had never been President, or Prime Minister, or Commander-in-Chief, or Dictator of that *great* country. But Alobi, the knowledgeable persona of Mazrui, in analyzing the "Igbo Question," speaks of "the verve and ambition of the Ibo [sic], the initial commitment to Pan-Nigerianism combined with the ambition to lead the rest of the population behind energetic Ibo [sic] initiative" (53).

Mazrui goes on to delineate brilliantly the distinction between Individualism, Collectivism, and Universalism (67ff.) upon which Chinua Achebe's commentary has already been invoked, and is right in marking in Okigbo the felicitous wedlock of individualism and universalism. But he misses the whole point when he asserts that the wedlock floundered at "the explosion of Ibo separatism" and thus charges Okigbo with "narrow sectionalism" (69). One cannot over-emphasize the fact that there never was a movement for "Igbo Separatism" in Nigeria. They *were pushed out*, for the duration of Biafra, from the Federation, and the declaration of independent Biafra was, thus, *not* a momentous conclusion of calculated Igbo separatism.

Okigbo saw himself as both man and poet. But his individualism did not lead him to egomaniacal compromises on principles. Thus, as Mazrui factually reports, he rejected the First Prize for Poetry at the Dakar, Senegal, Festival of Negro Art. But that was because he sincerely believed that to accept it was to subscribe to the prevalent Western ethnographization of African Art. He was convinced that the uncritical epithet "African" or "Negro" was used only to inferiorize and pejorate poetry or Art produced in Africa. He believed that art/literature should be evaluated by critical criteria which had nothing to do with geography or skin color.

But the move from an endorsement of Okigbo's universalism to a charge of base tribalism can only be explained in terms of "logical sophistry." In a finely crafted and thunderously delivered argument, the Counsel for Damnation (Prosecution), Apolo-Gyamfi, says, *inter alia*:

> When he refused the prize which fellow black people were awarding him, sharing in the pride of achievement, he was refusing to mix art with nationalism. However, this same young man who had proclaimed the universality of what is valuable, later put on a uniform, helped himself to a gun, and engaged in a fratricidal war. At the Festival of Negro Art in Dakar Okigbo had refused to dilute art with the milk of nationalism. On the desolate battlefields of Biafra he was to dilute art with the blood of tribalism. (70)

To say this about Okigbo is to expose one's ignorance of, deprecate the achievement of, and insult the memory of Africa's greatest poet. Okigbo was not a "tribalist," and until his death one of his greatest friends was the Nobel Laureate Wole Soyinka, a Yoruba, with whom he had contacts even in Biafra when it was still possible to do so; in the thick of the crisis he even found time and emotional disposition to call Ibadan from Enugu and ask about affairs at the Mbari Cultural Establishment, of which he was Secretary, and about his young friends Femi Osofisan and Kole Omotoso, both Yoruba. Above all, it must be repeated that his wife, Safinat Attah, is from the Royal House of Igalla, Northern Nigeria. Even though Okigbo understood that the genocide was perpetuated by "them" against "us," his assumption of the role of Company Commander was in response to the outrage against humanity; he was not going to war to kill people merely because they were Hausa or Yoruba. Moreover, like all Biafrans who believed that without Biafra the fate of the Igbo was sealed in Nigeria, Okigbo once told Chinua Achebe, in my presence, at their new Citadel Publishing House in Enugu, that "without Biafra, there can be no Citadel." This sad prophecy came too quickly to pass. But that was not his only prophecy for, as we shall soon see, the bulk of his prophecy, encapsulated in *Labyrinths With Path of Thunder*, is even now being meticulously played out in the orgiastic dance of repetition in Nigeria.

And for a highly learned African to refer to the Nigerian-Biafra war as "tribal warfare" (The Trial:71) is to confess that one is drowning (not swimming!) in the ideological and discursive rapids of the West. It is to be utterly ignorant of the movements of history and of the intersection of imperialism with "local" Third-World Politics and events. For Biafra was neither a tribe nor a village but a metaphor for a people's resistance to last-ditch attempt by Imperialism to maintain a strangle-hold on the economic-political throat of Black Africa. In the words of Chief Arthur Nwankwo:

> Biafra presented an irresistible opportunity to establish a modern African State bereft of all the traditional ills that plague most African countries. Biafra soon viewed itself as an opportunity to revolutionize the Black African from his stupor of psychological bondage and his psychological feeling of inferiority. It viewed itself as a potentially powerful African country with the best chance of political and psychological independence. It viewed itself as the best vehicle for shattering the myth of racism: the first black nation to be taken seriously in a world dominated by white people....Biafra viewed its own struggle as part of an international struggle by the black man to reclaim his confused soul from the cultural depredations of imperialism. (1972:109-110)

The victims, as always, were "natives" and the majority of the butchery was committed by indigenous manpower. But the lethal arsenal and technology as well as top-secret personnel were supplied by the West, to which most of the booty continues to return. But while Mazrui apparently senses the need to break this imperial strangle-hold (hence his endorsement of the collapse of the empire), he does not see the logical inevitability of fragmentation of the artificial geographical blocs created by Empire and for Empire's good: "But just because we permitted an empire to break up is not an adequate reason for permitting our respective countries to follow suit. Imperial disintegration is a good thing. Let us not permit it to become less good by allowing it to lead on to national disintegration. (*The Trial*:118)

National disintegration, of course, like any other kind of disintegration, is painful, but, as with other unions, may be preferred to a continued relationship that is fraught with potentially fatal abuse. And Okigbo, like most Biafrans, did not subscribe to disintegration *as such*. His involvement in Biafra and the war was a response to the imperative call to fight for guaranteed security of life of the people. In fact, Mazrui deviates into correctness here when he compares Okigbo with Lord Byron:—"Both Byron and Okigbo were poets who had died in their mid-thirties fighting for a people's freedom" (111)—and when he observes that "until 1966 Okigbo's own disenchantment with events in Nigeria was the disenchantment of a Nigerian rather than an Ibo" [sic] (125).

But then, in a passage that is reminiscent of the Andersonian concept of Nation, Mazrui describes the nation-in-the-making as "a potential work of art" in the sense of its being imagined, and accuses Okigbo of allowing himself to be "distracted from the image" (143). The trouble with this attribution of guilt is that it fails not to assign the agency of, but to locate the responsibility for imagining at the appropriate site: the image of Nigeria was an imperialist dream which the Nigerians themselves have failed to assume either because they have not taken the image/idea seriously enough, or because they have been prevented from doing so by "the Curse of the Trinity" (139):

> Yes, indeed, Nigeria came into being. Islam, Euro-Christianity, and indigenous tradition struggled to forge a new personality in a single nation. Nigeria was Africa in embryo. But super-imposed over this eternal tripartite tension was the mundane accident of three regions in a Federal Nigeria, each dominated by one of the three major tribes. The Curse of Trinity was chasing Africa to the very embryo of its Nigerian manifestation. (139)

It is thus not fair to charge Okigbo with the "crime" of "complicit distraction from the image" because, in all of his extant poetry, as we shall see later, what we have is a constant and consistent lament for primordial injustice and divisiveness which always activate and exacerbate "our dissonant airs" (CP:99), careless that:

> the secret thing in its heaving
> Threatens with iron mask
> The last lighted torch of the century. . . . (93)

Okigbo did not relent in his appeal to the unifying conscience of Nigeria, and when he had lived the oracle dry he had no choice but to paw the air howling his good-bye to the numinous and unattainable idea/image which he had loved so much. In the end, *The Trial of Christopher Okigbo* is a marred piece of work, for the verdict "not proven" (142), in the case of Okigbo, cannot be justified or sustained, especially as we have just been told that "ambiguity" is considered a crime or sin by the Elders of After-Africa (130), and yet that "in that very ambiguity [by his sentence] lies Okigbo's punishment" (144). Regarding the verdict "Not Proven" passed on Biafra itself, that too cannot be justified by the neo-colonial logic that it was better to prevent, *at all costs*, further fragmentation of African countries that might choose to go the way of a victorious Biafra, or by the more callous fact that more people got killed in the war than could ever have been slaughtered in "three decades of rioting in the North" (144).

Okigbo was one of those very many people killed in the war, thus bringing to an abrupt end a very short though completely fulfilling and fulfilled life. His description of the Watermaid could very well have been written by the poet about himself: "So brief [his] presence—/match-flare in wind's breath—/so brief. . . ." How could one have known? But in retrospect these lines resonate with the same prophetic ring that defines much of his poetry. In that connection, I recall Okigbo's visit from the war front to his brother Dr. Pius Okigbo's house in Enugu. He kept himself busy reading my most recent poems while I hurriedly prepared a meal of pounded yam and *Egusi* soup for him. After he had finished the meal and commented that the pounded yam was hard like stone (because in my haste I had failed to pound it to the right softness and "texture" by adding enough water), he said that he didn't care much for my "To Her That Won't Understand," but that he would help squeeze out the water from "Path of Freedom" (which echoes the title of his poem *Path of Thunder*) when he came back from the war. As if stung by a recognized mistake, he quickly corrected himself, saying: "*If* I come back from the war." He never came back, and the next thing we heard was the announcement of the death of Major Christopher Okigbo.

Nigerians rejoiced at this death, the credit for which was taken by the Federal troops. But *they did not kill Okigbo*. A reincarnation of his maternal grandfather (whose death had occurred in a similar circumstance and had been surrounded by the same mysteries, including that of the presence of a gun-shot wound in the neck) Okigbo could not—would not—have allowed the Federal troops to capture either himself or the strategic Opi Junction. What happened was that a Nigerian attack was being expected from the Northern sector and everyone was agitated including Okigbo, who refused to be sedated by his military doctors and threatened to shoot them if they did anything that would stop him from waking up before 5 o'clock the following morning, when he had planned a preemptive strike on the Federal forces. Knowing that Okigbo was a man of his word, these doctors chose their lives. But as part of the grand scheme to sabotage and bring down Biafra and force it back into the Federal fold, Major Okon, the commander of the 16th Battalion (whose duty it was to provide Okigbo and his Company with covering fire while they carried forays deep into enemy positions) had—apparently on orders from Army Headquarters (which later turned out to have been faked)—unaccountably withdrawn his troops, thus exposing Okigbo and his men to the enemy. Suspecting sabotage as well as the futility of his Company's entrenchment at the Opi Sector, Okigbo ordered his men to pull out, vowing to remain himself and to lose Opi Junction to the Federal troops only over his dead body. Okigbo could have escaped alive had he chosen to, but this treacherous withdrawal of the 16th Battalion on the "orders" of Headquarters overwhelmed him and he stood his ground. In fact, his twelve-year-old bodyguard who had refused to leave the side of his Commander, finally doing so only on the military orders of Okigbo, came back in one piece and told the most accurate and up-to-date story of Okigbo's last hours. Since Okigbo could not single-handedly have defended Opi Junction, he shot himself in the neck, and the Federal troops marched through (took) the junction announcing both the capture of the junction/sector and the killing of Major Okigbo.

Inside Biafra itself, an immediate high-powered investigation into the withdrawal of the troops of the 16th Battalion and, consequently of Okigbo's death, revealed a masterful *coup* which would have meant the immediate capitulation of Biafra, but which still resulted in the disorganized withdrawal of Biafran troops from the Republic of Benin (R.O.B.; [Midwestern Nigeria had been liberated by Biafran forces and declared an Independent Republic]), and the virtually unchecked advances, thereafter, of the Federal forces in other sectors. This was the beginning of the end of Biafra. The leaders of this coup, Ifeajuna, Alale, Agbai, and the one Yoruba commander in Biafra, Banjo, were rounded up and executed as Enugu, the Biafran capital, fell to Federal forces.

Regarding the exact place where Okigbo died, I believe that the controversy (Nwoga, 1984; J. P. Clark 1972) over mere cartography and location is unnecessary. Whether the soul departed from the body at Ekwegbe or at Opi Junction, my designation of the spot as Opi Junction assumes only a metaphoric or symbolic significance which honors the last recorded words of Okigbo, that "the Nigerians would cross [the Opi Junction] only over his dead body" (Nwoga 1984:14; Okafor 1981:24-30). The symbolism of the junction bespeaks Okigbo's resolve to defend his land and his people with his life; moreover, Opi Junction is a liminal metaphor for the junction/connection and disjunction/disconnection between Northern and Eastern Nigeria.

As already discussed, in Chapter I, this disjunction occurred not just between Eastern and Northern Nigeria, but among all the cultural sections of the country, accounting for the sharp cleavages which to this day have exerted strong centrifugal forces on the Nigerian polity. It was in that society that Okigbo was born in 1932 into a well-to-do but modest Roman Catholic family of Chief James I. Eze-Onyeligoluoda Okigbo, a school teacher and Headmaster, famous all over Awka, Onitsha, and Asaba Provinces in the present Anambra, Enugu, Imo, and Anioma States of Nigeria. The poet's mother, Anna Onugwaluobi, died when the poet was still very young, and though he was well cared for by his elder sisters and, later, by his step-mother who still lives in Ojoto, Okigbo remained ever hungry for love and friendship. But of greatest importance was the influence on him of Okigbo's surrogate mother (technically called Baby Sitter or Nanny), Eunice, whose good nature won her the poet's and everyone else's affection, and her integration into the Okigbo family was so total that to everyone she was/is "Auntie."

A very enterprising woman, who was later to engage in a full-
time trading business which kept her constantly on the road between
Elele (Port Harcourt) and Ojoto and environs, her lyrical disposition
must have made deep and lasting impressions on young
Christopher Okigbo, who later was to immortalize her in these lines:

Eunice at the passageway,
Singing the moon to sleep over the hills
Eunice at the passageway .... (CP 48)

It is possible that her lyrics quite early aroused Okigbo's own lyrical impulse.

Possessed of great mental and physical energies, Okigbo gave
his parents not a little bother. Vivacious restlessness was to continue
and to characterize the Okigbo that later became known to the
world. In a non-Christian family, such a child as Christopher would
have been branded *Ogbanje* and made to undergo all the rituals of
separation or severance from the spirit folk. But his was/is a
Roman Catholic family. Yet Okigbo continued to exhibit signs of
behavior that usually define an *Ogbanje*, such as an intense love
of solitude, a visionary inclination, a prophetic bent, extreme
idiosyncrasy, mystery, and other inexplicabilities. In fact, it is not a
simple coincidence that a contemporary and friendly associate of
mine at the University of Nigeria, himself a poet and painter:

Kevin Echeruo who died even younger and soon after Okigbo
. . . celebrated him as *Ogbanje*, one of those mysterious, elusive and often highly talented beings who hurry to leave the
world and to come again, or that Pol Ndu who died in a road
disaster, every gory detail of which he had predicted in a poem
five years earlier, should call Okigbo a seer. (Achebe 1978:v)

Dr. Catherine Obianuju Acholonu, another admirer of Okigbo and
serious scholar of his poetry, has devoted a full-length article to this
psychic aspect of Okigbo. Entitled "*Ogbanje*: A Motif and a
Theme in the Poetry of Christopher Okigbo," this authoritative
and informed piece begins with an assertion that:

In the poetry of Christopher Okigbo, myth and ritual are not
merely conscious exercise in symbolism invented by the poet

for rhetorical purposes, rather they are a spontaneous expression of the poet's existence; his belief in the reality of his object and his identification with karmic laws that guide nature. . . .

One such archetypal motif [à la Jung] is *ogbanje*. . . . A child is frequently referred to as *ogbanje* when his behaviour is ambiguous, when he is difficult to deal with and above all when there are indications of a dual personality. Christopher Okigbo, in his life time, was purported to have made references to the English word "changeling" as an equivalent of the Igbo word *ogbanje*.

Okigbo's life-style was a classical example of what the Igbo people refer to as *ogbanje*. (Acholonu 1988:103)

The same author, in an interview with Bob Njemanze, a close friend of Christopher Okigbo from 1965 until the poet's death in 1967, explores further the possibility that Okigbo might well have been an *ogbanje*. In Njemanze's own words,

I learnt the word "changeling" from Chris Okigbo.... Changeling is an English word that denotes a child (a fairy child) placed in this world by fairies in substitution for a human child. That is a changeling. Also Okigbo's girlfriend in those days . . . . always referred to Chris as *ogbanje*. Each time I wanted to talk to her about Chris, she would say, . . . "Bobo, please leave me alone, you and your ogbanje friend, Chris." Chris himself did not contest or object to *ogbanje*, rather he added a new dimension to it. His reference to the word "changeling" was a way of establishing that *ogbanje* was a universal phenomenon

I would say that Chris was everything that *ogbanje* connotes from what I hear people say of *ogbanje* in Igboland, which has nothing to do with my own personal beliefs. (Acholonu 1989:99)

The characterization of Christopher Okigbo by his elder brother, the renowned economist Pius Okigbo, would appear to lend credence to the *Ogbanje* hypothesis, for he remembers Okigbo's childhood as "absolutely turbulent . . . he was irrepressible as a child, a bit too energetic, somewhat mischievous, difficult to manage, yet very talented" (Acholonu 1988:103). I have no way of verifying or authenticating these mysterious matters, but I do know that when I lived with Chris Okigbo, I was always struck by a certain inscrutability, enigma, mystery, prevision, and love for solitude, which I could still apprehend behind his sheltering and unconditional love of his nephew.

Okigbo had his primary school education in many places, including Ekwulobia and Asaba, and wherever else his father's frequent transfers as a Catholic school headmaster took him. Nothing spectacular characterized this phase of the poet's life and it was usual that "nwa-headmaster" (the son of the headmaster) would be both revered and courted by his schoolmates, which ambiguous relationship would have secretly amused, and been exploited by, the young Okigbo, who was thus able to enjoy both the friendship of and distance from his mates. Anozie's comment on this stage of the poet's life is memorable:

> Everyone who knew Okigbo in the late 30s and early 40s when he was in the primary school, agrees that he was restless, very active and intelligent, ready to take a pugnacious stand at the slightest provocation from his mates. Something of a truant, too, he preferred outdoor games to sitting in the classroom. The lasting impact which the elementary school days had on him can be deduced from some of the anecdotes in his poetry, especially in connection with that village pedagogue, Kepkanly, transformed by Okigbo into a lively poetic character and symbol in *Heavensgate*. (Anozie 1972:7)

Kepkanly, no patronym as such, has in Okigbo's poetry been transformed from any particular historical reference to phenomenality, in those days when school teachers, brought up in the strictly disciplined tradition of the colonial-missionary order, some of them having also had the benefit of training and service in the imperial West African Frontiers Force, and all of them always heavily starched and ironed and "booted," would lead their pupils in regular morning drills aimed at producing a healthy, strong, and disciplined body for the better residence and operation of a sound mind. Such marching exercises would be done with great delight and trepidation, and to the barked commands, *Aka-Ekpe Aka-Nli* (Left-Right), issuing from the stern faces of the teachers. To the marching students and to any passers-by, what actually got heard was the elision, *'kep-'kanli*, which Okigbo's poetic and associative sensibility had no trouble transforming into an honorific and permanent homonym for the Phys. Ed. teacher!

Unfortunately, even this linguistic achievement used to constitute a major stumbling block to readers of Okigbo's poetry, who wasted no time in crying "obscurity." Hence, even Ulli Beier, that pioneering spirit who made it possible for the voices of African writers, including Okigbo's, to be heard, complained quite early that "the obscurity in Okigbo's poetry is of course deliberate. The book opens with the line 'Before you, mother Idoto/naked I stand.' Who is 'mother Idoto'? We shall never be told. Instead more mysterious names appear....from KEPAKLY..." (Beier 1984:43).

"Kepkanly" was not the only occasion when Okigbo succeeded in transforming a faintly-heard or misheard word or phrase into real poetic significance. In fact, I would go beyond Nwoga in asserting that even that early in his career, Okigbo was not simply making "linguistic jokes"; he was making an important political-cultural statement which I will presently elaborate. But first, the excerpt, "Passages," from *Heavensgate* (1962), which has been omitted from both the Heinemann (1971 and 1986) and the Africana (1971) editions:

> Bird of the sun on tree top sitting
> on fig tree top mourns under the lamp:
> *etru bo pi alo eshe anando we aquandem...*
> (quoted, Nwoga, 1984:16)

What is happening here must be of interest not only to socio-linguists, but particularly to those interested in the politics of language imposition/acquisition. For we are dealing here not with voluntary acquisition of language but clearly with imposition. The new language that the pupils were being made to learn was a language of distance, authority, power, and dread; it was also the language of strangers. To make matters no less easy for the pupils, who at their ages would still be learning their own languages, songs like "Little

Bo Peep Has Lost Her Sheep," which the italicized line above "translates," were taught them when they had hardly acquired the rudiments of the language sufficient to enable them to make sense of the lyrics or to appreciate the cultural baggage which the lyrics carried. Thus the line which has given critics so much headache, on account of which many of them have leveled their charge of "deliberate obscurity," "elitist jokes," and "private and privatist symbolism," apart from being an almost accurate reproduction of what the children actually heard/misheard, in its "nonsensicality," is metonymic of the cultural and linguistic havoc which colonial education achieved in the colonies: in spite of the many good things it did, colonial education still produced psychocultural confusion and linguistic displacement, whereby people not only were forced to despise their mother tongues, but many of them actually lost competence in them.

Anyone who went through colonial schooling in Igboland must be familiar with "Little Bo Peep Has Lost Her Sheep and Doesn't Know How to Find Them," which has been recaptured in Okigbo's poetry in a *Greek* way. The same process takes place in such ingenious rememberings and renderings as "*ah-pi an goyo yo-o-shi*" (happy and gushing), and:

> *ho-h ma-ge ma-ge*
> *we shal a si ma ho-h?*
> *we shal a si ma netifulai*
> *a nefa foge ma ho-h!*

> [home again, again
> when shall I *see* my home?
> when shall I *see* my native land
> I'll never forget my home!]
> or:
> *a rime-ba wa-na wa-na so-ja.*
> [I remember when I was a soldier],

which ex-soldiers from World Wars I & II, now teachers, nostalgically imparted to their pupils, and used as marching songs during regular morning school drills or during important "national" occasions like the Empire Day, or Queen Victoria's Birthday, when school children also marched and saluted the Union Jack of the Empire "whose sun never set."

So, I do not think that Okigbo was being facetious or deliberately obscure in the context under discussion. It is clear to me that Okigbo began to assume the serious political-cultural burden as poet of destiny the moment he began to take poetry seriously. Hence the remembrance of Kepkanly is not the simple childish/childlike gleeful recall of one funny, "half-serious half-comical primary school teacher" of the late thirties (*CP*: n.1, 22). Kepkanly is remembered as the personification of the imperializing enterprise: he was the agent of colonial education and psychological enslavement; he was the instrument of cultural imperialism and of forced religious conversion. It was Kepkanly who wielded the "red-hot blade" with which the "scar of the crucifix," the sign of the poet's initiation into Christianity and of alienation, was "inflicted." Even though this scar is external, it is permanent, and is associated not with pleasure or joy, but with pain and anguish. Fortunately, this misrepresenter of the mystery, whose teaching was a mere "gambit," this "Kepkanly that wielded the blade" "died from excess of joy when he received arrears of salary awarded by the Haragin Commission of 1945" (*CP*: n.1, 23). Okigbo's poetry is such a serious affair that for us to dismiss it simplistically as obscure because we chance upon a strange and perhaps initially incomprehensible or impenetrable construction is to be guilty of gross dereliction of critical duty, as is demonstrated in Paul Theroux's reference to the italicized line that set off these comments as "chinese-looking" (*CP*: vii-viii).

On completing primary schooling, Okigbo proceeded to Government College, Umuahia, a very meritorious achievement in those days when the whole of the Eastern Region had only three such schools, Afikpo and Owerri being the other two. At Umuahia, Okigbo continued to be the same vivaciously restless young man, playing active and other leading roles in every imaginable extra-curricular activity: he was a "member of the Arts Society and the Chess Club, [edited] a house magazine with V. C. Ike, and [played] the role of Defending Consul in a dramatic production of *The Trial of Hitler* " (Lindfors in Nwoga 1984:17). But according to Bernth Lindfors in the article "Okigbo as Jock":

It was in sports that young Okigbo really made his mark. In addition to starring on the school soccer and cricket teams, he played on the second eleven in hockey, came in third in the 220 yards in an intramural track meet, and captained his house boxing team scoring impressive victories in intramural matches in the 9-stone to 9-stone-7 division. There are detailed accounts in the school magazine [*The Umuahia Government College Magazine*] of most of the inter-scholastic and house matches played during the year, and Okigbo's name figures prominently in many of them. . . . In cricket his achievements were even more spectacular . . . In recognition of his prowess on the playing fields of Umuahia, Okigbo was honored his final year by being awarded school soccer colors and reawarded school cricket colors. (Quoted in Nwoga 1984:17-18)

Okigbo was clearly respected and admired by all for his meritorious activities outside the classroom. Yet these did not stop him from demonstrating that an active body could also be the habitation for a very able mind. For, contrary to Lindfors' estimate that "he does not appear to have been an outstanding student academically, [though] he did manage to win the Latin Prize in his final year" (17), Okigbo excelled academically. Academic prizes (including Latin ones) are not given to mediocre students who "manage to win" them; they are won by the best students. And in 1950, "a good Grade II pass on his Cambridge School Certificate examination" with distinctions in Mathematics, Physics, and Chemistry; credits in Biology, History, English Language, and English Literature; and a pass only in Geography was no mean achievement. If he was "in a tie for the fifteenth [place] among the twenty-six boys who passed the exam," that showed only the superior quality of that group of students, for the exam was set for, and taken by, students from all over imperial British Africa and possibly Asia. It is clear, then, that Okigbo was an outstanding all-around achiever and won the heart of everyone at Umuahia. He was even recognized for his sense of maturity and "entrusted with certain responsibilities: it is recorded that when a new wireless set was installed in the assembly hall on September 22, 1949, Okigbo was put in charge" (17). And the record-breaker was when one

Saturday morning he walked up to the School Principal's bunga-
low and knocked on the door. When the stern colonial educator
answered the door and wanted to know what "Master Okigbo's"
mission was that early morning, Okigbo simply asked to borrow
the principal's car. If the principal was struck by a thunderbolt at
this unheard-of insouciance, he did not show it, but proceeded to
fetch the car-keys which he gave to his sixteen-year old star-stu-
dent. Needless to say, the car was driven safely back to the principal after the fledgling driver had shown off his driving prowess
to the awed school community.

If Okigbo did not poeticize or immortalize any of his Umuahia
teachers, it wasn't because there were none there or because his
powers to lionize historical personages out of all proportion to
their real-life sizes had waned. After all even the Reverend Father-
Educator Flannagan, who did not have any direct influence on
him, but whose stern fame spread like wild-fire in the Eastern
Region of Nigeria from his base at CKC (Christ the King's College,
Onitsha), where Okigbo's brothers, Lawrence and Pius, went to
school, has been permanently immortalized as an archetypal emis-
sary of cultural imperialism. In this particular instance, Flannagan,
etched in a more tragic relief than the half-comical, half-serious
school teacher, *Kepkanly*, as representative of the infallible and,
the people were also taught, immaculate Pope, God's visible
viceroy on earth and in direct line of succession to St. Peter,
Flannagan carried out the mission of cultural-psychological imperialism to the last letter. Not only did he facilitate the political-
administrative work of the colonial administrator, but he made
sure that the people not only abandoned the religion of their
fathers, but also were forced to physically assist in the destruction,
by arson, of the shrines, sacred buildings, and paraphernalia of
ancestor worship (Egudu 1975). His watchword and credo:

> To sow the fireseed among grasses,
> & lo, to keep it till it burns out . . . (*CP*: 46)

Both Flannagan as a person and his activities as zealous bringer of
salvation and civilization to the benighted corner of the globe, were
rapidly replicated until all the gods of the people lay in state: "And

the gods lie in state / And the gods lie in state / Without the long-drum" (*CP*:50).

Given his precocity and allround ability, it surprised no one that Okigbo, the son of a famous school headmaster, and younger brother of Lawrence and Pius who had earlier distinguished themselves at CKC and thus blazed the trail, should be one of only ten students admitted from Umuahia to the Nigerian campus of London University, University College, Ibadan (UCI), in 1950. But even there, Okigbo would not abandon his many and variegated interests and concentrate on his medical studies. Instead, after two years he changed from medicine to Classics and Ancient History; founded and edited and published his own short-lived magazine; deepened his interest in music, especially jazz and piano, on occasion accompanying Wole Soyinka and Francisca Pereira at the piano during their public performances (Duerden & Pieterse, 1972:136); and starred again in sports. According to Lindfors:

> When he arrived at Ibadan, he naturally continued his athletic activities, quickly distinguishing himself as the best batsman on the cricket team in the 1950 and 1951 seasons, ably representing the University in the First Inter-University Sports Tournament held in March 1951, and trying "to build up a strong Football Club from the decrepit form into which it fell [the year before his arrival] owing to bad administration." However, he appears to have given up soccer late in his university career. . . . (Nwoga, 1984:19)

In spite of all these diversions, Okigbo graduated in 1956 with a B.A. (Hons.), Classics, albeit in the Third Class Division.

The meteoric ease which had characterized Okigbo's academic career should not obscure the profound complexity and turbulence of his nature. In fact, my belief that Okigbo was a true romantic would appear to be validated by the very course of his life, his boundless physical and intellectual energies, his keen sense of living, his restlessness and *wanderlust*, and his love and dread of water. Always seeking out challenges and adventures, when most people of his generation and attainment would simply have settled down in permanence, security, and growing wealth and power, Okigbo moved from one job to another, few, if any, ever giving him that sense of fulfillment. Thus, in the ten short years between 1956 and 1967, he had flirted with the Nigerian Tobacco Company, and the United African Company; served as Secretary in the Federal Ministry of Research and Information; taught Latin at Fiditi Grammar School; was the first Librarian at the premier university in Black Africa, the University of Nigeria, Nsukka; was the West African Manager and Nigerian Representative of Cambridge University Press; completed arrangements to join Wartrade, an Italian financial firm; established with Chinua Achebe the Citadel Publishing Company in Enugu, Biafra; and finally, was a distinguished, crack major in the Biafran Army, and posthumously honored with the Distinguished Service Cross of Biafra.

The more amazing thing about Okigbo's life is not the concatenation of these full-time occupations, which he combined with the serious commitment to poetry, but the fact that he performed each and every one of them meritoriously. I wish to comment briefly on just two of them which have received unjustifiable adverse assessments.

In an interview with Bernth Lindfors, Professor M. J. C. Echeruo, a poet and friend of Okigbo's, and my university teacher (whom I first met in Okigbo's company in Enugu, in the course of my escape from Ibadan to Nsukka, to which most Igbo students had transferred/escaped, during the crisis, from other Nigerian Universities), had described Okigbo's "career . . . in teaching [as] simply a failure" (Nwoga 1984:21). But as Bernth Lindfors has shown in "Okigbo as Jock," "The school annual, *The Fiditian* [for Fiditi Grammar School, where Okigbo taught High School Latin], is filled with information about the activities of this new teacher, who also served as Vice-Principal of the School" (Nwoga 1984:20). At Fiditi, Okigbo was Patron of almost all the Student Sports Societies; but he equally inspired the intellectual and cultural life of Fiditians. A true Renaissance man, Okigbo exemplified the felicitous wedlock of contemplation and action. And since Lindfors' research on this aspect of Okigbo's life remains the most thorough, I will quote him here again, at length:

Of course it would be an injustice to Okigbo to leave the impression that his energies as a schoolmaster were consumed entirely by sports. He was an enthusiastic Patron of the Senior Literary and Debating Society too; as the annual report of the Secretary of the Society makes clear:

> At the beginning of this school year, another energetic and virtuous leader was made the patrons [sic]. Mr. Okigbo, as the new patron is called, has set the progress in motion and has succeeded in influencing other educational giants to give lectures to boys. One of these is Dr. [Pius] Okigbo, brother to the patron.... The patron, encouraged by the interest of the boys and progress of the society voluntered [sic] to give a series of lectures on "Introduction to Poetry," which will come up in six series. The first is already given..

Later that same year a Prose and Poetry Society was formed at the School and Okigbo was called upon again to contribute his talents. (Nwoga 1984:21)

Of greater significance to us is the fact that Fiditi saw the coruscation of Okigbo's poetic genius.

The other of Okigbo's jobs that I wish to comment on is that as Cambridge University Press manager and representative. Paul Theroux (who is advertised as "Okigbo's old friend") has described, in his "Preface" to the Heinemann (1986) *Collected Poems of Christopher Okigbo*, a very warm and hospitable person who was also very irresponsible, with whom he drank and roamed Ibadan, and who virtually neglected his duties in order to roam the city and haunt the pubs with this wayfarer whom he had only just casually met, and whom he "had persuaded" to spend three or so weeks in his house. Okigbo did not touch alcohol, his only drink being Coca-Cola, of which he normally consumed a small bottle. And even though he occasionally went to night clubs where they played serious music—like *juju*—he was not a pub- crawler and, when he wasn't at home in Cambridge House (where I lived with him), he could almost always be found in his office at Mbari Club, working on his poetry or as Secretary of the Cultural Center.

Theroux says that Okigbo "seemed to [him] to resemble a mark of punctuation" (CP:viii), referring to the poet's size. Yet, everyone knows that Okigbo was far from diminutive. But more scathingly and relevantly he says in the same paragraph that Okigbo was so bored with his job at Cambridge "that he had stopped opening his mail. It simply accumulated, like fallen leaves. A man came with mail-bags full of proof copies and catalogues, and Okigbo dumped these on a table without glancing at them. They were piled high, they were months old, and many had fallen to the floor. 'There's no hurry'" (CP:x). This is not, cannot be the energetic and ebullient Okigbo that once lived; this one certainly is an emanation from Theroux's nightmare. As West African Manager and Nigerian Representative, Okigbo had working for him, besides a cook, steward, gardener, nightguard, houseboy, and mail-runner, a very capable administrative manager, who also did secretarial duties in the office. One would hardly suppose it was Okigbo's part to open the mail! And if the mail had not been opened for months, how did Theroux divine that the bags were "full of proof copies and catalogues"? Cambridge University Press would surely have gone out of business in West Africa with such a manager as Theroux has described! Okigbo was restless, not lazy; and the expression "There's no hurry" would not come from him in any circumstances. Okigbo was also highly systematic and very ordered. I remember the day after I had submitted my application forms at the University of Ibadan, Chris took me to his garage which served as warehouse for all the books that could not be contained in his office. These were stacked, ceiling-high, with not much room to walk around. Yet, with almost unthinking facility, he moved, retrieving all the books he thought I needed to read for the forthcoming concessional entrance examination to Ibadan. A careless person "irresponsible about petty details" (CP:vii), would not have arranged a garage-full of books, nor could he easily have located the fifteen books I needed, at my level, in the three subjects for the examination.

About the imposing and magnificently set and impeccably kept house, Cambridge House, Theroux throws out the following tidbits of gossip (and this in a "serious" Preface!): "Americans told me they hated the decor—'It's not African,' they said. It looked

Italian, something out of Fellini" (*CP*:x). If "the house was clean and very comfortable and it was obvious that Okigbo was very happy in the house" (*CP*:x), of what importance was it that Theroux or any American liked the decor or not? What qualified them to say what was "authentically African" or not? And what meddling business of theirs was it, anyway? But the traveling pundits and tourist-scholars have never stopped defining for Africans and the rest of the world what constitutes authentic culture and life. And because their word—however wrong-headed or misguided, or plain stupid—has always had the advantage of "Western microphones" (a virtual monopoly by the West over the communication media) and of the "authority" that comes from speaking unchallenged about Others, Theroux is able to pass off, as criticism of Okigbo's poetry, such an insipid insult as:

> He walked up and down, quoting poetry in his odd quacking voice. He had read Classics at Ibadan University. He quoted Virgil, he talked about Palinurus and Odysseus. He was jumpy and highly-strung. It made him a distracted and fitful writer. I think he was too fond of words like 'catechumen' and 'caparison' and 'panegyric'. It takes genius to use such words in any poem. He was [at] his best and most memorable at his simplest:
> We carry in our worlds that flourish
> Our worlds that have failed.... (*CP*:viii)

But it remains one of the sad tales of neocolonialism, and particularly of the politics of publishing in the "Third World," that a man who hardly knew Okigbo would be used to "sell" Okigbo's poetry with his importantly framing and thus "authorizing" Preface, in which not a single sentence can pass for sound scholarship or criticism, or even biography (see also Nkem Nwankwo, *Memoir* 1993).

Nor is that all. Of this most famous African poet (who was also his most magnanimous host during his escapades in Africa) Theroux says that "Characteristically—in a war that few people here [London] now remember—he [Okigbo] died fighting for his *village*" (CP:x; my italic). This is the conclusion of the last paragraph in which—Theroux must have forgotten that—he had just written that "Biafra was Igboland: one language, one culture, one people. There was every reason for it to exist as a sovereign state" (x). Of course, that whole sentence is false: Biafra wasn't all Igboland; and it wasn't one but many languages and cultures. For all his travels in Africa, which were characteristically touristic, Theroux was still able to escape the inoculation of sanity and balance of the hot tropics and so saw, like the imperializing agents before him, all lakes as puddles, all rivers as streams, all roads as bush paths, all houses as huts, and all nations as tribes or clans or villages. Okigbo did not "die fighting for his village"; he died fighting to save Biafra [a short-lived nation-state], Biafrans, and humanity threatened with genocidal extinction by the combined forces of neocolonial Nigeria and Britain and her allies.

Surely, Heinemann has done a disservice to Okigbo and his poetry through the use of this "authenticating" (really Orientalizing/Africanizing) voice of Paul Theroux. It is clear that Theroux hardly "knew" Okigbo, whose poetry is also clearly beyond his understanding, as is evidenced by his misreading of the few quoted lines in the "Preface," and by his not particularly original or distinguished readings of Okigbo and of African literature published elsewhere (Nwoga 1984:356-57 [Entries # 81-83]).

Thus, one cannot take seriously Theroux's assertion, in the closing paragraph of the "Preface," that Okigbo did not care for politics, but he was greatly attached to the past" (CP:x). Okigbo was neither obsessed with the past, which he understood in the same critical way as Soyinka and Achebe; nor was he a nativist (Appiah 1991). But he cared very much for politics, not in the sense of partisanship or *parti pris*, for he loudly detested the politicians and the ruins they wreak on society. But as populist poet-critic, Okigbo was concerned with politics as affecting and determining every facet of human life and the direction in which society careers.

When Okigbo was growing up, all through his primary, secondary, and university education, in fact, even after he started writing seriously, what mattered in Nigeria was not the fact that Nigeria was made up of a multiplicity of nations and subnationalities whose inability to get along together would later explode fratricidally, so much as the fact that all these nationalities were subjected to, and squirming under, a common and collective yoke of imperialism/colonialism. And if one looked beyond the "borders" of Nigeria, one also saw that the same fate was the lot of the black person in all of Africa. As poet of destiny, to whom his duties had clearly been delineated at birth (as successor to and reincarnation of the High Priest of Ajani, his maternal grandfather), it was obvious that his crusade would begin at that point where imperialism-colonialism had done the most deleterious damage: in the area of culture and most palpably in its religious manifestation.

If in growing up, children under colonialism and colonial education were fed deceit and confusion, it dawned on Okigbo quite early that that which had been white-washed over must be scraped and restored to its original, albeit inevitably disfigured, coloration. And that it had lain thus submerged and effaced for so long was no reason for continued forgetting. As poet of destiny, his duty was to be the vehicle of memory and an aid to the collectivity in their remembering. Thus, even in his Lagos-Ibadan/Fiditi poems, the gesture is to the mnemonic powers of poetry/poet, because Okigbo recognized that in the onerous task of cultural recuperation and rehabilitation which lay ahead for him, the people, his people, like a drenched or rain-soaked traveler who needed to determine where the rains overtook him before he could know where he dried his body and clothes, needed the poet/bard with all his powers of remembering and prophecy.

Thus if, according to Walter Benjamin (1968), "memory is the element of the epic mind that is derived from the muse" and "creates the chain of tradition which passes a happening on from generation to generation" (4-5), then the invocation of "memory" here, as a defining burden of the poet of destiny, is tragic because it carries with it all the implications and associations of the temporal-cultural disjuncture, a radical interruption of continuity, and a disruption of a people's way of life which is part of the subject of Okigbo's lament. It is thus to Okigbo's credit that, even as early as the Lagos-Ibadan phase of his career, he had already articulated a total view of his role as bard, as the vital link for his community between the past and the future in the confused flux of the present. He clearly recognized that his role had been complicated and made doubly arduous by those forces which would, but could not, make of his psychocultural tableau a blank, but which, failing to create a total *tabula rasa*, still managed to produce an over-inscription which distorted and effaced autochthonous cultural texts. It is no wonder, then, that the poem "Lament of the Flute," which articulates both this importance to the poet of destiny and the lament over the attempted cultural effacement, was written *both* in Ojoto, the poet's hometown, and in 1960, when Nigeria achieved "independence":

> Tidewash . . . Memories
> fold-over-fold free furrow,
> mingling old tunes with new.
> Tidewash . . . Ride me
> memories, astride on firm
> saddle, wreathed with white
> lilies & roses of blood . . .
> Sing to the rustic flute:
> Sing a new note . . .
> Shall I offer to *Idoto*
> my sandhouse and bones,
> then write no more on snow-patch?
>
> Sing to the rustic flute.
> Sing a new note. (*Collected Poems*:10-11)

If the tide did not quite wash away the marks, on ebbing it left "fold-over-fold free furrow," an overinscription and sublation. It is true that the cultural palimpsest could still be discerned, but the overall effect at this stage of the poet's career was more cacophonous than harmonious because the "new tune," though sung "to the rustic flute," results in what to readers like Paul Theroux "was a chinese-looking line that went *etru bo pi alo a she*" (vii-viii). I have already commented on Paul Theroux's Orientalizing reduction of this and other lines of Okigbo's poetry. One needs, however, to make two observations here: first, in the "final version" of his poetry collected by the poet himself about the middle of 1966 and published in 1971 by Heinemann after his death, the poet had taken care to expunge from his poetry this and similar imponderabilities in keeping with his avowed populist mission. Second, the apparent incomprehensibility of such lines is a major consequence of the "errors of the rendering" and a reflection of the cultural, psychological, and linguistic confusion which resulted, not merely from the collision of cultures, but from the forcible displacement and near-total submergence and effacement of the one by the other. As poet of destiny it was part of Okigbo's duty to correct and rectify these "errors of the rendering." In doing this he was very much like Walter Benjamin's "historian who stops telling the sequence of events like the beads of a rosary" (1968:263): "Instead he grasps the constellation which his own era has formed with a definite earlier one. Thus he establishes a conception of the present as the 'time of the now' which is shot through with chips of messianic time" (263).

In closing this chapter, since we have repeatedly referred to Okigbo as poet of destiny, and since the discussion of his poetic mission in the remaining chapters presupposes not only the poet's assumption of the awe-full role, but also our acceptance of him as such, it is in order here to meditate on Okigbo as poet of destiny. In a confident declaration of his credentials in the "Introduction" to his *Labyrinths with "Path of Thunder*," Okigbo leaves us in no doubt as to how he viewed himself as poet, and how he expected us to take his poetry, in which:

> a *poet-protagonist* is assumed throughout; a personage, however *much larger than Orpheus*; one with a *load of destiny on his head*, rather like Gilgamesh, like Aenas, like [Ahab] the hero of Melville's *Moby Dick*—like the Fisher King of Eliot's *Waste Land*; a personage for whom the progression through "Heavensgate" through "Limits" through "Distances" is like telling the beads of a rosary; except that the beads are neither stone nor agate but globules of anguish strung together on memory. (*CP*: xxvi-xxvii; my italics)

It is clear from this excerpt from the "Introduction" (Okigbo's poetic manifesto), that he conceived of his poetry in very serious terms, in his words in terms of "a live-die proposition" (xxiii). Therefore "for him, poetry is no mere aesthetic pastime, no simple celebration of verbal ingenuity, no indulgence of intellectual gymnastics. It is a sacred vocation espoused by persons who feel specially called and set apart from all other persons to carry the grave responsibility of speaking for their people" (Obiechina 1980: 8).

That is why, in spite of his own vast learning and close attention to details of technique, Okigbo was impatient with "academic versifiers" and took the trouble to distinguish between "art and craft," which is very important in Igbo aesthetics where *Nka* is not hollow craft or *techne*, but combines craftsmanship with the beautiful and the significant, functionality with sheer aesthetic rapture:

> Well, I think that there is some—that there is a great deal of difference between carving and sculpture, for instance, a carver is not naturally a sculptor, though a sculptor carves; you know carving is just a technique—it is just a method.
>
> In a sense artists are continually experimenting but I don't think that one should feel strongly attracted to experiment actually for its own sake. (Duerden & Pieterse, 1972:140-42)

So, in spite of the concern in Okigbo's poetry for technique, for beauty, for music and sense of rhythm, what gets privileged is the level of seriousness of the statements to which, according to him, it is possible to respond "without passing through [the] process of intellectual analysis, and I think that if a poem can elicit a response, either in physical or emotional terms from an audience, the poem has succeeded" (144). Given the intellectual level of the generality of his audience—that collectivity for whom he was the poet of destiny—it could not have been otherwise. This approach to poetry which "is to make one feel and then understand, rather than make one understand and then feel" (144) explains that incident when Okigbo read his poems in Yola, Northern Nigeria, to high school girls. Whether they understood his poetry or not, they *felt* the anguish embodied in it and *wept*. Such response is possible only with the poet of destiny whose at-one-ment with the people is total. His song is their song, and stirs the innermost recesses of their beings; the anguish of the beads of his rosary is their collective anguish; the poet of destiny is the people's eyes and tongue, their ears and their heart.

But this is a frightening and intimidating role for a poet to assume. And for us to accept him as such demands absolute faith in him. It is for that reason that Obiechina recommends a critical and skeptical examination of the credentials of the "poet-prophet, in much the same way as the Jews of old used to examine critically the personal credentials of their prophets" (1980:15).

I did insist earlier that a writer should be allowed to exist apart from his work. I still believe that, especially if such separation will prevent us from using genuine poetic images to draw fantastic psycho-sexual conclusions regarding the person of the poet-as-man (Fido 1986); and if that will allow the poet as spokesperson for his people to make necessary, if dangerous, political statements and pronouncements (Mazrui 1971). The first credential of the poet of destiny is his own word uttered in all seriousness and integrity. For one—poet or prophet—to declare that "I am who am" imposes grave responsibilities, and is not to be taken facetiously either by the poet or by his readers. As I have already mentioned, Okigbo from the outset delineates a formidable, larger-than-life poet-protagonist in his "Introduction" whose presence is unmistakable throughout his poetry and who, when matters assume dire urgency, discards the poetic mask and performs in person: wearing "my own mask, not ancestral." In doing so he is fully cognizant of the dangers and personal risks to his person, but that is part of the "occupational" hazard of the vocation of the poet-prophet: "If I don't learn to shut my mouth I'll soon go to hell, / I, Okigbo, town-crier, together with my iron bell" (CP:94).

But it is not only that the poet of destiny assumes the awesome role or that he is aware of that role. It is a role that is not achieved as such, but imposed; it is a destined role which one is assigned and must accept even before one gets "born." In Okigbo's case, he is not merely a successor to the priestly functions of his maternal grandfather; he is his reincarnation. Like the typical Ogbanje (or Abiku, a reincarnate being who repeats the birth-death cycle indefinitely), he was privy to this secret of generation and took great care not to flaunt it:

Secret I have told into no ear
Save into a dughole, to hold, not to drown with—
Secret I have planted into beachsand
. . . Secret I have covered up with beachsand (CP:26)

Reference had earlier been made to Acholonu's study of this aspect of Okigbo. In his own interview, also earlier referred to, Okigbo talks about his awareness of his awesome responsibility:

> Well, my maternal grandfather was the head of a particular type of religion which is intimately connected with my village and since I am a reincarnation of my maternal grandfather, I carried this on, and I began to show them my responsibilities in that direction as soon as I grew up; and even when I went to secondary school, I had to take something out of my pocket-money regularly to send home to my grandmother for my maternal uncle who was, as it were, standing in for me until I should grow up to carry on the various periodic rites which were connected with the worship of this particular Deity. And my "Heavensgate," is, in fact, designed to do that sort of thing—it is my own contribution to this. (Duerden & Pieterse 1972:145)

It was for reason of that same priestly-oracular conception of his role that Okigbo abjured the mundane fame which writers would kill to attain, and for which reason he actually once refused a First Prize in poetry: "I haven't got that kind of ambition, which some people may have, of becoming a great writer or something like that" (147). The path for the poet of destiny is cut differently. Hence, while writers wrangle over property and proprietary rights, Okigbo was even content to disclaim credit for his own poetry, for which he was merely acting as conduit from the well-springs of wisdom to his people:

> Well, I really don't think I can claim to have written it ["Lament of the Drums"]. All I did was to create the drums, and the drums said what they liked. Personally I don't believe that I am capable of saying what the drums have said in that first part: it's only the long funeral drums that are capable of saying it and they are capable of saying it only at that moment when they talk, then they've said it. They are not capable now or in the future of saying that. So, I don't think that I can claim to have written the poem; all I did was to cover the drums, and to create the situation in which the drums spoke what they spoke. (Duerden & Pieterse 1972:143)

Who, but "the prophet only the poet" (*CP*:25) "Elemental, united in vision / of present and future / the pure line" (22), would be capable of such self-effacing forthrightness? In another interview Okigbo reiterated this position:

> The poems have nothing to do with me. The poems live their own separate lives and when you've created a poem, written a poem it is just like creating something, I'm giving it life. It goes to one audience and speaks one language, goes to another and speaks a different language, goes to another person and remains mute and no message is delivered, . . . I've started writing through other persons. When I created the drums all I did was to create the drums and the message they deliver has nothing to do with me at all. It just happens that there might be some political tinge in the message of the drum and also the message of the silent sisters—there might also be some political tinge there—but the message has nothing to do with me, nor has it anything to do with my intention. (Duerden & Pieterse 1972:147)

It is interesting that even as Okigbo tries to dissociate himself from any intentional message of his poetry, and to refuse the credit for the "creation" of the poems, the frequency of the imagery of creation, of "giving it life," of "writing through other persons" begins to force a consideration of the poet in association with the divine in its creative aspect. That is in order, and the poet himself is not reticent about his role as oracle. In "Elegy of the Wind" there are these lines:

> And may my muted tones of twilight
> Break your iron gate, the burden of several centuries,
>   into twin tremulous cotyledons . . .

> Man of iron throat — for I will make broadcast with
>   eunuch-horn of seven valves—
> I will follow the wind to the clearing,

> And with muffled steps seemingly out of breath break
>   the silence the myth of her gate.

> For I have lived the sapping sprung from the bed
> of the old vegetation;
>
> Have shouldered my way through a mass of ancient
> nights to chlorophyll; . . .
>
> I have lived the oracle dry. . . . (*CP*: 90)

and in "Elegy for Slit-Drum," the identification is complete:

> the mythmaker accompanies us . . .
> Okigbo accompanies us the oracle enkindles us...
> Okigbo accompanies as the rattles enlighten us—.... (*CP*:96)

Clearly, Okigbo passes the first test "of the aspiring spokesman of the people and humanity" which is a demonstration of "his inspiration inclining him towards high seriousness, a sense of the understanding of the inner springs of himself as prophet-aspirant . . . a wholesome assimilation of the self and its interests to the broad, inclusive destiny of a people and the world of people" (Obiechina 1980:15).The rigorousness of that test is in direct proportion to the role, and as Obiechina goes on to elaborate the requirements,

> We must demand of our poet-prophet a clarity of view and personal integrity as reliable guides to our better understanding of the forces that tyrannize over us. In other words, we must seek to be reassured that the poet is of us, that he possesses adequate intellectual scope and breadth of sympathy to understand our problems, that he has the personal integrity to tell us the truth as he sees it and that he is sufficiently assimilated to our destiny to share our sufferings and agonies, our joys and hopes, our dreams and reveries. We must insist that he should adequately internalize these things in order to become the sensitive needle that probes and locates our emotional traumas, our anxieties and elations, our fears no less than our hopes and aspirations. We could not trust him otherwise. (15-16)

Okigbo passes the test not because he assumes our mundane and prosaic nature both as individuals and collectively. No, he still

145

retains the divine detachment and humble arrogance of his calling, which enable him to function with "sensitivity, intelligence and
integrity" as oracle, equipped with "poetic sensitivity and the
capacity for imaginative re-ordering of experience" for the opti-
mum benefit of the collectivity (17).

By way of conclusion, however, one needs to correct an
impression created in Obiechina's discussion: that of Okigbo's
role as poet of destiny having been "self-appointed" (20). No (sane)
man (or woman) in history has ever simply appropriated the awesome burdens inherent in that role. Quite distinct from false
prophets and opportunistic charlatans, the poet-prophet-oracle
has a destiny which he cannot escape, even if he had wanted to.
The poet of destiny is chosen; he does not choose. In Okigbo's
case, he assumed the inevitable cross and cup to the very end
when, were he simply one of us, he could have passed and thus
saved his skin/life. Thus, that apotheosis of the poet which
became known in Ibadan in 1966 when Okigbo's name began to
be mentioned regularly in terms of sainthood; when, even while
still living, he had attained "canonization," is played out when the
poet of destiny, on ascending the cross as it were, combined the
names and roles of Chris/Christ:

> A mock-grin on his face
> he lies abandoned at the confluence . . .
> for they said they wanted life
> and he gave his own:
>
> and the saint lay abandoned
>
> Unto his people he came a messiah
> and they knew him not
> We await another messiah. . . .. ("Without a Grave He Lies,"
> in Okafor 1981:24)

Unsurprisingly, Okigbo himself had asked about this fate of
prophets:

> Who would add to your statue
> Or in your village accept you? (CP:45)

It is this understanding of Okigbo as poet of destiny which enables me to refute Theroux's charge that Okigbo was not concerned with politics. It is not possible to extrude politics from Okigbo's poetry for his role as priest-bard-oracle made politics an imperative integer of his poetry. A double-sided agenda then, Okigbo's politics comprise a postcolonial critique which concentrated on the cultural axis, and a popular-national program which included the excoriation of the gastrocentric self-seekers; the lament over the unrealized political helmsmanship of Awolowo, a statesman and pioneer "nationalist;" a celebration of the sadly short-lived possibility of "national" sanity and direction; and the culminating prophecy of lost hope and of repetition for Nigeria. These aspects of Okigbo's poetry will constitute the subject of the remaining chapters.

CHAPTER V

OKIGBO'S POSTCOLONIAL AND CULTURAL POLITICS

The term "postcolonial" is both controversial and problematic, but it has been found a more innocuous critical category than the older paradigm "Third World," and a less politically incendiary term than "Neocolonial" and "Imperialist." But, since no problem is ever solved by getting swept under the carpet, nor an evil ever wished away by a willful occlusion of the terms that name it, the terms *neocolonial* and *imperialist* will also be used in this discussion whenever it is appropriate to do so. As for *postcolonial*, I will follow Ella Shohat's elaboration whereby the term designates "critical discourses which thematize issues emerging from colonial relations and the aftermath, covering a long historical span (including the present)" (1992: 101). An interesting thing about the enthusiastic embrace of the now-fashionable term by critics of literature and culture is that in its very problematicity, in its ambiguity, are concealed "doubts about its political agency" (100), since both critique and action are hamstrung by the impossibility of agreement regarding even the subject under discussion: the critical term and politics, postcolonial, is defined by a "dubious spatiality" whereby the tendency is to lump together, as if differences of geography, politics and other experiences do not matter, nor places as far-flung from one another as Nigeria, India, Jamaica, and Sri Lanka; and by a "problematic temporality," as if it does not matter whether we are dealing with a society which gained its "independence" from direct imperial rule in 1960, or that which did so 200 years ago, or even that (like Palestine) which is still shedding the blood of its youth in the struggle for emancipation and self-determination.

The same problematicity obtains when the discussion centers around the so-called "new" or "newly accredited" Literatures written in English as well as discourses on these. (Cultural-literary productions in other Europhone-colonial languages do not fall under our present purview.) Yet, no sustained interrogation of their belated accreditation nor of their delayed emergence has been done; nor has there been an equally serious contestation of the amalgamation of different discursive traditions into an undifferentiated epistemological monolith. Thus, to name only six from a proliferation of titles in a fashionable and lucrative disciplinary formation: H. H. Anniah Gowda, ed., *The Colonial and Neo-Colonial Encounters in Commonwealth Literature* (1983); Dieter Riemenschneider, ed., *Critical Approaches to the New Literatures in English* (1989); Dieter Riemenschneider, ed., *The History and Historiography of Commonwealth Literature* (1983); Reingard Nethersole, ed., *Emerging Literatures* (1990); Bruce King, *The New English Literatures* (1980); and Davis & Maes-Jelinek, eds., *Crisis and Creativity in the New Literatures in English* (1990).

Behind any consideration of "postcolonial" is a basic assumption—that the facts of empire and colony were and are an important determination, in both immediate and mediate instances, for the discourses and cultures of all the people involved on either the colonizing or colonized side of the momentous historical encounter. This dialectical view, which applies whether one is talking about Nigerian and Indian or about "English" and American Literatures, runs counter to the usual and complacent traditional disciplinary position which insisted (and often still insists) that English culture was neither affected nor shaped by its foreign and imperial policy. This recognition of the reciprocal (albeit unequal) impingement lies, in part, behind what I have referred to as the monumental and almost unwieldy epistemological monolith and, in part, behind the calls for a multi-disciplinary or even anti-disciplinary (Mowitt 1992) approach, which would study together cultural-literary products from both sides of the imperial divide: both have been largely influenced and mediated by imperialism. But this call has so far been mostly tentative because it recognizes that the profound and painful "truth and falsity" of race has been the public and secret motivation of imperialism as well as the foundational raw material and catalyst of the discourse of imperialism.

It is possible that this call, like the unreflecting celebration of hybridity, has not seriously considered the profound implications and reality of the continuing asymmetry in the arrangement of global power relations even though game-pieces keep getting reshuffled and participants in the power-game keep changing clothes. This call may perhaps be better understood in the light of that "realistic" position which sees imperialism as a beneficial evil; which also sees the imperialist as not totally devoid of humanity, nor the imperialized as not totally incapable of inhumanity. According to Edward Said:

> [there are] large groups of people who believe that the bitterness and humiliations of the experience that virtually enslaved them nevertheless delivered the benefits of a national self-consciousness, liberal ideas, and technological goods, benefits over time that seem to have turned colonialism into a much less unpleasant thing. (1993:18)

While the contestation of the dubious "benefit" of especially "a national self-consciousness" will wait until the next chapter, it is fair to observe that the position thus articulated balances the unilateral and unilineal view of the history of imperialism and colonialism which used to see only a drama of giving and of receiving, of doing to and of suffering, by one side and by the other, respectively. The unilineal view, mainly Eurocentric because it used to belong to the monopolistic writers and disseminators of "history," described a "history of one-way Western endowments and free handouts followed by a reprehensible sequence of ungrateful biting of that grandly giving 'Western hand" (Said 1993:22).On the other hand, according to Samir Amin:

Within left-wing ideological currents in the West, it is recognized that the colonization which accompanied European expansion favored European progress. If a few extremists only see the "civilizing role of colonization," that does not mean that this opinion is common to all of Western thought. Not everyone denies the brutality and devastating effects of the slave trade and the massacre of the American indigenous peoples. . . . [Despite its] recognition of the role of colonialism in the unequal development of capitalism . . ., the dominant view is based on a refusal to accept the principle that the centers-peripheries contradiction constitutes the fundamental contradiction of the modern world. (Amin 1989:113)

The corrective vision is aware that for the duration of a wrestling match, and that until the victor and the vanquished are determined, the two combatants remain entangled in each other's arms and embroiled in the dirt of combat. Yet, we know that as it started out, imperialism was a system of invasion, warfare, coerced, outrageous, abnormal and violent imposition, and the exploitation and expropriation of goods and resources—human and material—by European powers. As Said sees it, "there occurred ravages of colonial people who for centuries endured summary justice, unending economic oppression, the total distortion of their societies and their intimate lives, and a recourseless submission given to them as a function of unchanging European superiority" (Said 1993:22). Unlike other forms of warfare, imperialism was founded and propped up by an idiotic chromatic philosophy and complex of superiority which its "scientists" strove to authenticate, and which rationalized its binarism as a central act of civilization itself, an altruistically Promethean act of bringing light to the benighted regions and peoples of the world. Enabled by its material, technological, military, and piratical superiority, a handful of European nations thus were able to subdue and control 85% of the earth's surface and its people in the heyday of imperialism (Said 1979: 41; Ashcroft, et al., 1989:1).

But it is not as if the presumption and thinking behind that militarism and consequent control have receded into prehistory. As Edward Said explains it:

Always there lurks the assumption that although the Western consumer belongs to a numerical minority, he is entitled to own or expend (or both) the majority of the world resources, why? Because he, unlike the Oriental [or non-Western person], is a true human being. No better instance exists today of what Anwar Abdel Malek calls "the hegemonism of possessing minorities" and anthropocentrism allied with Europocentrism: a white middle-class Westerner believes it's his human prerogative not only to manage the non-white world but also to own it, just because by definition "it" is not quite as human as "we" are. There is no purer example than this of dehumanized thought. (Said 1979:108)

The sad fact of contemporary "history" is that the same "philosophical" and cultural anachronism which was used to "justify" imperialism now informs a lot of colonial discourse and colonialist/neocolonialist cultural productions which find it ideologically convenient to continue to propagate, perpetuate, and disseminate the binary myths of superiority/inferiority, benevolence/ingratitude, civilization/backwardness, enlightened/savage, rational/emotional, intellectual/physical, literate/oral, good/bad, and white/black, as if there cannot exist other possibilities, other grey or indeterminate zones.

It is that kind of superiorist refusal to even consider the possibility that there might reside some sense in the *other*, already castigated as inferior, which accounts for the interpretive outrage flaunted by Dennis Duerden in his "influential" book *The Invisible Present* (1975). In his rambling discussion in the chapter on "Time and African Art" which is littered with presumptions to intimate knowledge of African art and society, superior to that possessed by his European predecessors, Duerden, apparently unwittingly, perpetuates the gross misconceptions and false knowledges of Africa held by the West. After warning that "it is extremely important for an understanding of these societies to get away from the sense of the word 'symbol' used to describe identifiable objects existing in modern European art," and asserting that a typical African society "avoids the use of representations of objects as if they were symbols" (10), Duerden ventures into an area which interests us, and where he claims particular expertise and authority:

It appears, however, that the artist in nonindustrial African society, be he *poet, painter*, or *storyteller*, wishes to avoid making his symbols permanent, wishes somehow to prevent them from becoming universally accepted Symbols. It follows that when describing the uses of art in African society we should make it plain that it appears as if *generally accepted symbols are being used unintentionally and not state affirmatively that it is the intention of the artist to use such symbols.* (Duerden 1975:11; *my italics*)

One is at a loss as to the identity of the society under discussion here. But the assertions delivered with all arrogant apodicticity do not conceal a definite affiliation with Anthropological Darwinism. For one thing, the treatment of "symbols" here has resulted in a complete denudation of its meaning. For if, as according to the *Princeton Encyclopedia of Poetry and Poetics* (1993),

> a symbol is a device of the poetic art when it refers to something else in the poem; it is a power of poetic language when it refers to the way words and rhythms can evoke mystery; it is a function of the whole poem when it refers to the kinds of meaning a literary work can stand for; it is a form of therapeutic disguise when it refers to the ways in which a poem stands for the working out of the author's inner disturbance; and it is an index of cultural values when it refers to the ways in which man's products reveal his attitudes. (835)

then African art and artists, including Okigbo, not only understand symbols and symbolism very well, but also use them not "unintentionally." As for the question of permanence, that is pertinent only with regard to plastic arts, including architecture, where the artists simply obey the imperatives of ecology as well as their people's ways of life even as their "obsession" with impermanence reflects their cosmological understanding of the universe and of the transitoriness of everything within it. With regard to Okigbo, one of the charges against him had been, not that he does not use symbols in his poetry, but that his mastery of the symbolist craft, which enables him to appropriate symbols from both indigenous and exotic doxa, mixing these with his private symbolism, has left his readers often flabbergasted and obfuscated. In that early phase of his poetic career when that charge of obscurity can be sustained, Okigbo was simply being a true "universal" symbolist poet whose poetry was characterized, like the best of the Symbolist School, with "its overwhelming concern with the non-temporal, non-sectarian, non-geographic, and non-national problem of the human condition: the confrontation between human mortality and the power of survival through the preservation of the human sensitivities in the art forms" (Balakian 1977:10).

That was when Okigbo's moods were wont to be "impish," as Achebe would describe them in his "Preface" (Achebe & Okafor 1978:x), and when, exhibiting an "esoteric attitude" toward art, he preferred to move "in closed circles communicating solely with [his] own breed" (Balakian 1977:10). In an interview with Lewis Nkosi, Okigbo quickly proffered an explanation/rationalization for this "elitism" to the effect that "there are not many Nigerians who would read poetry and would take delight in reading poetry, and there are very few Nigerians who would read poetry that appears difficult. Somehow, I believe I am writing for other poets all over the world to read and see whether they can share in my experience" (Duerden & Pieterse 1972:135). That was Okigbo in 1962, master of the poetic symbol, whose "artistic vision, freed from national [even pan-African] ideals, focused on the relationship between the subjective, purely personal world of the artist, and its objective projection" (Balakian 1977:10), and who, by grafting the French and European branches of the Symbolist practice to the autochthonous poetic stem, contributed, in effect, to bringing Symbolism "to its apotheosis as an international literary movement" (ibid.; see also Moore 1965:41-50).

This elaboration has been necessary because Duerden has become so important and influential, and like Darwin and the orientalists before him, whatever he says gets widely disseminated; because he cites his "authenticating" connection with important Africans like Kofi Awoonor, Laz Ekwueme, and Wole Soyinka; because he generously devotes two long paragraphs in his book to a discussion of the whole of the poetry of Christopher Okigbo; and, not the least important, because the contestation of imperialist discourse and distortion/falsification is an onerous part of the politics of Postcoloniality.

In the truest Eurocentric arrogance and presumption to superiority, and in the most transparent discourse on Orientalism/
Africanism, Duerden seriously thinks that the African artist/writ-
er can only stumble into symbols "unintentionally." How can it be
otherwise when the whole non-occidental world has been judged
"incapable of representing itself," and when "Europe granted itself
the right to represent others...—and even to judge them" (Amin
1989:101). Yet, in the two paragraphs on Okigbo's poetry, what
stands out is neither Duerden's knowledge nor interpretative and
judgmental/evaluative ability, not yet his perspicuity. What stands
out is not just a deliberate misreading or misinterpretation of
Okigbo's poetry (which might well have proved impenetrable to
Duerden), but also a flagrant misrepresentation of a "prose" statement made by Okigbo to Serumaga, his 1965 interviewer. Okigbo
had simply observed, quite correctly, that

> the modern African is no longer a product of an entirely
> indigenous culture. The modern sensibility which the modern
> African poet is trying to express is by its very nature complex,
> and it is a complex of values, some of which are indigenous,
> some of which are exotic, some of which are traditional, some
> of which are modern. Some of these values we are talking
> about are Christian, some are non-Christian, and I think that
> anybody who thinks it is possible to express consistently only
> one line of values, indigenous or exotic, is probably being
> artificial. (Duerden & Pieterse 1972:144)

In another context, Ngugi had expressed exactly the same sentiments on the importance to cultural life and vitality of mutual and
coemptive "give and take": "Cultures that change to reflect the
ever-changing dynamics of internal relations and which maintain
a balanced give and take with external relations are the ones that
are healthy" (Ngugi 1993:xvi).

But as Duerden understands it, Okigbo has (in the response
cited earlier) "asserted that the mythic garments of cultures are
interchangeable" (Duerden 1975:100). Okigbo *did not* assert any
such thing! If we must retain the sartorial metaphor, what Okigbo
said was that the garments of culture are complexly woven with

many different and variegated braids, "some of which are indigenous, some of which are exotic." Okigbo went on to adumbrate his
position by referring to *actual* dresses and styles, but which
Duerden, armed with his peculiar monopoly over the use of "symbols," actually proceeded to *interpret literally!* If one may ask, how
American does one become because one wear jeans? And how
Nigerian can one's apartment become because one relishes *egusi*
soup and pounded yam in it? Understandably, Duerden comes
from a literalist society, one which has all but lost its sense of
metaphor and clings to its exclusive right to "rationality" and "rational philosophy" (Amin 1989:91). But the fact does not restrain
Duerden in his generalizations of African poets, painters, and sto-
rytellers as incapable of appreciating, understanding, and deploy-
ing symbols (Duerden 1975:10–11). Duerden belongs in a long line
of respected distorters, falsifiers, pontificators, and lucubrators.
Thus with the authority and dignity of "the expatriate expert" he
pronounces a final judgment on Okigbo's "Lament of the Drums"
which he condemns for mixing "Tamuz, Mesopotamian god of the
corn with Osiris of the Nile. Nevertheless, to throw light on the
ideographic language of African art the Mesopotamian and African
myths must be kept separate" (100). The arrogance in this pre-
scriptive/proscriptive pronouncement is both unmistakable and
characteristic, and goes to reinscribe the task of postcolonial contestation with strategic urgency.

This task must begin with an examination and interrogation
of the rationale and foundation of the unacceptable state of affairs,
the kind of exercise ably undertaken Said in *Orientalism* (1979)
and *Culture and Imperialism* (1993), and by Amin in
Eurocentrism (1989). This must be followed by the recuperation
and empowerment of all the marginalized, suppressed, and
silenced minority discourses. In this regard, Abdul JanMohamed
believes that the emphasis should be on the singularity of Minority
discourse unmediated by Western dominant discursive filter. The
important thing about this strategic singularity is not that it dis-
privileges the constituent differences of the epistemological monolith of the *Other*, earlier created/erected by the West, or that it
ignores the perversely intimate but unequal relationship between
the center and the peripheries; its importance lies in its disturbance

and attempted marginalization or de-centering of the center, in its attempted reshuffling of the masked prevailing asymmetrical power relations, and in its inauguration of and insistence on a reciprocal and multilateral dynamic (Jan Mohamed & Lloyd 1990: ix;1-16).

In his peculiar way, Okigbo, who was clearly ahead of his time, had—long before it was fashionable to engage in postcolonial critique—combined in his poetry the cultural concerns which now comprise the cultural-critical agenda of writers and theorists alike. Okigbo's postcolonial politics can be understood if we contextualize it within the general nativistic upsurge then prevailing in the Black world which gave rise to such trends as the Negritude Movement among the French-colonized Africans, and the more pragmatic cultural reinterpretation and rehabilitation among the English-colonized.

The most important effect of slavery, and latterly of colonialism/neocolonialism has been to leave on the African psyche a stamp of inferiority and servility, as well as a sense of cultural inadequacy and aping shame in relation to Western culture which, placed on the topmost rung of the Darwinistic hierarchy, has been *presented/represented* as superior. This "idea of European identity as a superior one in comparison with all the non-European peoples and cultures" has been identified as the sustaining pillar of European cultural hegemony (Said 1979:7). The obverse of this superiorist doctrine is that of primitivism which encouraged Africans who had invented nothing, who had not industrialized, who had not felt the need to colonize the moon, planets, and the stars, and who had produced no Homer or Shakespeare, to mimic and aspire to Westernism: "Imitate the West, the best of all possible worlds" (Amin 1989: xii). While among the English-colonized, this doctrine had quite deleterious effects, among the French-colonized there was a near-total submersion of the African in the French psycho-cultural stream. When, after the drunken joy of being called Black Frenchmen, the French-speaking Africans were roused from their cultural amnesia into sobriety by the falsity and hypocrisy of the policy of Assimilation, founded itself also upon Eurocentrism, they started the movement which sought to counter racism with a hyperbolic foregrounding of the virtues of blackness. Okigbo was born in 1932, the very year that this

Negritude Movement was inaugurated in Paris by African (and diasporic) intellectuals. This movement must have been histori- cally necessary, but soon became subject to strident attacks, espe- cially from Anglophone intellectuals—including Wole Soyinka who not only thought that it was not necessary for a tiger to proclaim its tigritude (it should just pounce and tear!), but, more impor- tantly, saw Negritude as having "trapped itself in what primarily was a defensive role":

> It accepted one of the most commonplace blasphemies of racism, that the black man has nothing between his ears, and proceeded to subvert the power of poetry to glorify this fab- ricated justification of European cultural domination. Suddenly we were exhorted to give a cheer for those who never invented anything, a cheer for those who never explored the oceans. The truth, however, is that there isn't such a creature. (Soyinka 1976:129);

and Okigbo who thought "there might not in fact be any cultural meet- ing points between the various black peoples of the world" (Duerden & Pieterse 1972:139) to justify the globalizing assumptions of Negritude. In fact, of Negritude poetry itself he had earlier said that:

> when you've read a lot about it you just hit through the whole pattern, you begin to have the feeling, or I begin to have the feeling that it is just like working a machine or, if you like, work- ing a *duplicating* machine, you think it is so easy to do. I don't know how much genuine feelings we have in a lot of negritude poems and the pity of it is that some of the negritude poets could still have been great poets in spite of negritude. (138)

Because the critique of Negritude has continued to emphasize its essentialization of Blackness, it is important to cite Okigbo's judi- cious appraisal of that program. When in a 1963 interview Dennis Duerden suggested that Negritude "starts with the idea that there's some sort of specific mental attitude that characterizes someone who's black—. . . this is what negritude seems to be saying; that all black people have some specific mental attitude" (139), Okigbo was quick to correct him:

I don't quite agree. I don't think this is what negritude seems
to be saying. I think that negritude seems to be saying that
*black people who have somehow felt a sense of alienation
are now looking for their roots,* which I think is a perfectly
legitimate thing to do. . . . I think too that on another side the
political equivalent of negritude tends to assert an African
personality. (139-40)

I have italicized part of the sentence in the quotation because it not
only represents a corrective on some misreading of Negritude,
but more importantly, it will be found to constitute a major part
of Okigbo's own postcolonial project. For even though the
Francophone and Anglophone programs appeared to be taking
different routes, their aims were the same.

Okigbo's contribution to the cultural rehabilitation of his society can be seen as a trinary endeavor. First he had to equip himself intellectually in order to confront a system which, first and
foremost, was grounded in an epistemology that was formidable,
albeit false and deliberately distorted; second, he needed to retrace
the exilic route and assume a vantage base at "home"; and third,
with the confidence and assurance of a reintegrated prodigal and
courageous wisdom of a poet of destiny, he could begin his critique.

Ironically, Okigbo's exile was part of his preparation. For,
even though it was not a path willingly "chosen," the exilic condition enabled his acquisition of Western education and immersion
in world cultures, which was to prove indispensable in this crusade.
His formal Western education ended with his study of the classics
and ancient history at the university. But, aware of the immensi-
ty of the task ahead of him, he stretched his natural inclinations
to their limits and became a truly voracious reader and polymath,
with the result that of the long chain of occupations he undertook,
it was only during his stints as teacher at Fiditi, University Librarian
at Nsukka, Manager at Cambridge University Press, and publisher at Citadel, that he found real happiness. In all of them he was
not only always among books, but he was a cultural worker directly involved in the production and dissemination of knowledge.

Given the amount of energy and zeal he invested in his
preparation, it was no surprise that in the end he became thor-

oughly familiar with most civilizations and cultures of the world, and could read, speak, write, and translate the major languages of the world including Latin, Greek, Spanish, French, Italian, Portuguese, Igbo, Yoruba, and English. In his own words:

> I translate from Latin verse into English verse or from Greek verse into English verse and *vice versa*. . . . I think that I have a fairly *good* knowledge of Latin, a working knowledge of Greek....
> In fact enough Latin to read and understand Latin poetry in the original, and understand before I translate—and in fact enough Greek to translate Greek poetry into English. (Duerden & Pieterse, eds., 1972:137)

What we have been describing here is not an exercise in mechanical translation. And, completely different from the juggling of card-indexes by "linguists" who thereby declare their mastery of "exotic" languages which they in turn, as Professors of African or Oriental Languages, distort and profanate (cf. Echeruo's "comment" on Austin Shelton's exemplary misreading/mistranslating of Igbo proverbs from which he then went on to "penetrate somewhat into collective rural Igbo thought" in *Conch* III. 2 [Sept. 1971]:63-66), Okigbo's was a serious and devoted commitment to the acquisition of the tools he would need in his life-task. The objects of his study were so thoroughly mastered and so completely assimilated that in his poetry it is useless to chase the elusive shadows of influence. The languages and cultures of the world were so subdued and possessed by him that no other poet or cultural worker could have been better equipped than Okigbo for his task. On the matter of influence itself, Okigbo had this to say:

> I think that I've been influenced by various Literatures and cultures, right from Classical times to the present day, in English, Latin, Greek and a little French, a little Spanish, but I think that in fact the question of influence is a very complicated thing. . . . It's often difficult to pin down an influence to a particular source. If those sources have become assimilated into the subject and have come together to form an integral whole it is very difficult to sort them out—to know where the Babylonian

influence ends and the classical influence starts, and where the classical influence ends, and where, if you like, the modern influence starts. I have been influenced, generally, by Greek and Roman poets and writers and also by modern English, French, Spanish poets. (Duerden & Pieterse 1972:145-46)

It must be mentioned here that as important as these influences, more appropriately intertextualities, were, that of music was special because it not only served as training-ground in versification, but provided for the composing poet a veritable vehicle of transport and inspiration, putting him in the right mood, that of rapture, excitation, and meditation, in which he was both a capable transmitter and composer, an efficient vehicle for poetry. For this particular purpose and reason, his music collection at Ibadan comprised only such titles that, being neither "highlife" nor "sentimental," it was difficult for me to understand or appreciate. But whenever Okigbo played these "classical" numbers, he became visibly radiant and happy and often "carried away" at the same time. In fact, Okigbo thought that music was a greater influence on him than poetry:

> I think that what has influenced me most is not in fact poets, but the composers, the musical composers are the people who have influenced me more than the poets. . . . Well, it is very difficult to explain, but take "Heavensgate": when the spell of the impressionist composers Debussy, Caesar Franck, Ravel . . . Yes, I think that the musicians have influenced me much more than—well, of course, it is the same thing except that the composer is working in abstract form and the poet is working with words. (Duerden & Pieterse 1972:137-38; Nwoga 1984:241-42)

We must remember, of course, that Okigbo's musical roots go both far and deep. There was, to begin, the almost primal influence of Okigbo's nurse, Eunice, who was given to constant lyrical outbursts; then there was his own mother who not only sang and played the organ, but had one at home which was still at Ojoto during my last visit there; there was the boyhood close attention to and imitation of bird-songs:

Bird of the sun on tree top sitting
on fig tree top mourns under the lamp:
etru bo pi alo she e anando we aquandem...

And when we were great boys
hiding at the smithies
we sang words after the bird—

Krastobiate
And we would respond,
great boys of child-innocence,
and in the flames burn
white buck and helmet
that had pulled us through innocence.
ebili malo, ebili com com, ebili te que liquandem . . .

still sings the bird
under the lamp
stale song the dumb bell
loud to me. (*Passages* . . . in Nwoga 1984:16-17)

Finally, Okigbo himself wrote music and played the piano, both of which he did with distinction, accompanying Wole Soyinka and Francisca Pereira "regularly in musical concerts at U.C.I.," and only giving up "writing music when I started writing poetry seriously. . . . I was writing music seriously up to 1956. I started writing poetry when I stopped writing music" (Duerden & Pierterse, 1972:136).

Paradoxical as it may sound, Okigbo's preparation could not have been complete without the alienating experience of Christianity, which Fraser questionably construes as a catalyst of the poet's "personal infidelity to the traditional gods" (Fraser 1986:106). He was born into the Roman Catholic family of James and Anna Onugwualuobi Okigbo. His father was not only an educator and school headmaster, but in those days, a school (head) teacher was also a worker in the Lord's vineyard, the Roman Catholic mission, and was always next in command to the Parish priest whose duties he filled whenever the priest could not, for any reason, make it to Sunday worship. Of his mother, wife of the first

Roman Catholic citizen in Ojoto-Uno, the remembrance is always in association with the church, the bible, and the organ:

> behind the bell-tower, . . .
> O Anna at the knobs of the panel oblong, . . .
> where the players of loft pipe organs
> rehearse old lovely fragments, . . .
> strains of pressed orange leaves on pages,
> bleach of the light of years held in leather:.... (CP:21)

The bell-tower is the one in St. Odilia's Catholic Church, Ojoto-Uno, and the "panel oblong" can equally refer to the pipe organ which his mother played or to a coffin, for the subject of the poem here is "festivity in black." The "light of years held in leather" refers to the leather-bound family bible. This then is the religious environment, the family, whose every child must be baptized in the church, according to the strict laws of the church whose powerful representative, "Liedan," at his "Holy See" in Adazi, known for his edicts and pronouncements and injunctions against everything traditional (Udechukwu 1984: 81) was immortalized in Okigbo's remembrance of the coming of "the first missionaries and invaders, scrunching their boots through the sacred places and clamping their alien law upon the land" (Moore 1984: 278):

> Behind the walled gods
> in market
> boots over mandos
> and byelaws thereto appended
> by Leidan,
> archtyrant of the holy sea. (Quoted in Moore 1984:278)

Of the baptism itself, which would ordinarily be welcomed with excitement and joy by the baptisand and marked with rejoicing and flurried preparation of post-baptismal entertainment by the family, it is significant that what Okigbo the poet's sensibility captures is:

> rank smell of olive oil
> on foreheads,

vision of the hot bath of heaven
among reedy spaces. (Quoted in Moore 1984:278)

As if that was not enough, the experience itself is re-presented in the most excruciatingly painful and terrifying of terms. And who else but the now notorious "alienator," Kepkanly, would wield the branding blade?

Scar of the crucifix
over the breast,
by red blade inflicted
by red-hot blade
on the right breast witnesseth
Mystery which I, initiate,
received newly naked
upon the waters of the genesis
from Kepkanly. (CP:22)

The important thing about this baptismal experience is that, notwithstanding its terror, it left only a scar, permanent albeit, but only physical and superficial; not psychical. It would, therefore, not hinder, in the least, the poet's impending mission. I therefore consider as unacceptable Anozie's reading which talks about "the Prodigal's implied failure to understand the value of Kepkanly's initiation—a failure which may mean a conscious or unconscious shirking of a heavy moral and spiritual responsibility" (Anozie 1972:116). The purpose of Kepkanly's initiation is the completion of the poet's alienation, which cycle being now complete, the poet is ready to return, like all repentant prodigals, if symbolically, home.

But Okigbo's retracing of the exilic route is a complicated and tedious process of "initiations" and purifications beginning with "The Passage," reaching the final acceptance of "Lustra," and climaxing with the celebration of "Newcomer," where he assumes his own mask, and is confident of the ancestral protection from Anna. Only then can he launch his crusade.

Okigbo then appropriately begins his return, his movement of reintegration in all contrition and humility. He had been forced to wander among alien and distracting orthodoxies and isms; his return now as repentant and supplicant cannot but be sincere:

Before you, mother Idoto,
naked I stand;
before your watery presence
a prodigal
leaning on an oilbean,
Lost in your legend.
Under your power wait I
on barefoot,
watchman for the watchword
at *Heavensgate*;
Out of the depths my cry:
give ear and hearken . . . (*CP*:19)

The nakedness of the returning prodigal implies humility, total surrender, and helplessness before the neglected deity to whose absolute power and authority the poet "on barefoot" submits. Distracted by nothing now, and consumed totally by his devotion, "Lost in your legend," the poet has confidence that his supplication will be heeded. As the poet instructs us in the footnote, Idoto is "a village stream [in Ojoto]. The oil bean, the tortoise, and the python are totems for her worship" (*CP*: 19, footnote 1). But symbolically, and even in actuality, there is a lot more than is given in the footnote. Idoto (*Ide-Oto* = Pillar of Oto) is not merely a village stream but the sustainer of life in that village for in it people swam, bathed, did their washings; and from it they drew their drinking and cooking water. It was also the domain of the water goddess, *Idoto*. The oil bean is that sturdiest of trees (*Ukpaka* = *pentaclatra microfillae*), stubborn in its rooted strength, and lining the sides of roads, in recent times has withstood the wrecked trials of automobiles whose drivers have been reckless and unwary. Its (oil-)beans which are violently scattered in thunderous explosions of the dry pods are a proteinaceous delicacy of the same name *ukpaka* (or *ugba*). Its grove which may not be entered carelessly except by the foolish is thus sacred to *Oto*, thus the name *Ukpaka-Oto*. The tortoise, on the other hand, is that eternal creature, paradigmatic, in folklore and real life, as a being of great wile and wisdom, resilience, duplicity, ubiquity, and divination. These traits have enabled it to survive great adversities the tales of which are told by the fragmentary appearance of the shell of this trickster-being. The python (*Eke*), in its slithering regality, symbolizes the connection or bridge between humans and the higher powers. It is for reason of this association with the god/man covenant that its name is hyphenated with the rainbow: *Eke-na-Ogwulugwu*. Both the tortoise and the python are thus, in Idoto mythos, beings whose liminality has equipped them to function as potent totems.

This explication enables me to reiterate an admonition to chasers after echoes and influences and allusions. As Okigbo himself has repeatedly told us, these are there, no doubt, but so fully assimilated are they into his poetry, that it is futile playing critical detectives with them. From wherever they may have been taken originally, the variegated intertextualities constitute the complex braid of Okigbo's poetic and cultural heritages. Moreover, why, for instance, do we need to invoke, like Anozie (1972), the *Old Testament* in order to understand or explain a self-sustaining cultural practice which predated the deleterious intrusion of Christianity? It is the very pandemic devastation visited on the indigenous culture by Christian cultural imperialism which has necessitated the present misery of the returning prodigal, who is asking for forgiveness, acceptance, reintegration, and empowerment to begin his crusade.

The python (*Eke*) is so sacred in Ojoto-uno that it roams the homesteads undisturbed. And should it be accidentally killed it is usually accorded expensive and elaborate funerary rites, while the culprit makes atonement as is appropriate to manslaughter or *female ochu*, the kind of fate that befalls Okonkwo in *Things Fall Apart* after he accidentally shoots Ezeudu's sixteen-year-old son during the old man's funeral (chapter thirteen). The python is to be distinguished from the boa-constrictor, *eke-ogba*, which Okigbo introduces later on in *Passage*, and which normally evokes terror and dread. Perhaps that explains why Theroux derails in his interpretation again and deserves the stricture of Anozie:

> On the rainbow passage already quoted here one Okigbo critic, Paul Theroux, himself a poet, has made the following remark: "The rainbow, the Covenant, is seen as a snake capable of both leading and destroying the poet. The symbol that will lead the poet is seen as the embodiment of good and

evil. The dual vision of Okigbo's occurs all through the journey; the saint would see only the rainbow, the profligate
would see the snake—but the visionary Okigbo sees both."
Paul Theroux's interpretation is based on the biblical premise
that the rainbow signifies the Act of Covenant (between
Jehovah and Noah) and the snake evil (because it invokes the
sin of Adam and Eve). Having thus implicitly assumed that
Okigbo was working from this Christian religious viewpoint
Theroux claims that the rainbow symbolizes good and evil and
therefore ascribes this duality to Okigbo's poetic vision. . . .
his assumption about the immediate symbolic role of the rainbow in the context—is wrong. (Anozie 1972:44)

Theroux's example illustrates how wrong-headed criticism can get
when it imposes a cultural-cosmological system arbitrarily on
another in an attempt to make sense of the cultural-literary products of that system. What concerns the poet here is the python-
rainbow and not the boa, even though the rainbow reminds the
poet of the dread-inspiring boa which he may or may not have
seen in growing up. In fact, a closer look at the structure of the
relevant poetic statement/sentence makes clear my point: the boa
functions only as a simile:

> Rainbow on far side, *arched like a boa bent to kill,*
> foreshadows the rain that is dreamed of (*CP*:20; *my italics*)

Moreover, the poet/prodigal whose single-minded physical-men-
tal attitude we have already seen in the earlier quoted first section
of *Passage*: naked, on barefoot, leaning on an oil bean, and consumed only with his present purpose—"lost in your legend"—cannot correctly be held guilty of "double vision."

Indeed, even this early, the poet's devotion and single-mind-
edness are beginning to pay off, and there is every sign and hope
that "out of the depths [his] cry" will be heard. This is because
unlike the ultra-violet rays which "foreshadow the fire that is
dreamed of," reminiscent of the apocalyptic devastation of the
fires of Armageddon, the rainbow here "foreshadows the rain that
is dreamed of," which will soothe the weary returning prodigal. As
if he had already been given the positive sign, he happily but heav-

ily withdraws in solitude to the "orangery" there to embark on extensive introspection, and also, like a truly repentant prodigal who had abdicated his filial duties, "to mourn / a mother on a spray." His acceptance and integration are not yet final but, at least, he has not been rejected and turned back; in fact, he has been allowed entry up to "the passage," where, as the wise hen newly arrived at new surroundings, he stands on one leg until it/he gets used to the new place; in Okigbo's case the "new place" is the old but estranged/defamiliarized *milieu*.

Passage *iii* continues the mood and atmosphere of bereavement and mourning of *Passage ii* by introducing:

Silent faces at crossroads:
festivity in black . . .
Faces of black like long black
columns of ants,.... (*CP*:5),

whose "festivity in black" is an oxymoronic suggestion of either the passing on, at a very ripe old age of the deceased, in which case his funeral usually becomes a festival; or the second funerary rites for one long dead, in which case the prodigal's fulfillment of a filial duty long abandoned could be instantiated. In any case, the procession leads to the "bell tower" of St. Odilia's where the "Christian" departed also had their "hot garden," the Catholic Church cemetery, which truly, not merely symbolically, after all life's journeys and races, represents the final destination, "where all roads meet." It is here too that the poet's mother was laid to rest, and in the poet's new mythopoetic order which transcends Roman Catholic sectarian exclusivism, she has assumed her place among the sanctified ancestors. In her own right, she can answer the cry/prayer of her son:

O Anna at the knobs of the panel oblong
hear us at crossroads at the great hinges (*CP*:5)

I have already commented on "panel oblong" and "great hinges" as equally capable of signifying both the coffin and the pipe organ. It is interesting how Fraser, in a strained and gallant effort to rescue Okigbo from a possible charge of atavism or paganism, always tries to underline the continuing presence of Christianity in—and thus the continuing relevance of Christian interpretation of— Okigbo's poetry. Thus he says that "The 'Anna of the knobs of the panel oblongs' may indeed be Okigbo's mother, *but she is also St. Anne*" (Fraser 1986:108; *my italics*). It is true that *naming* in the Roman Catholic tradition has always depended on the finite repertoire of names of saints. Indeed, in Igboland, until very recently, not to be called by one of the saints' names meant that one was not baptized, not Christian, and, therefore, pagan! Also, since all such saints' names were as a rule European/English, the Igbo having produced no saints, to answer a saint's/Christian name was to answer an English name: in colonized Igboland, Christianity and Englishness were interchangeable, but, definitely, not in the sense suggested by Fraser when he says that "at this juncture [of Okigbo's poetry] Christian and African religious initiations are made to fuse, to haunting effect" (Fraser 1986:108). Okigbo's mother was named after St. Anne but in this poem Okigbo was not thinking of St. Anne; Mrs. Anna Onugwualuobi Okigbo was already a respected ancestor, capable not only of answering prayers, but also of protecting her son from "them fucking angels" and saints and other mythological creations of Roman Catholicism. How can it be otherwise when Okigbo has shed all sartorial and other encumbrances associated with his alienation and exile and, as before the flaming forest, on holy ground stands both naked and unshod, the only sad reminder of his exile being the sign of that hot blade:

> Scar of the crucifix
> over the breast,
> by red blade inflicted
> by red-hot blade,
> on right breast witnesseth. (*CP*:6)

This is how Okigbo begins "Initiations," the second long poem in the *Heavensgate* sequence, about which two comments are in order. First, this position of the poem in the sequence has no historico-chronological significance because, as *remembering*, the events described took place before the penitential return of the poet-prodigal in *Passages*, but it does show the importance of memory to this poet who must recall and reenact the events that colluded to produce his present impasse. Second, it is important to note that here *"initiations"* are pluralized for they dramatize a series of initiations or junctures in the initiatory continuum: the alienating initiation into Christianity and the consequent abruption of his traditional allegiance; his initiation into poetry and into prophecy, from Jadum and Upandru respectively, but the two representing, in reality, a certain inseparability. It is, therefore, incorrect to describe the experience as the "three-fold initiation into three *distinct* and *potentially conflicting schools of thought*: the Christian/ individualistic, the professionally artistic and the ancestral folkloric" (Fraser 1986: 108; my italics). Igbo tradition-al individualism has always been predicated upon the overarching superordinacy of the collectivity, and the artistic has always been in the service of the group. Moreover, there should be no reason to bring in the notion of ideologically fractious and "conflicting schools of thought" here, since, in his definition of poetry as logis-tics, Okigbo conflates the notions of prophecy and poetry.

After the horrifying sadism of the imagery of the first stanza, reminiscent of the ordeal of the slaves during their translocation across the Atlantic, there is an almost redemptive ambivalence in the poet's attitude towards Kepkanly who had wielded that blade. The poet talks of:

> mystery which I, initiate,
> received newly naked
> upon waters of the genesis
> from Kepkanly.
> Elemental, united in vision
> of present and future,
> the pure line, whose innocence
> denies inhibitions. (*CP*:22)

So that alienating missionary ogre would appear to be also respon-sible for the poet's initiation into prophecy and bardic unity of vision: "Elemental, united in vision / of present and future." According to Anozie:

In the poet's imagination, therefore Kepkanly assumes the stature of a prophetic symbol, becomes a pagan god or bleeding Christ. From the mode of his death the poet learns or rather fails to learn one great lesson; the miraculous state of joy, the sheer psychic orgasm which the human spirit is capable of attainment at a moment of beatific grace and elevation. For at a moment such as this, death is seen not as an alienation of the spirit but as a fulfillment of the happiness so unexpectedly possessed and so independent of our free will. (Anozie 1972:52)

For about the end of that indigenous agent of the proselytizing missionaries, the poet has said:

and the hand fell with Haragin,
Kepkanly that wielded the blade;
with Haragin with God's light between them:
but the solitude within me remembers Kepkanly (CP:23)

The reason for this sudden death is explained in a footnote supplied by the poet: "Kepkanly was reported to have died from excess of joy when he received arrears of salary awarded by the Haragin Commission of 1945" (23,n.1).

The next but associated initiation (which, placed in close spatial-textual relationship with the one from Kepkanly, is made to contrast sharply with it) is that from John the Baptist, whose message, in the poet's view, is a mere "gambit." In its hypocritical impracticality, impossibility, even denial and negation of life itself, this gospel has been described as "barren orthodoxy, especially in its abstract morality ('life without sin')" (Obiechina 1980:25). If the sexual union which is the only enabler and guarantor of a new life is seen by Western Christian orthodoxy as sinful then the prescription of life without sex/sin is a proscription of life:

so comes John the Baptist
with bowl of salt water
preaching the gambit
life without sin, without
life; which accepted,

way leads downward
down the orthocenter
avoiding decisions. (CP:22; my italics)

This gambit doesn't have to be accepted or imbibed without question as the poet implies through the use of that conditional phrase,
"which accepted," which I have italicized in the quotation to call
attention to the poet's "cynical scepticism about the crux of
Christian values" (Anozie 1972:53). It seems to me that it is this
element of skepticism or honest doubt which needs to be emphasized as a possible legacy from Kepkanly and not, as Fraser (1986)
sees it, "an induction with the safe port of Christian commitment,
where the agonizing complexity of moral responsibility disappears
in a reassuring 'confluence of planes' corresponding to the 'orthocentre' [sic] of a triangle" (108).

The poet who criticizes the dissemination of the gambit
"which accepted / way leads downward / down the orthocenter
/ avoiding decisions" cannot be endorsing, much less delighting
in, the abdication of moral responsibility as Fraser suggests. But
Fraser's further elaboration on the concept of "orthocentre," if
unenlightening, at least, introduces an interesting perspective on
plane geometry which will be relevant to the second part of
"Initiations":

> An orthocentre is the point at which the perpendicular from
> the vertices of the triangle meet. "Ortho-," however, also sug-
> gests "orthodoxy," and hence a completely water-tight creed,
> such as the church supplies for weaker brethren, those who do
> not share the poet's compulsion to forge a personal spiritual
> vision. The symbolism of geometric figures seems to distill the
> angularity characteristic of those with blinkered minds, con-
> stricted either by the simplifications of Christian doctrine, by the
> petty bureaucracy of "fanatics and priests and popes / orga-
> nizing secretaries and party managers," or worse still, by the
> sheer rapacity of the social parasites: "brothers and deacons /
> liberal politicians / selfish self-seekers." (Fraser 1986:108-09)

But one fails to see how a poet who is presented here as happy
with his "induction into the safe port of Christian commitment"

can, in the same paragraph, be said to be possessed of a "compulsion to forge a personal spiritual vision." We know that Okigbo's sympathies were too large and broad for the constrictions of any of the known sectarian religions; his sympathies and consciousness were expansive enough to both transcend and accommodate them all. As Nwoga explains it:

> Both Christianity and traditional religion are conventional and Okigbo was not conventional. He was consistent in his interviews in denying absolute attachment to either religion and in acknowledging continuing influences from both. As he said to Marjory Whitelaw in 1965: "I think that over the years I have tried to evolve my own personal religion . . . So I don't think it would be right for me to say I am a Christian or I am a pagan. I think my own religion combines elements of both."
> . . . [Okigbo's] psychic consciousness transcends and can accommodate and use the myths of disparate religions. (Nwoga, ed., 1984:120)

Coming back to Fraser's sweeping definition of "orthocentre," then, we cannot accept his diminution of the social-political-critical implications of the poet's meticulous geometric elaboration as set forth in these lines:

> Or forms fourth angle—
> duty obligation:
> square yields the moron,
> fanatics and priests and popes
> organizing secretaries and
> party managers; better still,
> the rhombus—brothers and deacons,
> liberal politicians,
> selfish selfseekers—all who are good
> doing nothing at all;
> the quadrangle, the rest, me and you.... (CP:23)

The characterology elaborated here is both acute and interesting. For one thing it leaves no one in doubt as to the poet-critic's attitude towards the representatives of the different "shapes" and their overriding ideologies: thus the pope, as the beginning and end of all earthly (Roman Catholic) orthodoxy, figures here as an undistinguished member of the same class, the "Square," whose other members include all "fanatics and priests," as well as "organizing secretaries and party managers." Interestingly, Kepkanly, like Leidan of course, belongs here. And they are all "morons."

The next group whose sign is the "rhombus," and whom Fraser rightly calls "social parasites," comprises those elements in society whom I have already characterized as gastrocentric, monomanically preoccupied with the pursuit of "things" to tuck away either in the unsafe and decomposing recesses of their guts, or in the safe and criminally anonymous vaults of a Swiss Bank. They are also reminiscent of that group whose trait Thomas Carlyle had identified as "do nothingism."

In the single last line dealing with geometric categories, Okigbo does a most important thing as poet of destiny. That single line which not only proclaims his identity, but also declares his affinities, affiliation, and his politics, is the triumphant display of his credentials: I am of the people; I am one of the people; I am for the people:

the quadrangle, the rest, me and you . . . (CP:23)

It is for this reason that, in response to Anozie's consignment of the poet to that political flux between Liberalism and Christian Democracy:

In neither of these two poems ["Laments"] does the poet really feel like committing himself to any socio-political philosophy. (In fact Okigbo was somewhere between a Liberal and a Christian Democrat in political sympathies.). (Anozie 1972:135)

I had, on a previous occasion, dismissed that categorical pigeonholing as "wrong because it has no basis in fact" (Okafor 1980:9). In the context of Nigerian politics the terms "Liberal" or "Christian Democrat," if ever heard, mean absolutely nothing. Moreover, what louder declaration of a political stand does one need than the proclamation, in that one line quoted above, of the poet's populism? Indeed I had gone on to say that:

Okigbo's politics was not partisan, not *parti pris*, for his political party, if he had any, embraced all of humanity. Not the
glorified *homo sapiens eternitas* but the humanity of harsh
reality groaning under the studded boots of power-seekers,
the selfish self-seekers. Hence Anozie's consignment of
Okigbo in that political flux between Liberalism and Christian
Democracy is wrong because it has no basis in fact.
Okigbo was only committed to the civilization of community for
which reason he unsurprisingly aligned himself both intellectually and physically with the forces of change. This commitment finally led to his taking up arms to challenge the forces
of oppression and dehumanization. (Okafor 1980:9-10)

Okigbo's identification is with the people. He is engaged in the
present self-denying preparation only in order to be able and
empowered to serve them. It is not surprising, then, that the next
two agents of his "initiations" are deeply rooted in the lores of the
folk; they even belong to the class whom the deracinated elite
would have dismissed or derided as flotsam and jetsam of the
social order. In the words of the poet himself, Jadum is "a half-
demented village minstrel" and Upandru "a village explainer" (*CP*:
24,25). Socially undistinguished, but rootedly integrally to the
social-cultural formation, these characters significantly embody
the very qualities which Okigbo as poet possesses, the felicitous
fusion in him of which has accounted for his great stature as poet:
madness, poetry—minstrelsy, divination—prophecy.

Jadum, depicted here in pastoral and rustic circumstances, is
full of song and warning. If people are simply amused by, and
ignore, his cryptic warnings, they do so at their own peril. For
Jadum's madness is characterized by wisdom, great clarity, and precise knowledge. The burning of the incense in his house indicates
serious mystical pursuits, for only one committed to the higher and
deeper things would want to invoke and commune with the spirits. And because this mysticism equips him with higher and superior knowledge, he is in a position to understand the superficiality
and falsity, "the errors of the rendering," of dogmatic orthodoxy:

And this from Jadum,
(Say if thou knowest

a village where liveth
in heart of the grassland
a minstrel who singeth)
to shepherds, with a lute on his lip:
Do not wander in speargrass,
After the lights,
Probing lairs in stockings,
To roast
The viper alive, with dog lying
Upsidedown in the crooked passage . . .
Singeth Jadum from Rockland
After the lights.
And there are here
the errors of the rendering . . . (*CP*: 24)

The warning is both loud and clear. Those who dismiss it as the inco-
herent, and therefore, inconsequential, ranting of a madman from
the semi-arid grassland will very likely experience the same fate as
the heedless "dog lying / Upsidedown in the crooked passage."

I believe it is possible to read and interpret Okigbo's poetry,
complexly intertextual as it is, without losing our critical bearing
in our search for trails and scents of influence. Thus, while it is possible that "Rockland" echoes, and might well have been taken
from, Ginsberg's poem *Howl*, as Anozie thinks, the accuracy of
the geography of Jadum's Rockland leaves no one in doubt that
there is nothing exotic or even borrowed about it (see Anozie
1972:54-55). For Jadum's Rockland is *Agba-enu*, a term used to
describe the semi-arid, partly rocky, partly grassy terrain of the
uplands, including the Aguata Province, of Igboland. Okigbo's
father was once a school (head-)teacher in Ekwulobia in Aguata
Province, and Okigbo's poetic sensibility recaptures and remembers not only the geography but also the social-cultural history of
this place of his growing up. The present writer briefly lived in
Aguata during the Nigeria-Biafra war, and can attest to its aridity—for drinking water one went to one stream *Otalu (ota-alu =*
biter, the one that bites), whose notorious U-shaped valley made
access to and from it a very daunting trial of one's faith and
endurance; the hilly and undulating landscape; the rocky terrain;
the preponderance of speargrass (speargrass = *Ata*), which gave

that province its name *Agu-ata* (= speargrass bush/land). This sub-Savannah vegetation was conducive to lucrative livestock farming, as well as to the luxuriation of vipers! The metaphoric landscape of this poem is, indeed, homespun, as is made clear in Egudu's discussion of it, which also reiterates the poet's skepticism about hollow Catholic Christian orthodoxy. According to Egudu,

> This poem is literally about the minstrel "Jadum," a madman who is known by that name. "Aguata" is the name of the county in which he lives. This county is in Awka Division of the East Central State of Nigeria. Thematically, the poem satirizes the Catholic priests who dragged the poet into Catholicism in his childhood and whose preaching means to the poet nothing more than the rantings of a madman "Jadum." The validity of this interpretation can be fully realized by reading all five poems that make up *Initiation* (sic). (Egudu 1984:244-45)

The poem truly contains Okigbo's critical attitude towards "theoretical christianity, the dogmas which all manner of charlatans push and behind which they perpetuate atrocities against their neighbours and Mankind" (Obiechina 1980:35), but thematically it is concerned with an important phase in the chain of *initiations* (plural) which the poet has embarked upon.

The next and closely related initiation is that which the poet receives from Upandru, "A village explainer" (*CP*:25, poet's footnote 1). But Upandru is not merely a villager who has acquired linguistic competence or who is "steeped in the use of words" much like the famous masters and "eaters" of words in Achebe's *Things Fall Apart* (Anozie 1972:56). Upandru belongs in a long line of explicators whose calling connects them to the very core of language as such, to the *logos* itself. It is for that reason that their role is, properly speaking, *divination* which, on a deeper level, attempts the explication of human destiny. An important item in the diviner's paraphernalia of divination is the shell of the tortoise. And if we recall the earlier reference to that ubiquitous and sagacious character in Igbo folklore, *Mbekwu* (the son of *Aniga*), in our discussion of Idoto, we can easily understand the relationship between the explainer/diviner and the trickster whose duplicitous indeterminacy and liminality enable him to act as a link between transcendence and mundanity, between discourse and destiny.

Upandru's explication/divination, *Igba Afa*, is the same thing as the more widely known Yoruba *Ifa*. In both instances, *Fa* and *Afa* refer to Fate, and its divination or explication is the function of the explainer who is thus "the sole agent of interpretation and hence mediation between man, on one hand, and the Book of Fate (*Fa*/*Afa*]) on the other" (Gates Jr. 1988:24). Henry Louis Gates' discussion of Legba, the trickster/linguist, is thus important for our understanding of Upandru. In this discussion the linguistic function of Legba as divine linguist is elaborated thus:

> To Legba was assigned the role of linguist between the kingdoms of gods and gods, and gods and men. Whereupon, in addition to the knowledge of the "language" of Mawu-Lisa [the primal god], he was given the knowledge of all the "languages" spoken by the other gods in their separate domains. (Herskovits, *Dahomey*, quoted in Gates 1988:23-24)

Gates goes on to say that:

> Legba, then stands as the discursive, or textual, principle itself; . . . Legba "is a creator of discourse, for his every movement is . . . a 'raid on the inarticulate,' a foray into the formless, which simultaneously gives shape to the dark and fearsome and new life to structure always in danger of becoming a skeleton." Legba is discourse and discourse upon a text. Legba . . . is the divine reader, whose interpretation of the Book of Fate determines precisely what the book says. The interpreter governs meaning. . . . (24)

Villagers would go to the explainer, then, for he, Legba/Upandru, alone, can read the divine text of Fate "because of the several stages of mediation and translation that occur in rapid succession in Fa divination. A supplicant's query is answered by a cryptogram" (24).

Appropriately then, immediately after the introduction of Upandru as the mysterious and enigmatic embodiment of hidden, "screened," texts and their meanings, we have a staging of a linguistic *agon*, or *stichomythia*, between the poet and the explainer, whose resolution yields the definition of poetry as "logistics," involving "'roads,' or 'pathways,' or 'courses' . . . which lead the supplicant through the maze of figuration," out of the "jungle of ambiguity that is the language of" (24) divination, of poetry itself:

And this from Upandru:
Screen your bedchamber thoughts
with sun-glasses,
who could jump your eye,
your mind-window,
And I said:
The prophet only the poet.
And he said: Logistics.
(Which is what poetry is).... (*CP*:25)

The excited arrival at this definition of poetry, after the cryptogrammatic test or *agon* with Upandru, is not a facile achievement. For Okigbo's "logistics" does not imply simple, mechanical movement but is a whole complex of hermeneutic procedure with which no simpleton, but only the madman/the prophet/the poet can deal. It is a ratiocinative and affective, and imaginative and intellectual exercise whose almost hyperbolic implication is captured in the image of "jumping the mind-window." Thus the very suggestion that the poet's enthusiasm at Upandru's wise reply "leads him to a kind of anti-climax in the pseudo-academic equation of poetry with logistics" (Anozie 1972:56) cannot be entertained at all.

In the same way, Anozie's reading of the next stanza, in which "the whole of the traditional Ibo ritual of castration is invoked . . . and [in which] the image suggests that the ram is left in a state of oestrus pain and heat [, whereby] . . . the poet-exile can see through the imperfections of his initiations—'the errors of the rendering'" (57) is unacceptable: In the stanza:

And he said to the ram: Disarm.
And I said:
Except by rooting,
who could pluck yam tubers from their base? (*CP*:25),

there is no suggestion of diffidence at all. The poet, having already arrived at the brink of initiation into, and at a definition of, poetry, is defiant and un-afraid and challenges Upandru to disarm him, the ram! In the Igbo folkloric *doxa* to which Anozie refers, the ram is asked to "remove" that thing hanging pendulous between his hind legs, to which he replies that one doesn't simply or easily "remove" a yam tuber. Only by "rooting," by painstaking and patient and expert "digging," can one "pluck" yam tubers from their "base," their deep anchor in the soil. In other words, far from exhibiting "oestrus pain and heat," even though the poet's initiations are far from over, for "there are [still] the errors of the rendering," the audacious poet is satisfied with his progress so far.

Taken together, then, the poet's initiations from Jadum and Upandru represent his solid "identification with the community, especially with its folk-outlook that leads to the recognition of the importance of individuals, be they ever so demented, grotesque or waggish" (Obiechina 1980:28). Indeed, Obiechina goes on to underline the importance of his grassroots and folk identification as having:

> the effect of locating the poet close to the centre of his people's folk-imagination which takes in everyone and everything which stimulates its responses. In the peculiar interactions, derivable from initiation rites and in which the individual is bound more closely to the group and the group more closely to the individual, no experience is too trivial, no action too inconsequential; each experience, action, speech and gesture helps to provide the emotional scaffolding that sustains the communal world from which the artist draws to enrich his sensibilities and the texture of his work. (28)

So, the poet's initiations so far have, piecemeal, block-by-block as it were, provided material for the "scaffolding" of his imminent enterprise. Clearly, they have been insufficient; but they have not been marked by "imperfections," as Anozie suggests (Anozie 1972:57).

Hence the poet embarks on another initiation, this time specifically into poetry and mystical vision. Constructed obviously as a lover's invocation of his mistress, "Watermaid" is devoid of banal carnality or mundane eroticism, except perhaps in the one sense in which mystical union is sometimes seen in orgasmic terms. The lover-beloved structure has misled some critics into reading the poem as dealing "with the secrecy of love and the loneliness of a boy waiting in vain for the arrival of his girl friend" (Egudu 1984: 341). But, clearly, the subject of this poem is mystical whose fruit is poetic sight/insight and vision, illumination and inspiration.

Thus, though the thrust of this project is hardly aesthetic, it is in order, with respect to this poem on vision, insight, and poetic initiation, to begin by dismissing Anozie's assertion that "'Watermaid' is a poor visual but a good lyrical realization of poetic intuition" (Anozie 1972:58). One does not need to be a poet to function as a critic, and it is amazing how one can read a poem which depends so heavily on visual as on other senses for its total effect, a poem whose first stanza begins:

Eye open on the sea
    eyes open, of the prodigal;
    upward to heaven shoot
where stars will fall from (CP:26),

and describe it as "a poor visual realization." The same poem goes on to invoke the "beachsand," breaking "salt-white surf on the stones," "lobsters and shells," "sunbeaten beach," "man with woman," "armpit-dazzle of a lioness," "white light," "moonlight," "match-flare," "mirrors," and "gold crop sinking ungathered." It appears to me that such close concatenation of concentrated visual imagery deserves closer visual-critical attention.

Moreover, even though the belief is rampant that "the Watermaid is reputed to bring wealth and other favours to her favourites," what Okigbo does in this poem is not, as Obiechina suggests, simply "to appropriate the existing belief and turn it over to the service of poetry" (1980:28-29). But he correctly notes that the poet's "encounter with the Watermaid is . . . a private experience with wider implications" (29). One of such implications is epiphanous, for in the poem the poet, for the first time, reveals the secret of his close connection with the mysteries, his long-standing relationship, as *Ogbanje* or changeling, with the spirit-world whose actual or mythological manifestation is the Watermaid or Mammy Water, the "white queen":

> Secret I have told into no ear
> save into a dughole, to hold, not to drown with—
> Secret I have planted into beachsand
> now breaks
> salt-white surf on the stones and me,
> and lobsters and shells
> in iodine smell—
> whose secret I have covered up with beachsand .... (*CP*:26)

The phenomenon of *Ogbanje* (Yoruba: *Abiku*), whereby a child with strong mystical ties with them of the spirit-world, enacts a repetitive cycle of coming and going, of being born and prematurely and often suddenly dying, has two variants. The terrestrial variant, simply called *Ogbanje* has his/her (its) secret or life-oath (*Iyi-uwa*) buried in the earth. The process of retrieval of this secret, usually in the form of smooth stones or pebbles, alone or in combination with other items, is accomplished with the aid of an experienced diviner, and with the cooperation of the changeling. For one reason or another, the changeling may change his/her/its mind and wants to live on, on earth, hence its cooperation in locating the "dughole." The retrieval of the secret severs its ties with the other world, and it lives, much like the character, Ezimma, in Achebe's *Things Fall Apart*, who represents the most adequate fictional exemplification of the phenomenon (1986:56-61; also 67-76).

The maritime or lacustrine variant is a more intractable case, if only because retrieval of the secret from a lake or river is a more tricky exercise, and, therefore, involves series of complex and often futile rituals and sacrifices of placation of the Watermaid. Those changelings associated with the "white queen" or goddess of the Waters, or Watermaid, are called *Ogbanje-mmili* (*mmili* = water) and maintain an ambivalent (fascination/dread) attitude towards water in the forms of lakes, streams, rivers, or seas (see Acholonu 1988;1989).

But whether terrestrial or maritime, the *Ogbanje* are the mysterious, enigmatic beings who live as if in a hurry to make their exit from this world. If Okigbo had not died in the war, it is quite conceivable that he would still have left quite early, by some other inexplicable and sudden way. Another remarkable trait of the *Ogbanje* is its (his/her) brooding withdrawal and reclusion which the uninitiated see as shyness or aloofness, arrogance or disconnection. But such solitude is indispensable to him/her who must commune with, or await the visitation of the Spirit-Queen. Characteristically such visitations are painfully brief but illuminating/illumining:

> Bright
> with the armpit-dazzle of a lioness,
> she answers
> wearing white light about her;
> and the waves escort her,
> my lioness,
> crowned with the moonlight.
> So brief her presence—
> match-flare in wind's breath—
> so brief with mirrors around me
> Downward . . .
> the waves distil her;
> gold crop
> sinking ungathered. (*CP*:27)

This poem is full of pain and regret because the ecstatic visit is too brief and tantalizing to be satisfying. Almost onanistic, the visit falls just short of delivery of the full gift of poetic inspiration; the "gold crop" comes teasingly within reach, but sinks "ungathered." Even then, all is not lost for the poetic recapitulation of the rare experience results in "some of the most splendid poetic evocations of the collection" (Obiechina 1980:29). Hence, the poet does not descend into unrelieved dejection: if so much has been lost, so much has been gained in abundant recompense; partial fulfillment is, perhaps, better than no fulfillment at all; the poet counts his blessings all the same:

And I who am here abandoned,
count the sand by wavelash abandoned,
count her blessing, my white queen.
But the spent sea reflects
from his mirrored visage
not my queen, a broken shadow.
So I who count in my island the moments,
count the hour which will bring
my lost queen with angel's ash in the wind. (CP:28)

Even though the queen appears to have been "lost," such loss is only momentary, and the poet has been able to learn, through his initiations so far, that the crucial thing is the ability "to clutch at this hour" however fleeting and evanescent it may be. Thus, even in the apparent disorientation of the intense experience, the poet is excited by possibilities, albeit inconclusive and "broken":

The stars have departed,
the sky in monocle
surveys the world under.
The stars have departed,
and I — where am I?
Stretch, stretch, O antennae,
to clutch at this hour,
fulfilling each moment in a
broken monody. (CP:29)

For even the feelings of isolation, almost desolation, and abandonment are all necessary to the maturation and preparation of the poet for the task ahead. And he is almost there; for the visit of the Watermaid, however brief, is a rare gift which is not given to the many, but is reserved for the qualified and "almost" ready. Moreover, the poet who has cultivated solitude all his life knows that it constitutes part of the strength of the pathfinder. As Obiechina (1980) points out:

Part of the lesson of this initiation is that isolation is the burden which all special and inspired people have to bear—

priests, poets, prophets and even philosophers. The very intangible nature of their concerns brings them face to face with despair and loneliness of their situation away from the din and bustle of the world of ordinary people. Initiation into the cult of poetry is . . . a retreat into loneliness and isolation, into areas where the best reward may be a flitting or fragmentary vision which if not captured opportunely is soon lost. (30)

Okigbo recognizes the critical importance of capturing opportunely the precious but transient coruscation of vision and inspiration, even if all that means is "fulfilling each moment in a / broken monody" (CP:29). A poet that is so cognizant of the evanescence of illuminations as well as the transience of inspiration/visitation cannot, therefore, be said to be "probably *unaware* of the present limitations of his power, of the unsatisfactoriness of his 'limitation' [for which reason] *the poet has ventured too precociously* to arrest the Muse's coquetry" (Anozie 1972:58; my italics).

It is because the poet is fully aware of his "limitations," aware also of the incompleteness of his initiations without a ritual cleansing, that he undertakes the purification of the next phase in *Lustra*:

So would I to the hills again
so would I
to where springs the fountain
there to draw from
And to hill top clamber
body and soul
whitewashed in the moon dew
there to see from
So would I from my *eye* the mist
so would I
thro' moon mist to hill top
there for the cleansing
Here is a new laid egg
here a white hen at midterm. (CP:30)

The poet has arrived here at the climacteric finale of the tortuous, tantalizing, and protracted quest for mystical grace, vision, clarity, and empowerment. But he cannot achieve this final state with even the tiniest encrustation of impurity or imperfection. The process involved here goes beyond the mere ablution suggested in "The Passage" by the figure of the naked prodigal standing before the "watery presence" of Mother Idoto. The present ritual of cleansing involves both "body and soul" to be effectual. The highest point in this most serious quest, the retreat or withdrawal, has a long antecedent history, involving prophets and sanctified persons, whose isolation took them to the wilderness or mountain tops, the latter representing both the source and origin of waters and of inspiration and the vantage point for visual and spiritual clarity and illumination. The ascent to hill-top is arduous, even excruciating, but the "clambering" must be endured for the result is snow-white or white-washed purity of both body and soul; it exceeds the abluent effectivity of hyssop! But not only must the body and soul be thus purified; the obscuring mist must also be completely dried from the eyes.

In this state of achieved purity and clarity the poet is ready to make an acceptable sacrifice which in all religious experience is the culminating re-establishment of the cosmic ties between man and God (Douglas 1966). The items of sacrifice here are suitable for the occasion, the egg representing freshness, purity, and the mysterious possibility of life; the "white hen at midterm" symbolizing purity because she has not yet been "known" by a cock:

> Here is a new laid egg
> here a white hen at midterm (CP:30)

These items of sacrifice fulfill the condition of acceptance and of reconnection of the severed bond between the higher powers and man, for they contain that most essential element: blood. The paradox of sacrifice is that in shedding blood (through death) life is given or made possible. The supplicant or community "offers" the blood of an animal or sometimes one of its members to mollify the Powers who, in turn, revitalize that community, restore social harmony, and reestablish the broken cosmic bond. Usually, the more dire the occasion, the bigger, and, therefore, higher the animal in the evolutionary hierarchy, and the more efficacious the sacrifice. But in this case, where what is involved is the purification and empowerment of an individual, a hen suffices. In these "modern" and "civilized" times, the religions of the world have not abandoned this practice; they have only, in symbolic substitution, replaced humans with animals, and in some cases replaced blood and flesh with unleavened bread and red wine.

Since Okigbo is after an integrated vision, his sacrifice cannot be complete without the "vegetable," which is not necessarily indigenous, component. So he adds:

> vegetable offering with five
> fingers of chalk . . . (CP:31)

The chalk here is *Nzu*, a white or off-white type of clay which is quarried, molded, and baked into "fingers." Above all else, it is an Igbo religious symbol of purity and cleanliness. Okigbo's "vegetable offering" thus makes his sacrifice complete; it does not necessarily replace Christian or other forms of sacrifice as is implied in Egudu's "he . . . has got all the necessary items for an indigenous kind of sacrifice: 'vegetable offering' and 'fingers of chalk'" (Egudu 1984:347). As far as Okigbo is concerned, and this is a lesson from deep mystical vision and awareness, all gods, Christian, indigenous, and otherwise, are the same, are only different manifestations and nominations of the same higher power. So his ascent to hill-top is for unified—not "divided"—vision. And even though he continues to be critical of Christianity as distorted and misrepresented by fanatics and morons, there is nothing here to suggest that he privileges one type of vision over another. If anything, in spite of the mockery of the drunken priests and celebrants, the affinity between Christ and Chris (which has already been marked) is not repudiated in the present remembrance of Christ, who "was silenced":

> The flower weeps, unbruised,
> for him who was silenced
> whose advent dumb-bells celebrate
> in dim light with wine-song:
> *Messiah will come again*
> *After the argument in heaven*

Messiah will come again . . .
Fingers of penitence bring
to a palm grove
vegetable offering with five
fingers of chalk....(CP:31)

The acceptance of his sacrifice, which marks the end of this phase of the poet's life-journey, is appropriately heralded by "thundering drums and cannons" and the release, in ecstasy, of spirit. In this instance which combines the overpowering ecstasy of Pentecostal release with the wonder of ascension, the invocation of the long drums and cannons is significant. Usually deployed only when important people make their exit from this to the other world, the drums and cannons invoke not death as a finality but death as both release of spirit and the passage and acceptance of spirit into the higher, ancestral realm. Thus, Okigbo's sacrifice having been accepted,

Thundering drums and cannons
in palm grove:
the Spirit is ascent. (CP:32)

No longer a prodigal, this finally accepted, reintegrated, and empowered poet is careful to memorialize the occasion with his own indelible "signature," the imprint of his palm with its five digits. This is also significant for the other reason that the number five, the pentagon, unlike the constraining and inhibiting square or rhombus that we have already met, represents liberation, of self and vision:

I have visited;
on palm beam imprinted
my pentagon—
I have visited, the prodigal . ..
In palm grove,
long-drums and cannons:
the Spirit in the ascent. (CP:32)

This admission into the limited circle of the called and empowered is a rare achievement and the moment calls for festivity. But it carries with it grave responsibilities and the poet-priest, fully aware of this, begins seriously in *Newcomer* with a worship which includes a premiere officiating, as in a first mass said by a newly ordained priest, in which the poet-priest is free, for the first time, to don his "own mask," and to pray directly to Anna—ancestral Mother as "guardian angel"—to protect the poet "from them fucking angels." There is no confusion of theologies here: in Igbo religion, the ancestors are a living reality, and part of their duty is the protection of those still living on earth. And, even though, as was observed earlier, Anna must have been named after St. Anne, her reality and role are different, for the poet, from those of christomythological mediation. The excitation of the moment collocates the symbols of his alienation: "bells of exile," the "angelus," and "guardian angel;" connects "remembrance of calvary" with a past "age of innocence"; but, above all, the mature, responsible, and humble poet-priest knows that it is first:

> Time for worship—
> softly sing the bells of exile,
> the angelus,
> softly sings my guardian angel.
> Mask over my face—
> my own mask, not ancestral—I sign:
> remembrance of calvary,
> and of age of innocence, which is of...
> Time for worship:
> Anna of the panel oblongs,
> protect me
> from them fucking angels;
> protect me
> my sandhouse and bones. (*CP*:33)

But the festivity and hilarity and celebration that are appropriate to this occasion are tempered by a certain premonition, perhaps of the realized dangers inherent in the new status. Hence "Newcomer II," which deals with "birth" and is appropriately dedicated to Mrs. Georgette Okigbo, is not simply a nativity poem to welcome Uzoamaka (now Dr.[Mrs.] Uzoamaka Udekwu), the daughter newly born to the poet's elder brother, Pius, and his wife, Georgette.

Taken as a whole the poem is a synthetic structure which deals with arrivals and integration: the arrival of the poet at the state of grace, poetic illumination, purity, and acceptance; the gestation and birth of a new poem, and of a new daughter, herself a synthesis of "white" and "black" cultures and genes (her mother being Belgian). But the arrivals are given "such synthetic welcome" as the diction, which is deliberately ambivalent and paradoxical, indicates. Hence the arrival takes place in May, the second month in the loveliest season of the year, but in the early morning when it is not simply cold but bitingly so. The arrival is in Spring/May when all nature's wardrobe should be renewed, but the draper "has sold out fine green garments." At this time when everyone and everything in nature is newly and freshly and colorfully attired and bedecked, the smile that is seen is a painted, false one. Finally, the arrival is "at the cock's third siren" which, together with "behind the bulrushes" suggests betrayal and treachery (Izebvaye 1984:321). Okigbo's death, as we have seen, was as a result of treachery and betrayal, and his poetry, especially *Limits*, is echoic of betrayal, treachery, and martyrdom. But the presence here, in a poem of jubilation, of the motif, makes it a cautionary tale and prophecy of the fate of the poet-messiah:

> In the chill breath of the day's waking,
> comes the newcomer,
> when the draper of May
> has sold out fine green garments,
> and the hillsides have made up their faces
> and the gardens, on their faces a painted smile:
> Such synthetic welcome at the cock's third siren;
> when from behind the bulrushes
> waking, in the teeth of the chill May morn,
> comes the newcomer. (*CP*:34)

In the same way that Christ's betrayal by his own disciples, pertinently here by Peter of the third crow/siren, did not deter him, this premonition of danger or betrayal does not deter Chris. His jubilation is given full reins in "Watermaid III," which also contains one

of the most arrogant synaesthesias in Okigbo's poetry: "Listening
to incense"!:

> I am standing above the noontide,
> Above the bridgehead;
> Listening to the laughter of waters
> that do not know why:
> Listening to incense —
> I am standing above the noontide
> with my head above it;
> Under my feet float the waters
> Tide blows them under . . . (CP:35)

Okigbo is now poised, ready, even eager to begin his mission, his
preparation finally achieved. Because this mission is cultural and
political, it is public duty that is motivated by a bardic, even prophetic impulse. And to talk of Okigbo's poetry, even up to *Heavensgate*
alone, as having "a peculiar sense of matured 'arrival,' relatively
speaking," as being "still too self-centred, too personal, not to say
subjective or erratic to permit of a clear penetration by any reader" and as "not necessarily a bardic impulse but *a way of looking
at life as a song*" (Anozie 1972:62) is to trivialize matters of grave
cultural importance. Okigbo was a lover, writer, and producer of
music, it is true, but his present mission is too serious to be
described in Anozie's terms italicized in the above quotation.

Having now overcome his deracination and alienation from
his cultural moorings, which the conjuncture of colonialism, colonial education, and cultural imperialism had produced, and having,
after a protracted retracing of the exilic route through a series of
penitential and purificatory ordeals, achieved acceptance, reintegration, and empowerment, the poet launches his cultural crusade.
And, sustained by those same forces—Reason, Truth-seeking,
Patriotism, Pity—which were said to have been the firing genius
of S. T. Coleridge (Woodring 1961:45), whom Okigbo admired,
the poet exclaims:

> Suddenly becoming talkative
> like weaverbird
> Summoned at offside of

dream remembered
Between sleep and waking,
I hang up my egg-shell
To you of palm grove,
Upon whose bamboo towers
Hang, dripping with yesterupwine,
A tiger mask and a nude spear . . .
Queen of the damp half light,
I have had my cleansing,
Emigrant with air-borne nose,
The he-goat-on-heat. (CP:39)

The excitement of this passage is unmistakable. So too is the declaration of readiness. In an almost surreptitious deployment of that beautiful imagery from Soccer, "offside," the poet is both called to order and reminded of the urgency of the task at hand; but it is obvious too that in his excitement he had not had an uninterrupted sleep. The reference to "yesterupwine," "tiger mask," and "nude spear" here is very appropriate for they symbolize energization, bravery, and readiness as in an unsheathed and drawn spear, respectively. And as if to dispel any doubt as to this qualification for participation, he declares to the goddess of intrigue and calculation of that grey dawn hour when most effective military, especially guerrilla incursions are launched, when apparently, in a prophetic or proleptic canniness, Okigbo would also launch his most devastating blows on the forces of carnage: "I have had my cleansing. . . / The he-goat-on-heat." Confident and bold and eager, the poet is almost arrogant in his new state of readiness: like "the he-goat-on-heat" he is not only ready and willing but anxious to begin. A sexual imagery here is quite evident, as in many other places in Okigbo's poetry. So, if I do not get into a discussion of "the sexual imagery of Okigbo's poetry," it is not because one is unaware of its presence or unappreciative of its importance. It simply means that, because in the poet's sensibility sexuality is not a distinct domain but an integral part of his whole being, the important thing becomes the nature of the poetic service to which the sexual symbolism is put. In the present instance that service is cultural and political.

But the poet's excitement, as well as the urgency of the situation, does not result in unrealistic expectations and overestimation of the poet's ability. He recognizes that his reintegration and empowerment notwithstanding, as a newly-called he still needs (like a seedling) both more time and more nourishment "to grow to sunlight." Appropriately then, in a botanical metaphor which Anozie (1972) thinks "is couched in the languages of the Bible" (74), the poet thirsts for the sunlight without which the sustaining photosynthesis cannot take place:

> For he was a shrub among the poplars,
> Needing more roots
> More sap to grow to sunlight,
> Thirsting for sunlight,
> A low growth among the forest. (CP:40)

But this recognition of his limitations is only a sign of the poet's present maturity, for he knows that his calling entails a continuous and continuing preparation and state of readiness. The modesty and realism of the quoted lines are, therefore, "no case of self-denigration" (Obiechina 1980 40). His continued preparation includes serious and deep introspection and "feeling for [his] audience":

> Into the soul
> The selves extended their branches,
> Into the moments of each living hour,
> Feeling for audience...
> And out of the solitude
> Voice and soul with selves unite,
> Riding the echoes,
> Horsemen of the apocalypse;
> And crowned with one self
> The name displays its foliage,
> Hanging low
> A green cloud above the forest. (CP:40)

The poem which started as an articulation of the poet's diffidence and tentativeness here ends with an apocalyptic optimism. A combination of the extirpation of ponderous foreign influences—

"Straining thing among the echoes"—sincere and deep intro-spection, and a committed concern for his audience results in the poet's present sense of purpose, unity or integration of the "selves," and achievement. About this deep connection between introspection and the social, it is interesting to consider what the poet himself had to say on a different occasion, actually in an interview with Marjorie Whitelaw:

> I believe that any writer who attempts a type of inward explo-ration will be exploring his own society indirectly. Because the writer isn't living in isolation. He is interacting with differ-ent groups of people at different times. And any inward explo-ration involves the interaction of the subject with other people. And I believe that a writer who sets out to discover himself, by so doing will discover his society. (Nwoga 1984:253)

Neither the fact that he has not quite found his audience, nor that he recognizes the near-insurmountability of the obstacles con-fronting the acolyte, constitutes sufficient deterrence against launching the campaign. The only thing needed is great caution, deliberateness, and prudence:

> Banks of reed.
> Mountains of broken bottle.
> & the mortar is not yet dry . . .
> Silent the footfall,
> Soft as cat's paw,
> Sandalled in velvet in fur,
> So we must go, eve-mist on shoulders
> Sun's dust of combat,
> With brand burning out at hand-end
> & the mortar is not yet dry . . .
> Then we must sing, tongue-tied,
> Without name or audience
> Making harmony among the branches. (CP:41)

The repetition here of imagery from military campaigns, nearly accurately depictive of guerrilla and commando raids, underlines the kind of urgency with which the poet views his crusade. The "eve-mist on shoulders" recalls the earlier quoted "damp half light," while "dust of combat" reconnects with "he-goat-on-heat" and "a tiger mask and a nude spear": again, they are all sadly proleptic of Okigbo's own eventual participation in war. But for now, what matters is the present "crisis point" where it is important to mark the subtle coalescence of the military and cultural urgencies, as well as their resolution in "Limits IV" in terms of poetry. Thus the poet tells us:

And this is the crisis point,
The twilight moment between
 sleep and waking;
And the voice that is reborn transpires,
Not thro' pores in the flesh,
 but the soul's back-bone.
Hurry on down —
 Thro' the high-arched gate —
Hurry on down
 little stream to the lake.... (CP:41)

The tempo of the acceleration here, of the hurrying to the point of climactic resolution, cannot be checked; is, in fact, almost precipitous, for the poet must rush to the insistent call of the creator/destroyer who, like the mythological Spider of initiation rites, must stitch/sew up the bodies of initiates after they had just been dismembered. It is therefore significant that "Limit IV" (which is said to have been composed after the poet's experience of surgery under general anaesthesia) refers not to a hospital bed, but to "near the altar" where the poem as sacrifice will be finished/presented:

An image insists
From flag pole of the heart;
Her image distracts
With the cruelty of the rose . . .
Oblong-headed lioness—
No shield is proof against her—
Wound me, O sea-weed
Face, blinded like strong-room—
Distances of her armpit-fragrance

Turn chloroform enough for my patience—
When you have finished
& done up my stitches,
Wake me near the altar,
& this poem will be finished . . .(CP:43)

On "waking up" then, the poet will not only have become finally and completely reconstituted, but the mortar will also have become dry. The period of tentativeness and protracted preparation is over. If one may appropriate a very ingenious metaphor from General Yakubu Gowon which he contrived during the Nigeria-Biafra War, Okigbo's cultural "police action" is now on the verge of transformation into full-scale "military campaign."

Interestingly this campaign begins with the delineation of the terrain by the poet. This terrain is characteristically ambitious in its scope and extends beyond Igboland, Nigeria, and Africa, to encompass even the oriental victims of imperial avarice, rapacity, and despoliation. The common denomination in all these cases is that the ravage had been both deliberate, calculated, and total. But in all these cases too, Okigbo's optimism envisages a recovery, even regeneration or rebirth, which to him "is no new thing either":

On an empty sarcophagus
 hewn out of alabaster,
A branch of fennel on an
 empty sarcophagus . . .
Nothing suggests accident
 where the beast
Is finishing her rest . . .
Smoke of ultramarine and amber
Floats above the fields after
Moonlit rains, from tree unto tree
Distills the radiance of a king . . .
You might as well see the new branch of Enkidu;
And that is no new thing either . . . (CP:44)

In his comment on this quoted poem, Obiechina (1980) thinks that:

The apparent lack of secure confidence is visible and pushes the poet into using an elaborate framework based on oriental mythology. Mesopotamian and Egyptian images sound impressive but do nothing to enhance the development of a personal voice and vision, and hardly help the reader, in spite of the explanatory notes by the author, to obtain more than a precarious and flighty sense of the poet's meaning. Those who accuse Okigbo of deliberate mystification and obscurity bordering on pedantry might find the opening part of this sequence real munition to support their accusation. (41)

But it hardly seems to me that a suggested identification of the poet with the "legendary King of Uruk in Mesopotamia, and first human hero in literature" or with Gilgamesh (see the poet's note on *CP*:44) is indicative of diffidence or "lack of secure confidence" on the part of the poet. More importantly, however, it seems to me that the incorporation of Mesopotamian and Egyptian mythologies at this crucial stage of the crusade, far from being a pedantic and sadistic infliction of obscurantist torture on the less polymathic of his readers, is Okigbo's strategic postcolonial device of demarcating his field of "combat," by locating in history the source of the cultural, and eventually, political and economic, disaster which has been the lot of Africa and the Third World. The ravaging and plunder, the appropriation and despoliation which left even the sarcophagus empty, the devastation of the non-white, non-Western world by the West, which in turn accuses the non-Western world of having contributed nothing to World civilization, did not begin with latter-day (*circa* 19th-century) Western adventures into the "darker regions" of the world. The loot and plunder of the quoted poem had, in fact, built the Hellenic or Greek civilization which has only recently, actually from about the Renaissance on, been appropriated as the founding kin of European civilization (Bernal 1987).

As Samir Amin (1989) has shown, "'Hellenomania' and the construction of the myth of Greece as the ancestor of the West'" laid the foundation for Eurocentrism which, he claims, is "a recent mythological reconstruction of the history of Europe and the world" (viii, ix). This Eurocentric project succeeded not only in establishing "a nonexistent historical continuity" between Greece and Europe (xi), but also in so widely disseminating that historical "knowledge" that it passes today as common knowledge, even among the highly educated. If the corollary project of the orientalization and inferiorization of the rest of the world, the white-Europeans' *Other*, has been at the root of the plight of "the rest of us" (Chinweizu 1975), it is only proper that Okigbo's crusade begins by pointing to the source of the contamination of the stream. With that diagnosis accurately achieved, it is hoped that half the "curative" job will have been done.

In performing that thankless task, Okigbo is not unaware of obstacles and stumbling blocks placed in his way even by the supposed beneficiaries of his mission. These do not just keep looking away as in Michael Thorpe's earlier quoted poem; they do not stop at piling "banks of reed / Mountains of broken bottles" on his path; like many oppressed peoples in history who have yearned and prayed for the messiah, they will not only not recognize him when he walks among them but will publicly disgrace him:

> He stood in the midst of them all
> and appeared in true form,
> He found them drunken, he found none
> thirsty among them.
> *Who would add to your stature,*
> *Or in your village accept you?* (CP:45)

The happy thing is that, in spite of the suicidal inclination of the people, the prophet, like Christ, like Enkidu, rises again from the dead reenergized for the task in hand:

> And from frame of iron,
> And mould of iron . . .
> For he ate the dead lion,
> & was within the corpse—(CP:46)

And that is the point. For the poet needs this revitalization to be able to confront the "fleet of eagles," the despoilers who now troop into the land, devastating and plundering it, while all the time

distracting the people with the cross and the promises of heavenly utopia. As the advance troop or vanguard of imperialism,
Christianity, personified by white cassocked and bearded zealots,
softened the hearts of the people, taught them to contemplate the
crucifix and the bliss of life in God's gold-paved kingdom, persuaded them to turn the other cheek even to their imperializers,
and to turn their eyes from material things and from all things of
the evil world. Meanwhile, as they did so, the looting went on. In
the words of one Isaac Delano, a Christian nationalist quoted by
Coleman (1958):

> The word "Christ" has always been identified here with the
> British Empire . . . [and] the general feelings are that the
> Missionaries have been the front troops of the Government
> to soften the hearts of the people and while people look at
> the Cross white men gather the riches of the land. (108)

The same source had correctly marked the close ties that existed
between Christian missions and the imperial and colonial governments: "Christ and Western Civilization came together; no one
could distinguish one from the other. Collar and ties, or the Bible"
(108). It is this "missionary-government conspiracy" (108) which
made it possible for the missionaries to embark on the total
destruction of the indigenous people's culture and religion without fear of their aggrieved onslaught; the long hand of the imperial military was never far behind the "indignant" and "righteous"
cleansers of the pagan world:

> And to the cross in the void came pilgrims;
> Came, floating with burnt-out tapers;
> Past the village orchard where
> Flannagan
> Preached the Pope's message,
> To where drowning nuns suspired,
> Asking the key-word from stone;
> & he said:
> To sow the fireseed among grasses,
> & lo, to keep it till it burns out . . . (CP:46)

It is hardly surprising that this fire of both "faith" and cultural destruction will continue and spread unchecked until it burns out. It is also hardly surprising that with the devastating might of the imperial military behind it, the "fleet of eagles," the Christian agents of imperialism, led by Reverend Fr. Flannagan, will regale in their deleterious achievement. So, as in the earlier scene ("Fragments V"), where the despoliation was also systematic, deliberate, and thorough—"nothing suggests accident,"

> where the beast
> Is finishing her rest . . .
> Smoke of ultramarine and amber
> Floats above the fields after
> Moonlit rains, from tree unto tree (*CP*:44),

here the eagles rampage and ravage unchecked, and resplendent, holding "the square / under curse of their breath." The poet/Sunbird who has already assumed the full bardic role as foreseer and voice of warning "repeats" to his people:

> "A fleet of eagles,
> over the oil bean shadows,
> Holds the square
> under curse of their breath.
> Beaks of bronze, wings
> of hard-tanned felt,
> The eagles flow
> over man-mountains,
> Steep walls of voices,
> horizons;
> The eagles furrow
> dazzling over the voices
> With wings like
> combs in the wind's hair
> Out of the solitude, the fleet,
> Out of the solitude,
> Intangible like silk thread of sunlight,
> The eagles ride low,
> Resplendent . . . resplendent;

And small birds sing in shadows,
Wobbling under their bones . . ." (CP:47)

In an imagery that is reminiscent of the "banks of reed" and "mountains of broken bottles," those obstacles that the poet-prophet had had to overcome, this poem recreates a hyperbolic scene of devastation. The eagles of prey, whose beaks are hard and sharp like bronze, and whose wings are powerful like hard-tanned felt, "flow" over their victims, pile upon pile of human corpses, "man-mountains," which stretch, as far as the eye can see, to the "horizons." In the same way, the wailing that is reminiscent of the lament at Ramah, "steep walls of voices," does not perturb the fleet who, in meticulous military post-campaign fashion, comb the place for possible survivors, depicted here as overwhelmed by dread and terror:

"And small birds sing in shadows,
Wobbling under their bones . . ." (CP:47)

After this extended warning the Poet/Sunbird/Prophet/Blind Dog is exhausted and squats to catch his breath. But the urgency of the situation hardly allows him that luxury. The imperial enemy is unrelenting and must not be given any quarter. In a warning which the "blind dog howls" at Eunice/his people, one is reminded of that situation in Achebe's *Things Fall Apart* (chapters 15-18) where the people reject the advice not to admit the white man into their midst. In their foolish generosity and hospitality, but also in their wishful dream that the "evil forest" would take care of the missionaries, they had allowed them to settle there. The germ once planted, its germination and spread is now part of history. In the case being discussed here, however, it would appear that, in spite of the advice/warning:

Give him no chair, they say,
The dawn's charioteer,
Riding with the angry stars
Toward the great sunshine (CP:48),

the "visitation" came to be, and the "visitors" did not really care for anyone's hospitality or welcome. They came with malevolence in their hearts and thus deserve the full working out on them of the curse of the poet/prophet: "*Malisons, malisons, mair than ten*." The original context of this malediction on the eagles has been traced by Nwoga to the poem "The Laverock's Sang" in William Cadenhead, *Flights of Fancy and Lays of Bon-Accord* (1853). There we have the two lines:

Malisons, malisons, mair than ten
That harrie the rest o' the heavenly hen.
(Nwoga 1984:101)

It would appear that, the groundwork having been done by Flannagan and his ilk, including local agents like Kepkanly, the present incursion is achieved with little or no assistance from anyone. It proceeded with methodical precision and was completed in almost no time, with only the putrid smell of destruction, despoliation, and desecration trailing these eagles of imperial havoc. It is significant that this poem ("Fragment X") ends in the same way that "Fragments V" began, by creating a close link, an identity, indeed, between "the twin-gods of the forest," the tortoise and the python, totems of Idoto, and "the twin gods of Irkalla" the Sumerian queen of the underworld. The same abomination and despoliation which included even the theft of mummified corpses (of the Pharaohs) in "Fragments V" will be reenacted in "Fragment X" with the same systematic thoroughness and rapacity:

And to us they came —
Malisons, malisons, mair than ten —
And climbed the bombax
And killed the Sunbird.
And they scanned the forest of oilbean
Its approach; surveyed its high branches . . .
And they entered into the forest,
And they passed through the forest of oilbean
And found them, the twin-gods of the forest . . .
And the beasts broke —

Malisons, malisons, mair than ten —
And dawn-gust grumbled.
Fanning the grove
Like a horse-tail-man,
Like handmaid of dancers,
Fanning their branches.
Their talons they drew out of their scabbard,
Upon the tree trunks, as if on fire-clay,
Their beaks they sharpened;
And spread like eagles their felt-wings,
And descended upon the twin-gods of Irkalla
And the ornaments of him
And the beads about his tail
And the carapace of her
And her shell they divided. (*CP*:49)

That Western interest in its *Other*, which included the plunder and devastation of Mesopotamia and Northern Africa, has run its full circle by extending the beaks and talons of imperialism to the rest of Africa. No louder statement of this common fate can be made than the poetic fusion of the twin-gods of the oil-bean forest and the twin-gods of Irkalla. In both cases, as in all other imperialized situations, the same pattern is observed: invasion, conquest, survey, control, occupation/domination, plunder/booty, sowing of secular fireseeds to ensure political instability and economic stagnation, and withdrawal/remote control (which latter has been described by some as neo-colonialism).

It is my conviction that, in spite of the anguish, agony, and the lament of Okigbo's poetry, the real driving force of this poet and his poetry is divine optimism. Hence the total devastation of "Fragments X," in which the Sunbird was an early casualty notwithstanding, what we have in "Fragments XI" is lament, not over the desecration and despoliation of the gods as such, but over the neglect by the people of their funerary duties to their slaughtered gods:

And the gods lie in state
And the gods lie in state

Without the long-drum
And the gods lie unsung,
Veiled only with mould,
Behind the shrinehouse. (CP: 50)

But in spite of such culpable cultural neglect, and, in spite of the attempted obliteration of indigenous cultures by imperialism/colonialism, the gods, together with their cultures, reassert themselves:

Gods grow out,
Abandoned;
And so do they . . . (CP:50)

The apocalyptic climax of this resurgence, echoic of the archetypal ritual of death and rebirth, is the excited reappearance of the Sunbird who cannot remain "dead," its duties still undone:

But at the window, outside, a shadow:
The Sunbird sings again
From the limits of the dream;
The Sunbird sings again
Where the caress does not reach, (CP:51)

The resurrected Sunbird sings now beyond reach of the talons of the beasts, and it is significant that his song is "Of Guernica." If the song of the Sunbird now celebrates the artistic achievement of Picasso (Anozie 1972: 96), it does so because Picasso, unlike his ancestors who refused to acknowledge the plundered roots of their civilization, not only acknowledged the African sources of his greatness, but also embodied the same serious social conscience which Okigbo exemplifies. Thus, it seems to me then that, more importantly, Guernica is invoked here by the poet because, like Fragments, it also deals with senselessness and barbarity, and with the same anguish visited by power and dominance upon victims:

Of Guernica
On whose canvas of blood,
The slits of his tongue
cling to glue . . . (CP:51)

This close reading also refuses to accept Anozie's interpretation which identifies the victims as the beasts of "Fragments X." If we look closely at the structure of stanza 4, we can see easily that "the beasts" is the subject of the verbs "broke," "grumbled," and "fanned," etc.; the beasts are doing the deeds of despoliation, but clearly do not break into the malediction which is functionally separated from the rest of the stanza by both the italics and the parentheses:

> And the beasts broke—
> *Malisons, malisons, mair than ten*—
> And dawn-gust grumbled
> Fanning the grove. . . . *(CP*:49)

But Anozie (1972) thinks that the tragedy which is the subject of the poem is presented "as it dramatically filters through the unschooled consciousness of the 'beasts' (the naive common folk who simply cry, '*Malisons, malisons, mair than ten'* . . ." (96). The efficacious malediction is being pronounced by the Sunbird, on behalf of the "folk," on the despoilers, *not* the despoiled. Finally, the invocation of *Guernica* in the last stanza of "Fragments XII" is appropriate because it prepares us for the "jubilee dance above the carrion" with which *Silences* will begin. The canceling out is, therefore, not (literally) complete.

CHAPTER VI

THE PEOPLE AND
THE DILEMMA OF NATION

The last chapter ended on a paradoxical note. It celebrated the resurrection of the Sunbird; but it also invoked Picasso, whose *Guernica* is a lament over the tragedy that had befallen mankind. Far from celebrating the glories of war, the anguish compressed in this painting properly anticipated for our present discursive purpose, the "dance above the carrion." As was indicated in that chapter five, the invocation of *Guernica* is less a tribute to the artistic achievement of Picasso than a statement of a common concern for brutalized humanity shared by both artists. The horse in Picasso's painting represents those with the power to make and mar, while the groaning victim is mangled and groaning humanity. That last stanza of "Limits XII" becomes, then, another loud declaration by Okigbo of his oneness with the people: "the quadrangle,—the rest, me and you," the groaning victims of Picasso's painting.

It is this identification with the people that defines and motivates Okigbo's politics. Thus, concerned as he was for the freedom of man (and woman), he lamented—throughout his poetry—the subordination and exploitation of the masses by the stupid, gut-driven, and visionless "leaders." Although the tone of

"Limit XII" is almost ecstatic, on account of the imminence of the resurrection of the unsung gods of "Limits XI," what would have amounted to a celebratory euphoria is immediately foreclosed, because what the gods faced, after lying unsung and abandoned, was the despoliation and emasculation of mankind, which is the subject of *Guernica*, and of *Silences*, where:

> For the far *removed there is wailing*:
> For the far removed;
> For the Distant . . .
>
> *The wailing is for the fields of crop*:
>
> The drums' lament is:
> They grow not . . .
>
> *The wailing is for the fields of men*:
>
> For the barren wedded ones;
> for perishing children . . .
>
> *The wailing is for the Great River*:
>
> Her pot-bellied watchers
> Despoil her . . .
> (CP:66)

The prophecy contained in these lines would be lived out to the letter in the crises immediately preceding the Biafra-Nigeria War. And it seems to me that that war was the final vindication of Okigbo's populism, his identification with the people (the "quadrangle"), for it enabled him to project his ideals into a practical arena, and there to die for the people:

> A mock grin on his face
> he lies abandoned at the confluence
> by the armed hands and unarmed hearts;
> for they said they wanted life
> and he gave his own: . . .

Unto his people he came a Messiah.
(Okafor, "Without a Grave He Lies," in Achebe & Okafor
1978:21)

It is this total identification with the people which accounts not only
for the subject matter (that of social-political criticism), but also for
the aggrieved, impatient, and almost tragic tone of *Silences*. As
an excoriation of the gastrocentric politicians, *Silences* reminds us
of their delineation in Achebe's *A Man of the People* (1966),
where, in a "chop-chop" political culture, they are characterized
only by greed, slothfulness, "Selfish Self-seeking," and the manipulation and exploitation of the people. Okigbo saw these politicians as intellectually empty, entirely unimaginative, and without
any vision whatsoever. With Brothers and Deacons, they are the
Rhombus in his characterological geometry:

> the rhombus—brothers, and deacons,
> Liberal politicians,
> selfish self-seekers—all who are good
> doing nothing at all; . . .
> (CP:23)

And in the world of the imagination they are as good as lost for,
while prophets and martyrs and lunatics occupy a dignified
pedestal, politicians, together with traders, princes, and advocates
of Negritude roam the jungle:

> On the stone steps on the marble
> beyond the balcony
> prophets martyrs lunatics
> like the long stride of the evening
> At the clearing dantini
> in the garden dillettanti;
> vendors princes negritude
> politicians in the tall wood . . . (72)

But the present situation is complicated by the presence of the
long fingers of those holding and operating the "remote control"(of
neo-colonialism) from across the seas. By playing the tunes for the

comprador, quisling elite in their "dance above the carrion," the "Scavengers" (local and foreign), much like the destroyers and predators of Ayi Kwei Armah's *Two Thousand Seasons* (1973), exacerbate the helplessness and hopelessness of the people. It is this hopelessness which Okigbo tries to expose in the "Lament of the Silent Sisters'" echo of the suspiring nuns of G. M. Hopkins' "The Wreck of Deutschland."

As in the poem by Hopkins, the atmosphere of "Lament" is that of doomed futility, impotence, and helplessness. This atmosphere is reinforced by the sequence of images of emptiness and ineffectuality: golden eggs that are empty of albumen; compass and cross that make no difference in a storm to Captain and nun alike; absence of anchorage, shank, or archway. In such a situation the question "How does one say *No* in thunder . . ." has no resolution or response, only a stifled and "anguished cry of Moloch." It is interesting to note that the only activity going on in this doomed site is that of the scavengers: "They comb the afternoon the scavengers / For scented shadows above the underrush— . . . /In this jubilee-dance above the carrion" (CP:55). Characteristically, the nuns, like the deluded many, still look for answers in the wrong place: "The cross to us we still call to us,/In this jubilee-dance above the carrion" (55).

In an antipodal arrangement of the stanzas, alternating between Crier/Poet/Prophet and the Chorus/people, in which the Crier clearly acts as the people's guide, the people have apparently become aware of, and incensed by, the self-centered "scavenging" and looting of the common wealth, in which each vulture, even before he has had his fill, is overtaken by yet another vulture, in a short-lived, but continuous relay of banditry:

Chorus: This shadow of carrion incites
and in rhythms of silence
Urges us; gathers up our broken
hidden feather-of-flight,
To this anguished cry of Moloch:
What cast-iron steps cascading down the valley
all forged into thunder of tanks;
And detonators cannoned with splintered flames,

	in this jubilee-dance of fireflies!
Crier:	They struck him in the ear they struck
	him in the eye;
	They picked his bones for scavenging:
Chorus:	And there will be continual going to the well,
	Until they smash their calabashes.
Crier:	So one dips one's tongue in ocean, and begins
	To cry to the mushroom of the sky: (56)

Whether the people, who had earlier been presented as foolishly clinging on to the ineffectual "cross" in their desperation, are responsible for this crop of reckless political leadership or not, they are now acutely aware of the tragic consequences of the self-aggrandizing dance of death which has made mockery of the hard-won (paper-)independence, as well as the touted promises of a post-independence good life, and even threatened social order itself. In a desperate cry which, like the rhetorical question "How does one say No in thunder . . .", despairs of an immediate answer, the poet emits the hyperbolic articulation of the people's helplessness:

So, one dips one's tongue in ocean, and begins
To cry to the mushroom of the sky.(56)

The sense of cosmic despair and futility contained in this closing couplet of "Lament II" is carried over to "Lament III" where it is even reinforced by the self-characterization of the chorus/people as "dumb-bells outside the gates." This sense of hopelessness is exacerbated by the collocation of paradoxes in the first two stanzas of "Lament III." For if the tragic cultural amnesia of "hollow seascapes without memory" would appear to be compensated for by "sand banks sprinkled with memories," and by the fact that "we carry / Each of us an urn of native / Earth," that compensation would appear to be nullified immediately by the association of urn with death/cremation, and by the fact that the "double handful" of earth/ash "we spread" are "To the nightairs of our silences / Suffused in this fragrance of diverse melodies." These melodies, rather than resolve into harmony, actually anticipate the "dissonant airs" of "Elegy For Alto" (99). That is why they become here

211

"our swan song / This is our senses' stillness" (57). Nor is it consolation enough for the chorus to observe, in a quasi-philosophical generalization, that human nature is normally composite of good and evil, success and failure: "We carry in our worlds that flourish / Our worlds that have failed" (57), because the Crier's retort, while repeating the fatalism of the swan—song motif, not only likens "our senses' stillness" and "the sigh of our spirits," to the blood-curdling shriek of the archetypal beast of courage and strength, the ram, but also cosmicizes the shriek in a clear reference to the "cry to the mushroom of the sky" and "No in thunder." Surprisingly, but encouragingly, the articulation of this cosmic analogy is given to the Chorus who may then, correctly, be construed as seeing eye-to-eye with the Crier:

> Unseen shadows like long-fingered winds
> Pluck from our strings
> This shriek, the music of the firmament . . . (57)

It seems to me that this convergence of purpose accounts for the apparent resolve of "Limit IV." Even though the picture of possible doom remains, I would read the interrogations of the last two lines optimistically, for they clearly indicate the Crier/Chorus' full apprehension of their common plight. If, as Nwoga says "the impending social debacle is transformed at the end into the threat of utter drowning (and) the 'Sibylline Chambers'" evoke "the original theme of fake and failed promises, for the sibyls were prophetesses, sorcerers and witches of early Rome" (Nwoga 1984:126), then the present apprehension noted above will surely enable the Crier/Chorus to resist the temptation to drown, and to answer "No" to that ominous question: "Will the water gather us in her sibylline chamber?" In the same way, the last line of "Limit IV" becomes a rhetorical question whose answer is given in the affirmative, capable finally of cathartic transformation of "our silences" and "our souls' stillness" into action: "And our silences fade into galloping antelopes?" In elaborating this reading, I am aware of what Nwoga calls "Okigbo's fascination with death and martyrdom which he would further 'celebrate' as the achievement of the pure self in 'Distances'" (Nwoga 1984:126).

But in doing that I have been guided by the divine optimism which I have discerned as the defining principle of Okigbo's poetry and life mission. Indeed, as Okigbo himself said in his "Introduction," *Silences* is an attempt by "two groups of mourners [to] explore the possibilities of poetic metaphor in an attempt to elicit the music to which all imperishable cries must aspire" (CP:xxiv). In the end, martyrdom, it must be remembered, is both positive and optimistic, because it contains within it the hope, nay, certainty, of redemption. Okigbo's "fascination with death" has nothing of the usual association with mortal finality.

It is for that reason that I see "Silences V" as a project of optimistic import. On one level, it mentions for the first time a projected major prose work, *Pointed Arches*, which, had it not been lost in the war, would have been the culmination of Okigbo's life's work. In a letter written to Anozie, Okigbo had said that:

> *Pointed Arches* is neither fiction nor criticism nor autobiography. It is an attempt to describe the growth of the creative impulse in me, an account of certain significant facts in my experience of life and letters that conspired to sharpen my imagination. It throws light on certain apparently irreconcilable features in my work and life, and places them in a new perspective. I am hoping for publication by 1970. (Anozie 1972: 21)

But, on another level, there is a happy resolution of the silences and stillnesses and shadows of the earlier sections into voices, sounds, music, melodies, and forms. This resolution brings together the vitally indispensable bardic organs of the poet/prophet: ears and eyes with which he also apprehends music/prophecy, memory, and beauty:

Alternatively Crier:/Chorus:

Yellow images:
Voices in the senses' stillness . . .

Pointed arches:
Pieces in the form of a pear . . .

Angles, filaments:
Hosts of harlequins in the shadows:
And bearded Judas,
Resplendent among the dancers . . .

I hear sounds as, they say,
A worshipper hears the flutes—

The music sounds so in the soul
It can hear nothing else—

I hear painted harmonies
From the mushroom of the sky—

Silences are melodies
Heard in retrospect: (CP:59)

The poet is still the visioner and voice of warning, the seer, hearer, and speaker, the bard of his people. It is clear that, in spite of the enormity of the task ahead of the bard, because the poet/prophet and his people are now one in their disillusionment at the turn of socio-political events, the poet can now speak with the voice of the people, with greater clarity and urgency, and with more direct social-political relevance. But the poet is also aware not only that the cosmic question "How does one say No in thunder?" has not yet been resolved, but that matters have become exacerbated by the introduction of the element of betrayal: "And bearded Judas/Resplendent among the dancers" (59).

With this one image of betrayal, Okigbo is able to bring together, for compressed poetic treatment, the strands that constitute the messy conjuncture that was post-independence Nigeria and Africa. Thus in the "Lament of the Drums" whose immediate inspirations were the assassination of Patrice Lumumba, the first Prime Minister of the Congo, and the imprisonment of Awolowo and, soon after, the death of Segun, his eldest son, Okigbo is able to denounce the treachery, betrayal of trust, collusion between indigenous comprador politicians and imperialism, and barbarism. As Obiechina puts the matter:

What these events did was to sharpen the awareness that political independence brought with it unforeseen dangers more threatening than those predictable atrocities of colonialism. The unleashing of barbaric violence on the little-suspecting people and the cynical strategies of neo-colonial imperialism to destroy real independence and replace it with puppetry sound the alarm that the great drama which opened with the colonial incursions was about to reach its climax. (Obiechina 1980:54)

We had earlier made reference to the Western Nigerian crisis of 1962 whose culminating act was the incarceration of Chief Obafemi Awolowo, the Leader of Opposition at the Federal House. Okigbo saw this imprisonment as the beginning of national tragedy because, without the wisdom of this political wizard, his unashamed ethnic prejudice notwithstanding, the country, manned by "some strange Celaeno and her harpy crew" would only continue the jubilee-dance of fireflies, the dance above the carrion, until they drove it to utter chaos. Awolowo was a pioneer combatant in Nigeria's anti-colonial struggles, and had demonstrated his helmsmanship as Premier of Western Nigeria.

It is possible that Okigbo had forgotten or, in his large-hearted nationalist accommodation, had forgiven Awolowo for his fraudulent manipulation of the 1951 Western Regional elections which had resulted in his becoming Premier. This fraud has been seen as the "death-blow" to the dream of Nigerian "nationness." As Chinua Achebe puts it:

As a student in Ibadan I was an eye-witness to that momentous occasion when Chief Obafemi Awolowo "stole" the leadership of Western Nigeria from Dr. Nnamdi Azikiwe in broad daylight on the floor of the Western House of Assembly and sent the great Zik scampering back to the Niger "whence [he] came." . . .No matter how anyone attempts to explain away that event in retrospect it was the death of a dream-Nigeria. . . . That dream-Nigeria suffered a death-blow from Awolowo's success in the Western House of Assembly in 1951. (1983:5)

As far as the pan-Nigerian Okigbo was concerned, that Awolowo
was Yoruba was among the least important considerations. Okigbo
believed in the destiny and possibility of Nigeria and, perhaps,
saw in Awolowo the only promise of rational national leadership
in a land full of robbers, anyway.

But Awolowo was found guilty of treasonable felony for his
part in the plan to overthrow the Federal Government. Whether
his participation in this plan was motivated by his overriding ambition to be Prime Minister, or by a more altruistic, nationalistic
dream to give Nigeria a sense of direction, no one can say now
for certain. But he was prevented from escaping "through the
door-way with an attorney," and imprisoned for ten years.

In a fuller elaboration of the earlier reference to the "bearded Judas," Okigbo describes Awolowo's fate as a classical rape of
justice, betrayal, and martyrdom:

> For we sense
> With dog-nose a Babylonian capture,
> The martyrdom
> Blended into that chaliced vintage. (CP:61)

Whether or not Awolowo's action and fate could, in fact, be
described as heroic martyrdom, he was seen by many as a fated
political scape-goat, whose internment exposed Nigeria in all its
unseemly nakedness:

> Lion-hearted cedar forest, gonads for our thunder,
> Even if you are very far away, we invoke you:
>
> Give us our hollow heads of long-drums . . .
>
> Antelopes for the cedar forest, swifter messengers
> Than flash-of-beacon-flame, we invoke you:
>
> Hide us; deliver us from our nakedness . . . (61)

And in a deft manipulation of the classical figure of Palinurus,
Okigbo achieves an identification of Awolowo and his son, Segun,

the latter a victim of an automobile accident of very suspicious nature, just at the time of his father's ordeal:

> Palinurus alone in a hot prison you will keep
> The dead sea awake with nightsong . . .
>
> *Silver of rivulets this side of the bridge,*
> *Cascades of lily-livered laughter,*
> *Fold-on-fold of raped, naked blue—*
> *What memory has the sea of her lover?*
>
> Palinurus, unloved in your empty catacomb,
> You will wear away through age alone . . .
>
> Masks and beggar-masks without age or shadow:
> Broken tin-gods whose vision is dissolved . . .
>
> *It is over, Palinurus, at least for you,*
> *In your tarmac of night and fever-dew.... (63)*

According to many believers in the cause of national sanity, the dignified tears which Awolowo shed both at his sentencing and at the news of his son's tragedy, were enough vindication of his innocence or, at least, the rightness of his "treasonable" cause:

> *Tears of grace, not of sorrow, broken*
> *In two, protest your inviolable image;*
>
> *And the sultry waters, touched by the sun,*
> *Inherit your paleness who reign, resigned*
> Like palm oil fostered in an ancient clay bowl;
> A half-forgotten name; like a stifled sneeze.... (63-64)

With this formidable Leader of Opposition safely removed from the scene, the scavengers were, as it were, unmuzzled, whose rampage Okigbo described thus:

> Nothing remains, only smoke after storm —
> Some strange Celaeno and her harpy crew,

Laden with night and their belly's excrement,
Profane all things with hooked feet and foul teeth. (63)

Yet, that man, as an intrepid actor in the struggle for independence, was partly responsible for securing the loot, or national cake, for which the "harpy crew" were now scrambling, while he was left, alone and unloved, figuratively unclothed, in a hot prison. Okigbo begged:

Fishermen out there in the dark—O you
Who rake the waves or chase their wake—
Weave for him a shadow out of your laughter
For a dumb child to hide his nakedness.... (64)

This prayer, like those of others, fell on deaf ears. And neither the rage and anger of the people at the mismanagement of affairs or miscarriage of justice, nor their dream/fear of exile/escape, could avail anything. The people, personified in "Lament IV" as the Drums, were reduced to impotence and mere lament:

So, like a dead letter unanswered,
Our rococo
Choir of insects is null
Cacophony
And void as a debt summons served
On a bankrupt (65)

Consequently, the social-political cauldron, under the chefmanship of the robbers, continued to boil. It was to know no abatement and, indeed, escalated in 1964/1965 when it threatened to boil over and engulf the whole country. In effect, the lament of "Lament V," though chilling in its effect, is only a presagement of events yet to happen: "we are talking of such common places,/and on the brink of such great events . . ." (70), of such dire proportions:

For the far removed there is wailing:
The wailing is for the fields of crop:

The wailing is for the fields of men:
The wailing is for the Great River:
Her pot-bellied watchers
Despoil her . . . . (66)

It was a surprise to no one that a country, (mis-)led by such
an unimaginative, scrambling, scavenging, and "lost" breed, would
lack all ideological compass, all sense of direction, and that her
leaders, in their gastrocentrism, megalomaniacal upmanship, and
crude ethnicism, would push her to anarchy and chaos. With this
despised "crew," politics, far from being a process of nationwide
socialization and community building, became the only motive
force for personal socio-economic aggrandizement (Okpaku, ed.,
1972: 38). This would account for the frequency of that peculiar
Nigerian brand of frivolous "carpet-crossing" and purchase of
political opponents by the ruling parties both in the Regional
Houses of Assembly and in the Federal House of Parliament. It
also trivialized and travestied elections and censuses, which were
usually rigged and manipulated for the sole purpose of securing
and clinging on to political control, power, and wealth. In all this,
the masses were remembered only during election-campaigns,
when they were fed with election promises. Okigbo asked:

Today—for tomorrow, today becomes yesterday:
How many million promises can ever fill a basket (CP:94),

for he believed that political promises were all empty, and that,
conversely, morality was empty until all empty stomachs had been
filled.

But the people continued hungry, neglected, and were driv-
en to cynicism and apathy which almost amounted to "national"
despair, while the people entrusted with the leadership of the
country continued to blazonly rape it. It is that same class whom
Wole Soyinka despises in *Season of Anomy* (1973):

The Sweet-toothed ones alas lacked all moderation
No man-made laws restrained them

They milked the cocoa-tree in a mass operation
They drained the nectar, peeled the gold
The trees were bled prematurely old
Nor green nor gold remained for the next generation. (35)

In the same way, writing in 1983, Chinua Achebe talks, in his anatomy of Nigerian politics, of the breed of irresponsible leaders whose recklessness amounted almost to hatred of the country. His analysis can apply just as aptly to any period in the history of Nigeria:

> The fear that should nightly haunt our leaders (but does not) is that they may already have betrayed irretrievably Nigeria's high destiny. The countless billions [of Naira/dollars] that a generous Providence poured into our national coffers in the last ten years (1972–1982) would have been enough to launch this nation into the middle-rank of developed nations and transformed the lives of our poor and needy. But what have we done with it? Stolen and salted away by people in power and their accomplices. Squandered in uncontrollable importation of all kinds of useless consumer merchandise from every corner of the globe. Embezzled through inflated contracts to an increasing array of party loyalists who have neither the desire nor the competence to execute their contracts. Consumed in the escalating salaries of a grossly overstaffed and unproductive public service. And so on ad infinitum. (1983:2-3)

One does not need any further authenticating corroborations of the activities of the "cursed dullards" whom Okigbo despised and excoriated. For they virtually created in Nigeria a political culture and (dis-)order very much like that in Shakespeare's *King Lear* where, the old stable order having disintegrated and lying in ruins, the new one, which could not properly be called an order, tottered dangerously towards complete chaos (Muir 1965: 49). For this their crime, for the politicians, "there will be a continual going to the well,/Until they smash their calabashes." (CP:56).

Okigbo knew that these "robbers [could still] strip us of our thunder" (65), and that their penance was no panacea for the national quagmire. Yet, he also knew only too well that in his outspoken desire for change and betterment of the (dis-)order lay inherent danger. As a result, he was at one stage content with a "stifled sneeze":

> Then we must sing, tongue-tied,
> Without name or audience,
> Making harmony among the branches. (41),

for as he realized:

> I see many colours in the salt teeth of foam
> Which is no where to face under the half-light
> Wild winds cry out against us
> We shall swallow our heart in our stomach. (58)

Okigbo thus sought refuge in symbolic silence. But it was not to be for long. Nor for long will the careering along the path of stone be for the country led by "Celaeno and her harpy crew." They could not save the country which stood in dire need of salvation. It surprised no one, then, when in the small hours of January 15, 1966, the army struck. Okigbo sympathized immediately with the forces of change and possible social-political revolution. In fact, he had earlier prayed for such a deliverance:

> Lion-hearted cedar forest, gonads for our thunder,
> Even if you are very far away, we invoke you:
>
> Give us our hollow heads of long-drums . . .
>
> Antelopes for the cedar forest, swifter messengers
> Than flash-of-beacon-flame, we invoke you:
>
> Hide us; deliver us from our nakedness . . .
>
> Many-fingered canebreak, exile for our laughter,
> Even if you are very far away, we invoke you:
>
> Come; limber our raw hide of antelopes . . .

Thunder of tanks of giant iron steps of
   detonators,
Fail safe from the clearing, we implore you:
We are tuned for a feast-of-seven-souls.... (61)

And when, indeed, they came, in answer to the unsilent prayers of
many, Okigbo, like most Nigerians, celebrated the apparent cessation of the misrule of "Celaeno and her harpy crew," of the death-
dance of the country above the carrion, and welcomed the army:

Fanfare of drums, wooden bells: iron chapter;
And our dividing airs are gathered home.

This day belongs to a miracle of thunder;
Iron has carried the forum
With token gestures. Thunder has spoken
Left no signatures: broken

Barbicans alone tell one tale the winds scatter. (89)

I have italicized the second line of this quotation to emphasize the
point that, as the nationalist poet-critic Okigbo saw this military
intervention, its most important and most immediate impact was
the infusion, for the first time in the history of Nigeria, of a new
sense of unity, of transethnic cohesion among Nigerians. No matter that, before long, divergent, even spurious and, above all, mischievous and divisive interpretations would be made, the most
damaging being that made by the Northern cultural section, on the
loving advice of their British mentors, that the military coup was
a purely Igbo irredentist affair, it was clear that, for most Nigerians,
this coup inaugurated the end of ethnic politics in Nigeria: "And
our dividing airs are gathered home."
   Very short-lived though it turned out to be, the prospect of a
sane national course, away from the "path of stone," inculcated
in all sectors of the country an ebullient euphoria. Even though
there was sincere sorrow over the loss of some innocent lives, for
which Okigbo sent "Condolences . . . from our swollen lips laden
with / condolences: . . . condolences from our split-tongue of the
slit drum condolences. . . . condolences to caress the swollen eye-

lids of the bleeding mourners" (95), there was no sympathy for the now discredited political leadership which had brought the country to the precipice of shameful disintegration:

> Parliament has gone on leave
> the members are now on bail
> parliament is now on sale
> the voters are lying in wait—
>
> the cabinet has gone to hell
> the timbers are now on fire
> the cabinet that sold itself
> ministers are now in gaol— (95-96)

The national mood was that of irrepressible elation, and in four lines that evoke a national festival and celebration, we are given the mental picture of a whole nation congealing into a dance ensemble, parading through the streets and highways of the entire country, with Okigbo as lead-dancer/singer:

> The mythmaker accompanies us
>   *(the Egret had come & gone)*
> Okigbo accompanies us the oracle enkindles us
> the Hornbill is there again *(the Hornbill has had a bath)*
> Okigbo accompanies us the rattles enlighten us— (96)

The poet is mythmaker, the repository of the collective memory and repertoire of the narratives of the people; he is the oracle through whom the spirits speak to the people, and from whom the people divine their destiny; he is the rattle, that symbol of inspiration and authoritative pronouncements; he is the enlightener; but above all he is Okigbo the person, one of and one with the people: he is now completely subsumed within the collectivity, which fact is even grammatically demonstrated by the sociologization of the personal pronoun "we/us." It is in order here to evoke Obiechina, with whom I share many interpretive insights, and whose reading of the present poems both validates and authorizes mine:

The nature of the situation itself requires a lifting of the masks and the revelation of the true resonance of the natural voice. The lyrical persona whose self-conscious individuality up till now controlled the poetic inspiration is now overridden by the social persona that absorbs the deeply felt fears and anxieties of a whole people. The "us" which increasingly supplants the "I" of the earlier sequences symbolizes this acceptance of the destiny of the individual within the larger, inclusive destiny of the group. The poet's assertion in "Elegy of the Wind" that he had lived the oracle dry on the cradle of a new generation marks a significant, near-total submergence of his individuality within the wider, collective interests of the entire people. The mythmaker, Okigbo, whose outlook is objectified in the unique role of community poet can no longer stand aside from "us," the collectivity, now hemmed in by immense possibilities of both salvation and damnation. The poet is lost in the people. Okigbo, the poet "Accompanies" us, the people, and his rattle music unifies the emotional aspirations of the people. (1980:65-66)

Thus, when the people, the Nigerian collectivity, wanted to know the full details of what actually happened, since the details were still kept as "state secret" from the people: "For barricaded in iron handiwork a miracle [was] caged" (CP:89), Okigbo, the outspoken articulator of the wishes and desires of the people, characteristically asked that the true fact be made public. It was the people's right to know, and the revelation of the "truth" would also dispel the fear of those who might be persuaded by the unpatriotic interpretations and rumors then rampant:

Bring them out we say, bring them out
Faces and hands and feet
The stories behind the myth, the plot
which the ritual enacts. (89)

But, apparently, because of logistical difficulties, lack of coordination, and, possibly, because of sentimental and ethnic reasons, the January Revolution had been only partially successful. The political leadership of Eastern and Mid-Western Regions was virtually

224

unscathed, while their Northern, Western, and Federal counterparts were summarily dispatched. This lopsided execution remains the strongest arsenal in the ethnopolitico-rhetorical armory of those who believed, and still believe, that the January coup was as ethnic as any other putsch or political legerdemain that has ever occurred in Nigeria. Because of this partial success, the coup leaders could not establish or exercise effective control beyond Kaduna and, in a matter of days, a mock or Kangaroo session of the National House handed over the political leadership of the country to General Ironsi who was, clearly, neither ready nor equipped for the hypocritical decorums of diplomacy and the duplicitous burdens of government. It is this liberal soldier of the old order, as inheritor of the coup and government, whom Okigbo mock-eulogized in "Elegy for Slit-Drum," in which is also capsulized the poet's contempt for tyrants, be they Leidan, that "archtyrant of the Holy Sea," or the hard-drinking General, soon to be famous or notorious for unimplementable decrees:

> The General is up . . . the General is up . . .
> Commandments . . .

> The General is up the General is up the General is up—
> condolences from our twin-beaks and feathers
>   of condolences:

> the General is near the throne
> an iron mask covers his face
> the general has carried the day
> the mortars are far away— (96)

It was clear to the poet that the assumption of the leadership of this new government by someone who was not part of the plan for socio-political change and regeneration, who was an entrenched part of the old, decadent order, forebode ill for the society. His celebration of the change, was, therefore tempered by fear, dread, anxiety, and caution. Thus he talked of "condolences quivering before the iron throne of a new conqueror: . . . / condolences with the miracle of sunlight on our feathers. . . ." (96).

This new conqueror, brought up in the best British military tradition of royalism and loyalism, actually saw the leaders of the January Revolution in treasonable light, and was openly willing to succumb to the sectional clangor for blood and reprisal, for the heads of the now-imprisoned coup leaders, who nearly gave Nigeria freedom. Okigbo reminded the new leadership that the:

> Thunder that has struck the elephant
> the same thunder should wear a plume—condolences
>
> a roadmaker makes a road
> the road becomes a throne
> can we cane him for felling a tree—condolences . . .
>
> Thunder that has struck the elephant
> the same thunder can make a bruise—condolences. . . . (97)

If the reminder and the warning contained in the poem did not avail, Okigbo offered what amounted to his last nationalistic plea for peace, harmony and mutual forgiveness. While offering "condolences to appease the fever of a wake among tumbled tombs" (96), Okigbo noted the futility of hypothetical speculations and questionings. The "elephant" had already fallen and it paid no one to brood

> forever over its fate:
> the elephant has fallen
> the mortars have won the day
> the elephant has fallen
> does he deserve his fate
> the elephant has fallen
> can we remember the date—(96)

In the interest of unity, peace, reconciliation, and (possibly) national progress, Nigerians were advised to bury the hatchet:

> we should forget the names
> we should bury the date
> the dead should bury the dead—
> condolences (97)

But the sectional cry for blood would not be quelled. Ethnic blood, they said, must have ethnic blood, and the scrambled political equation at the center must be solved or resolved, before peace and normalcy could return to Nigeria. All the decrees of appeasement and unification promulgated by Ironsi were "null cacophony" and, while the worst was yet to come, Nigeria began to witness orchestrated rituals of blood and carnage, which the assassination of Ironsi and the seizure of political power in July 1966 by the Northern Sector did not, or would not, check. What was happening now reduced the dance of fireflies and the dance above the carrion to mere child's play. In spite of his full awareness of the dangers inherent in outspoken criticism of political (especially undisciplined military) regimes, which fear he had earlier expressed openly—

> If I don't learn to shut my mouth I'll soon go to hell,
> I, Okigbo, town-crier, together with my iron bell. (94)

—it was clear to Okigbo, as voice of the people, that he must stake and risk all, or else lose the very reason for his being and calling. In the face of the rape of humanity that was going on, he could not abandon the people by keeping silent:

> White light, receive me your sojourner: O Milky way,
> let me clasp you to my waist;
> And may my muted tones of twilight
> Break your iron gate, the burden of several centuries,
> into twin tremulous cotyledons . . .
>
> Man of iron throat—for I will make broadcast with
> eunuch-horn of seven valves—
> I will follow the wind to the clearing,
> And with muffled steps seemingly out of breath break
> the silence the myth of her gate....
> I have lived the oracle dry on the cradle of a
>   new generation. (90)

His "broadcast with eunuch-horn of seven valves" notwithstanding, that repetitive ritual pattern of sanguinary extirpation of infidel "stranger" elements from their midst by Northern bands, which

I had prosaically attempted to sketch in chapter one, is here endowed with poetic vividness and pathos, capsulized in the image of the dripping blood of excruciating circumcision:

> The Chief priest of the sanctuary has uttered
> the enchanted words;
> The bleeding phallus,
> Dripping fresh from the carnage cries out for
> the medicinal leaf . . .
>
> O wind, swell my sails; and may my banner run
> the course of many waters;
>
> The child in me trembles before the high shelf
> on the wall,
> The man in me shrinks before the narrow neck of
> a calabash,
> And the chant, already all wings, follows
> In its ivory circuit behind the thunder clouds,
> The slick route of the feathered serpent.... (91)

It is the same blood-thirst whose orgiastic savagery and unprecedented barbarity Wole Soyinka captures in *Season of Anomy,* where:

> twenty miles from Irelu a woman was dragged from her bed, sliced open at the belly. She was not even dead when they left her guts spilling in a messy after-birth between her thighs . .. The assailants stuffed her mouth with a roll of court orders she had served on them and set the grotesque cigar alight. The antelope's hoof, symbol of the Cartel manipulated party, Jeku, inspired the idea of amputation of their agents in Aro-Oke. They were hunted down one after the other, a foot was hacked off at the ankle and stuffed into their mouths. A family of twenty, three generations in all wiped out in a noon of vengeance. An agent on the run from mob rage had fired wildly into his pursuers felling two, fled and barricaded himself in his own house. He was still scrabbling for more cartridges when they came upon him, a huge wave borne sole-

ly on pain and rage. Up the stairs fled all the inmates of the house, seeking imagined safety. The mob set the stairs alight, shot and cut down every being in the house who leapt or tried to creep into the safety of the bushes even on broken legs. A nursing sister, niece of the agent drove into the blood-crazed arms of the mob as she returned from work. Recognized, the yet unsated avengers raised her, she flew from arm to arm, was swung back and forth and into the flames. (1973:109-110)

This senselessness and carnage continued until Nigerians went to a war of unprecedented venom and ferocity, which lasted for thirty long months, but which did not succeed in fulfilling its genocidal intentions, and which also did not succeed in resolving the primordial tensions and cleavages plaguing the country. Even as we approach the last chapter of this book, as Nigerians remain unsure as to how the constituent sections of the country would coexist, one hears rumbles of threats and counter-threats, clearly reminiscent of the first indigenous crop of rulers boasting their borrowed powers:

The elephant ravages the jungles
the jungle is peopled with snakes
the snake says to the squirrel
I will swallow you
the mongoose says to the snake
I will mangle you
the elephant says to the mongoose
I will strangle you. (CP:97)

Those shots that disrupted the uneasy sleep of Nigerians that early morning of January 1966 can be said to have let loose a horde of winged, mischievous beings who can no longer be controlled or contained; to have inaugurated a more hardy and more pernicious version of the dance above the carrion, and of the fireflies, whose virtual invincibility and irreplaceability are ensured by their monopoly over the means of violence and political control in Nigeria. But it is not as if the poet of the people did not foresee and warn against this impasse. He did, but no one paid heed then:

Now that the triumphant march has entered the last street
corners,
Remember, O dancers, the thunder among the clouds . . .
Now that laughter, broken in two, hangs tremulous
between the teeth,
Remember, O dancers, the lightning beyond the earth . . .

The smell of blood already floats in the lavender-mist of the
afternoon.
The death sentence lies in ambush along the corridors of
power;
And a great fearful thing already tugs at the cables of the
open air,
A nebula immense and immeasurable, a night of deep
waters—

The drowsy heads of the pods in barren farmland witness
it,
The homesteads abandoned in this century's brushfire wit-
ness it:
Magic birds with the miracle of lightning flash on their
feathers . . .
The arrows of God tremble at the gates of light
The drums of curfew pander to a dance of death;

And the secret thing in its heaving
Threatens with iron mask
The last lighted torch of the century.... (92-93)

That "secret thing" refers to the military which, since its first taste
of the intoxicating wine of political and economic power in Nigeria
in January 1966, has found it both irresistible and addictive. It has,
therefore, remained inebriatedly mired in politics ever since, reluctantly relinquishing power only once, from October 1979 to
December 1983. In effect, that "last lighted torch of the century,"
a model democracy, called Nigeria, which was celebrated all over
the world in 1960, as Britain's legacy to political economy, as well
as its compensatory atonement for whatever atrocities it might
have committed in the name of colonialism and the sustenance of

the imperial sun, has remained a precarious potentiality. Instead of functioning, in the words of the Random House Dictionary of the English Language (1987), "as a source of illumination, enlightenment, guidance, [and example]" to other ex-colonies, the political trajectory of Nigeria, that "last lighted torch," has continued to evoke a particular transitive sense of the verb, "to torch: to subject to the flame or light of a torch, as in order to burn, etc.," and a sinister connotation of the slang variant of the same verb: "to set fire to maliciously." One begins to wonder—especially as no single ex-colony of Britain has known peace, stability, or progress—if the refusal of Nigeria to metamorphose from a mere geographical expression into nation or, at least, to a viable, if not enviable, nation-state, has more or less to do with the "malicious" or mischievous intent of the creators of the polity, than with the intractability of the ethnic blight and the insatiability of the cavernously avaricious (mis-)leaders of that country.

When that fratricidal crucible exploded into full-scale war, against which Okigbo had so loudly warned, the jingoistic slogan of the Federal Government had been "To Keep Nigeria One Is a Task That Must Be Done!" That war ended after thirty months of carnage in favor of Federal Nigeria, but because it was waged by leaders whose primordial blinkers were hardly hidden, its successful resolution did not result in fairness and justice (cf., Wole Soyinka's parody of the Federal Military Government's War Cry: "To Keep Nigeria One, Justice Must Be Done," quoted in Gibbs 1980:12), nor in the inculcation in the people of the consciousness of nation, of the sense of "nation-ness" (Anderson 1991:3). Indeed, even though the nation-state has been maintained as political structure, this maintenance has remained a very uncertain achievement because the "sub-nationalisms" which constitute the nation-state do not only harbor the dreams of one day "shedding this subness" (3); they are even now actively canvassing for relatively separate, autonomous, albeit, cooperative existence. This was made clear in the different Position Papers formulated and reformulated by the different cultural sections in anticipation of a Constitutional Conference that turned out to be still-born. Even before that conference had been convened, at which these positions would have been discussed, "All over the country, ethnic nationalists and champions are emerging" (Okonta 1994:21). It is interesting that in a clear *deja vu* of history, among the most prominent subjects being touted were, (and still are), "the continued existence of Nigeria as a corporate entity, . . . a fundamental restructuring of the power equation in the country" (22), and "revenue allocation, power sharing and ethnic nationalism," as well as "injustice, exploitation and marginalisation" (23). But a common thread which runs through the various ethnic nationalities in the Southeastern and Southwestern parts of the country is the strong feeling that the Nigerian Federation as is presently constituted can neither move the country forward nor bring out the best in its constituent parts (25).

One is hardly surprised that in such a cacophonous situation, even when people were still "talking about talks before the talk," there had been reported cases of vociferous altercations degenerating into serious physical fights, a drama reminiscent once more of those ominous lines by Okigbo:

> The elephant ravages the jungle
> the jungle is peopled with snakes
> the snake says to the squirrel
> I will swallow you
> the mongoose says to the snake
> I will mangle you
> the elephant says to the mongoose
> I will strangle you (CP:97)

In this latter-day version of the "jubilee" dance of "ethnic nationalists and champions," what gets seriously foregrounded is the paradoxical tension between "the objective modernity" of the Nigerian nation-state and the "subjective antiquity" of the cultural sections, to appropriate Anderson's theorization (1991: 5). I have already virtually overstressed the primordial importance of attachment to cultural sections as that bane which has made the evolution of nation impossible in Nigeria. As Anderson defines it, nation "is an imagined political community—and imagined as both inherently limited and sovereign" (6). In this formulation, it is asserted that, even though members of such a community have lost the intimate directness of "primordial villages," "yet in the minds of each lives the image of their communion" (6). Anderson's attempt (6) to distance himself from Gellner (whose definition "'Nationalism is not the awakening of nations to self-consciousness: it invents nations where they do not exist'" is faulted for assimilating "'invention' to 'fabrication' and 'falsity,' rather than to 'imagining' and 'creation'" notwithstanding), his isolation of three crucial elements of nation, as defined, is important in the present discussion. Of the three qualities of nation: "limited" because it "has finite, if elastic, boundaries, beyond which lie other nations;" "sovereign" because "nations dream of being free. . . . The gage and emblem of this freedom is the sovereign state;" and community (7), it is this last attribute which is crucial, by default, to the Nigerian situation. According to Anderson, a nation:

> is imagined as a *community,* because, regardless of the actual inequality and exploitation that may prevail in each, the nation is always conceived as a *deep, horizontal comradeship.* Ultimately it is this *fraternity* that makes it possible . . . for so many people, not so much to kill, as *willingly to die for such limited imaginings.* (7; my italics)

In spite of the present conflict between Nigeria and the Cameroons over a large tract of territory which Nigeria ceded to the latter in order to secure its cooperation and support against Biafra, Nigeria's borders/boundaries can be said to be largely unproblematic; in spite of the dependence of the country on Westminster and the Western Metropoles, as well as on the MNC's and their comprador political elite, Nigeria's sovereignty can still be largely asserted; but *Nigeria is not a community* because its people are not connected by "a deep, horizontal comradeship" and "fraternity." Moreover, even as that latest war "to keep Nigeria one" had demonstrated, people were not willing to die for the country as such, in the sense of "colossal sacrifices" which Anderson speaks about. As if to underscore this fact, the conspicuous and most important "cenotaphs and tombs of Unknown Soldiers," which adorn City Squares in Nigeria, are those that pay empty "ceremonial reverence" (9) to the Nigerian soldiers who died in the wars of the British Empire, not to those conscripts and vandals, many of whom went in to loot and amass wealth, to settle old personal and ethnic scores, to avenge the deaths of their cultural/political leaders, or even to stop the mad military/political ambitions of upstart comrades, who died in the Nigeria-Biafra War.

So, while I admire Anderson's elegant theorization, it does appear to me that it has very limited applicability to the Nigerian situation. Perhaps Chatterjee's meditation on nationalism, which is an excellent critique of and corrective on Anderson's, may prove more relevant to us.

In this book, *Nationalist Thought and the Colonial World: A Derivative Discourse* (1986), Chatterjee begins by elaborating on and critiquing John Plamenatz's distinction between "'two types' of nationalism," one "western" and the other "eastern," the latter referring to instantiations "in Eastern Europe, in Asia and Africa, and also in Latin America" (1). The implication of the radical distinction between the two types of nationalism is that whereas the "Western" nations felt culturally equipped to reach the standards of development and civilization, "universal" or "common" standards which were set, in the first place, "for the rest of the world by France or Britain" (1), the "Eastern" nations were "drawn into a civilisation hitherto alien to them" and forced to adapt to "success and excellence" as defined by "these cosmopolitan and increasingly dominant standards" (2). A sad fact of the colonial experience is the paradoxical attitude towards these "alien standards": hostility to the alien is combined with the desire and aspiration to emulate and, dreamlike, even surpass it. At the same time, a love of identity-bestowing "ancestral ways" is joined to a desire to repudiate them as an obstacle to the attainment of alien standards of modernity. No wonder "eastern" nationalism is said to be "disturbed and ambivalent" (2) for it "simultaneously rejects and accepts the dominance . . . of an alien culture" (11).

Chatterjee identifies Eurocentric epistemology, which dichotomizes in order to inferiorize, subjugate, and control the other, as lying at the root of "the liberal-rationalist dilemma in talking about nationalist thought" (2). In this binary scheme, the terms Western, good, liberal-rational, pure, classical/model, progress, democracy, and freedom are evaluatively positive terms contrasted with Eastern, evil, deviant, illiberal-irrational, impure, and other negative attributes of unorthodox nations which, because they "are culturally incapable of acquiring the values of the Enlightenment" (10), stand in dire need of reequipment and transformation (2, 3). Yet, as Chatterjee points out, the narrative of "classical," "orthodox," "model," and "Western" nationalism has not necessarily been the story of freedom and liberty:

> [The liberal-rational] historiography accepts nationalism as an integral part of the story of liberty. Its origin is coeval with the birth of universal history, and its development is part of the same historical process which saw the rise of industrialism and democracy. In its essential aspects, therefore, nationalism represents the attempt to actualize in political terms the universal urge for liberty and progress. And yet the evidence was undeniable that it could also give rise to mindless chauvinism and xenophobia and serve as the justification for organized violence and tyranny. Seen as part of the story of liberty, nationalism could be defined as a rational ideological framework for the realization of rational, highly laudable, political ends. But that was not how nationalism had made its presence felt in much of recent history. It has been the cause of the most destructive wars ever seen; it has justified the brutality of Nazism and Fascism; it has become the ideology of hatred in the colonies and has given birth to some of the most irrational movements as well as to the most oppressive regimes in the contemporary world. . . . nationalism and liberty could often be quite irreconcilably opposed. (2-3)

With regard to the national question in the "Third World," Chatterjee marks its connection with colonialism, for the assertion of national identity was constructed as a weapon in the war against colonial imposition and exploitation. Except in such cases as Nigeria, where atavistic collectivism and solidarity was patently false and forced, for which reason it was short-lived, the general outcome of the confrontation between "the modernizing, Westernizing" trend and the "assertion of traditional cultural values" was always already determined in favor of the former (18). This historical determinism does not necessarily devalorize

"atavistic nationalism" which, if construed "as part of a movement of the people to regain its pride and self-respect [as well as
freedom from imperial domination], it has a constructive aspect"
(19). On the other hand, Horace Davis, whom Chatterjee discusses, thinks that "belligerent, aggressive, chauvinistic nationalism is a menace and thus irrational from the point of view of
humanity as a whole" (19). The lofty idealism of Davis's
Eurocentric humanism fails, however, to account for the fact that
the imposition of the colonial yoke on sections of "humanity as a
whole" by a section of that "humanity as a whole," was inherently unjust, irrational, violent, aggressive, and chauvinistic. One
remembers here Fanon's convincing justification of violence when
used to end the violence of colonial imposition (1967:passim).

Unfortunately, even before the colonial structure had been
indigenized (not dismantled) in Nigeria, the atavistic "unity" of the
cultural sections, which had been temporarily arranged and precariously maintained for the duration of anticolonial struggle, had
begun to degenerate into (truly atavistic) disunity. For instance, the
Regional Houses were controlled and populated exclusively by "sons
of the soil," members by blood of the cultural sections in the
Regions. It has been pointed out how the brazen fraud in the 1951
Western Regional election which virtually "took" Zik's victory from
him, sang the *nunc dimittis* of that country (Achebe 1983:5). At
the Federal Houses, the election and membership were not a function of merit, ability, or nationalistic fervor of the parliamentarian
or Senator, but of his cultural Section (and thus political party) of origin. This cultural-sectional determination of the compositional structure of the Federal Houses, as well as the compromised (im) balance
of power between a Northern Prime Minister and a Southern
Governor-General (later President), both made visible and ensured
the perpetual precariousness of the nation-state and the impossibility
of the emergence of true nationness.

It is true that nationalism, as Horace Davis points out, is a
"process," "a movement," and "not a thing, even an abstract
thing" (Chatterjee 1986: 19). But the refusal or impossibility of the
emergence, which I have just referred to, may be directly related
to the absence of persons who would relegate ethnicity to secon-
darity in order to enable the imagining of community (ibid.;

Anderson 1991:6); to dream it into being; to construct and to build it. Since the 1950s when the "'nationalist' leaders . . . forsook nationalism in favour of the quick returns of tribalism" (Achebe 1983: 20), Nigeria has never had another chance to build a viable community.

But whether we talk about building, or "inventing" with the connotations of fabrication and falsity, or creating and imagining, in the end, when all the quibbling over semantics is over, it will be seen that we are all talking about the same thing. In fact, Chatterjee's perceptive observation is cogent:

> What if we look closely, at the substantive differences between Anderson and Gellner on 20th century nationalism? None. Both point out a fundamental change in ways of perceiving the social world which occurs before nationalism can emerge: Gellner relates this change to the requirements of "industrial society," Anderson more ingeniously to the dynamics of "print capitalism." Both describe the characteristics of the new cultural homogeneity which is sought to be imposed on the emerging nation: for Gellner this is the imposition of a common high culture on the variegated complex of local folk culture, for Anderson the process involves the formulation of "print language" and the shared experience of the "journeys" undertaken by the colonized intelligentsia. In the end, both see in third-world nationalisms a profoundly "modular" character. They are invariably shaped according to the contours outlined by given historical models: "objective, inescapable, imperative," "too-marked deviations . . . impossible." (Chatterjee, 1986: 21)

I have here italicized the word "impossible" because what characterizes the Nigerian situation appears to be impossibility even more than mere refusal. I had earlier referred to the limited applicability of Anderson's "modular" insights to the Nigerian case. It appears to me that that inapplicability is broader than it would seem. If one considers "industrialism," for instance, its rudiments, together with a truncated or lopsided modernity, came to Nigeria in the wake of colonialism; "print-capitalism" developed soon after the establishment of printing presses by the missionary establishment and by the colonial administration. Since then several Nigerian languages have been reduced to graphological fixity and some permanence in orthographies, modified and disfigured, albeit, to varying degrees. The production of the printed text in these indigenous as well as English languages has not had any significance in terms of national cohesion. For one thing, the degree of illiteracy in Nigeria is scandalous, and it does not matter whether one is considering the two hundred and one indigenous languages or English: mass literacy has remained a distant utopia mouthed only during electioneering campaigns of decades past, and appearing infrequently in programmatic Government White Papers. Enforced successfully in Awolowo's Western Nigeria, mass literacy as a goal was not systematically applied across the country. The result was that even the Universal Primary Education (U.P.E.) program introduced by the Military turned out to be a huge national joke, with thousands of uneducated market women turning teachers overnight in order to supply the first, but unforeseen, need of a "revolutionary" educational program. Moreover, there has not been any serious or concerted attempt to develop a supraethnic medium of communication which would obviate the need for the continued use of a colonial language, and circumvent the problem of imposing one of the Nigerian languages on the rest of fractious cultural sections, whose neurotic fear of domination, be it cultural, political, or linguistic, has remained characteristically Nigerian. Finally, apart from the International Fanfares and Jamborees of Waste, the most famous/notorious example of which was "Festac 77," there has never been an attempt by the successive rulers of Nigeria to create or forge a National or State or High culture which would articulate with, and begin to influence, "the variegated complex of local folk cultures" which, working subtly with the suggested "transethnic tongue," would have attempted a unification of the different cultural sections, transforming them into effective interlocutors with the statal-systemic axis. Consequently, the dream of "cultural homogeneity" remains a dream in Nigeria.

In sum, neither the creation of the colonial state of Nigeria in 1914, nor the "independence" of that state in 1960, nor, yet, the periodic parcelization of the country into unviable fragments called "states," has succeeded in superseding the centrifugalities of ethnicity and cultural sectionalism. In effect, as of 1997, the nation-state remains precarious, while the consciousness of nation, of nation-ness, remains a dream which people have continuously forgotten to remember whenever they wake up. It is the tenacity of that cultural-historical amnesia which accounts for the fact that the much touted Constitutional Conference turned out to be merely a grand replay of the 1956 Conference; the resort to physical confrontations in 1994 even during the "talks before the Talk" was a reenactment of the insanities of the "cabinet that sold itself." What Okigbo said of the situation as far back as 1966 applies just as aptly now in Nigeria, where always:

> . . . we are talking of such commonplaces,
> and on the brink of such great events . . . . (CP:70)

It is a sign of the times, as well as inadvertent vindication of the warnings and prophecies of Okigbo, that a national magazine became sufficiently bold and brazen to declare on its front-cover:

> "Get Set for the Worst"....
> "February is Nigeria's Most Critical Month"....
> "The Nation May Grind to a Halt"....

and to litter the inside-pages with such show of frustrated courage as "Abacha's New Political Economy Portends Danger on All Fronts," "Are Our Leaders Mad?," "A Revolution is Knocking," and "The Party Is Over" (*The News*, 14 February, 1994). If the charade seems to have gone full-circle, and prepares to begin all over again, it is sad, for we have been warned by the poet after he had "lived the oracle dry" that, for us, as for our leaders, "there will be a continual going to the well, / Until they smash their calabashes" (CP:56). If Nigerians did not heed Okigbo's warning before the first national impasse, there is no evidence that they will now revisit his warnings and prophecy of, in order to avoid, the repetition of that historic impasse. So, as Okigbo foretold:

An old star departs, leaves us here on the shore
Gazing heavenward for a new star approaching;
The new star appears, foreshadows its going
Before a going and coming that goes on forever.... (99)

CHAPTER VII

A PROPHETIC CONCLUSION: POET, NATION, DEATH

Immediately preceding *Path of Thunder*—that apogee of Okigbo's poetic trajectory, that climacteric summation and capsulization of his poetic-prophetic statement—is *Distances*. *Distances* is the poet's *Song of Sorrow*, a sequence full of tears and warning, whose dismal and lachrymose atmosphere provides a most logical transition into thunder, eclipse, and prophecy of repetition.

Unfortunately, many extant readings of *Distances* have either missed the interpretive mark or emphasized the wrong thing. In this necessary discussion of the prelude to the poet's farewell, I wish to briefly indicate five of such readings before undertaking my own, which, like a discursive vine, will be intertwined very closely with the poet's text.

Philemon Gomwalk sees *Distances* as a celebration, at the end of the poet's spiritual quest, of "the final consummation of the protagonist's acceptance—his final homecoming" (in Nwoga, ed., 1984: 205). The relevant paragraph of his essay reads as follows:

> From the beginning of *Distances*, the protagonist is converted from "flesh" into "phantom," the only form in which he could retain his spiritual purity and so warrant the ultimate union he had so much desired with his goddess (the oblong-headed lioness) and the attainment of ultimate creative illu-

mination from the poetic Muse. The spiritual quest in *Distances* then assumes a "survival of the fittest" endeavour, of which only the stronger can "laugh the effervescent laughter / the open laughter" at the end. And this "open laughter" is quite evident from the tone of the final consummation of the protagonist's acceptance—his final homecoming:

> I have entered your bridal
> chamber; and lo,
> I am the sole witness to my homecoming.
> (Nwoga 1984:205)

It is not necessary to respond individually to the readings being cited here. The interpretive departure or divergence of my reading will directly or indirectly address what I think are grievous misinterpretations. In Anozie's book, *Distances* is correctly but uninsightfully said to be a sequel to *Siren Limits*. The poet himself had said so; he had also repeatedly referred to the organic connection among all his poems: "Although these poems were written and published separately, they are, in fact organically related" (CP: xxiii). In fact, Okigbo goes a little further than this surface expression of organicism to indicate a relationship between *Siren Limits* and *Distances* which amounts to interchangeability:

> *Limits* and *Distances* are man's outer and inner worlds projected—the phenomenal and the imaginative, not in terms of their separateness but of their relationship—an attempt to reconcile the universal opposites of life and death in a live-die proposition: one is the other and either is both. (xxiii)

But as Anozie goes on to elucidate,

> In terms of our own response to and analysis of it, for example, the theme of *Distances*—note taken also of the fact that this poem is a sequel to *Siren Limits*—can be stated briefly as follows: the spiritual quest after a receding symbol, and the progress towards its final apocalyptic illumination. Analogically, this theme is treated by the poet as the experience of sex and its orgasm. (Anozie 1972:151)

The chapter from which this excerpt is taken ends with a reiteration of the theme of *Distances* as a "spiritual-cum-artistic quest" (170). In refuting this, Egudu declares that *Distances* is crucially a narrative of cultural retrieval, a nativistic repudiation of Christianity, and an embrace of indigeneity:

> *Distances* is essentially concerned with a spiritual journey from "foreign" Christ to native Idoto, a journey from the Christian theory of salvation effected after death to the indigenous state of purity and bliss attainable in life. For Okigbo could have reasonably argued using the words of Kofi Awoonor, that salvation is here with us and not somewhere beyond this world:
> Who says there is a resting place elsewhere?
> It is here with us.
>
> For Okigbo's protagonist, therefore, the resting place is that "home" which is under the matronship of the Water-Goddess. The process through which he arrived back at this "home" in spite of those "shadows distances labyrinths violences" which are created by Death and the Christian world seen in a vision, which hindered his progress and distracted attention from his quest—this process recreated as a dream vision, seems to me to be the essential burden of *Distances*. (Nwoga 1984:153-154)

Annemarie Heywood's study of Okigbo's poetry as "ritual" is a piece of illuminating scholarship. It is also a sober rebuke on Anozie whose "modish academicism and ideological cant" make his "critical tool kit" so "grotesquely inappropriate" that his readings of Okigbo's poetry are both "arbitrary and unhelpful" (208). Through a recourse to "anthropology, mythology, and comparative religion" (212), and deriving much insight from Joseph Campbell and Mircea Eliade, Heywood locates "the key to Okigbo" in ritual:

> I mean *poetry as ritual*, poetry which is in itself a ritual instrument. The words on the page do not function to body forth a reality beyond them, and to be grasped through them: they *are* the reality and the experience in sensible form. . . . Ritual

does not communicate or express; it enacts, invokes, or conjures. . . .

Generally speaking, Okigbo uses language eloquent yet uncommunicative, concrete yet not "natural," private yet impersonal; its texture is richly sensuous, both directly by virtue of its sound and rhythm and patterns, and indirectly by virtue of its evocative power. Such is the medium of revelation and ritual. . . . "Throughout history," Mircea Eliade observes, "sensory activity has been used as a means of participating in the sacred and attaining to the divine." That, to my mind, is the key to Okigbo. (212)

A little later in the same article, as she attempts an analysis of an "impenetrable" stanza from *Distances*, Heywood talks of "a passage that deals with the approach of ritual dissolution and detachment from 'all the forms / [which] were formed after our forming'" (214). This "ritual dissolution," which will be thematized presently in my reading, actually also serves to make unnecessary any response to such readings as have located the burden of *Distances* in cultural atavism or in the celebration of the survival of the stronger in a Darwinian struggle.

The last reading of Okigbo which I cite here, by Gerald Moore, himself a scholar and poet, is also the most incisive. The essay itself begins with an insightful generalization which applies acutely and precisely to Okigbo's poetics:

The visionary writer does not journey into the past but into himself, where he encounters the gleams and fragments of many pasts and many possible futures. Loneliness is essential to his journey and he must not expect to report to us more than a metaphor of what he found there. The visionary must construct a symbolic language which gives meaning to his isolation and thus connects him with those who will listen. . . . For what is unique in him is ... the readiness to develop his life in that direction. By so doing he re-enters the world of myth. . . . (274)

But in the middle of a very useful discussion of Okigbo's poetry, even Moore slips into a particular misreading, of a simple word "anti-hill" as "anthill," which has also characterized the other readings already

cited. It seems to me that that single misreading is capable of changing the whole semantic thrust of the sequence, and accounts for the
view of *Distances* as a celebration, and as a happy return or consummation. Okigbo's use of *anti-hill* in the "final version" of his
poetry is deliberate and represents an antithesis to "anthill," and to
the "hill-top" of *Lustra*, where ecstatic delight and rejoicing were
in order. The full stanza where the word occurs reads:

> Miner into my solitude,
> incarnate voice of the dream,
> you will go,
> with me as your chief acolyte,
> again into the *anti-hill* . . .
> (CP: 69; my italics)

In spite of the use of "again" which suggests revisitation of an
already visited place, it seems to me that both the circumstance
and the terrain have changed. For even though the poet talks here
of "homecoming," and later deals with "consummation," it is clear
that the solitary homecoming is not a very happy one, not an
occasion for rejoicing: to achieve the homecoming, the transformation "from flesh into phantom" has to take place first, "on the
horizontal stone" which, it is true, suggests "the operating table
on which the poet passes from waking to dreaming, and the altar
on which his reunion is to take place" (Moore 1984: 284). But the
"horizontal stone" also recalls "marble slab," so that we could also
be talking about "grave stone" or tomb-stone. Hardly an occasion
for rejoicing, this homecoming is accompanied by serious communion of spirit with "a bowl of incense," which, by becoming "a
nest of fireflies", recalls for us the tragic "dance of fireflies" which
has hardly ended. Moreover, this homecoming is a regression to
the primordial womb, to "the birthday of earth," not through illu-
minated pathways, but "through some dark labyrinth" (CP: 69).

This kind of "home" and "homecoming" is quite resonant with
the general atmosphere of gloom and disaster which will quickly build
up from a simple "ambush" by death, to real carnage where Death,
personified as "chief celebrant," "bathed her knees in the blood of
attendants; / her smock in entrails of ministrants" (71). This atmosphere is such that "the wind," ordinarily welcome and soothing in

normal evenings, is, on "that evening," an ominous dealer in "bandages," usually associated with wounds, sores, surgery, blood, death:

> It was an evening without flesh or skeleton;
> an evening with no silver bells to its tale;
> without lanterns, an evening without age or memory—
> for we are talking of such commonplaces,
> and on the brink of such great events.... (70)

"Such great events" have already been clearly indicated by the cold and freezing, deathly images. Even though the whole poetic journey had earlier been associated with solitude and anguish, here the cry of the poet is not only "scattered," but also smothered by "anguish and solitude;" the same agency will "smother" the dancers who at the same time are "lost among their own snares." The occasion here is quite different from that in "Elegy for Slit-Drum" where, in the last chapter, I had talked about the poet as mythmaker and rattle, imagined as leading a celebratory procession of his people. Here where "the interstices" are "reddening with blood," the chief celebrant is "Death herself" "in smock of white cotton." "Smock of white cotton" would indicate priestly purity as well as eerie ghostliness. But the closely related "cotton wool," suggested by the overall atmosphere, is usually associated with the traumatic activities of the Emergency Ward of a hospital; it is also the thing with which the nostrils, and often ears, of dead persons are plugged. Evocative of, but clearly different from the scene in Wole Soyinka's *Idanre* (1967), where the drunk and crazed Ogun butchers his own men, the scene here has "Death herself / in a cloud of incense / paring her fingernails," unperturbed by the severed and falling heads of her own dutiful ministrants: "like cut fruits; . . . numerous as locusts." But she does not just stand unconcerned; as if in ritual gesture of ablution:

> She bathed her knees in the blood of attendants;
> her smock in entrails of ministrants.... (CP: 71)

In such a situation of chaos and unreason, one wonders how the "line of pilgrims/bound for Shibboleth" can be described as "an enthusiastic pilgrimage moving in a strictly hierarchical order

towards the same Holy of Holies—the 'white chamber inside'"
(Anozie 1972: 152), when the poem describes the line of pilgrims
as "scattered," in total disarray! It is true that the poet-as-priest has
"the crucifix / the torn branch the censer," but the pilgrimage
which stretches "from Dan to Beersheeba" directs us to a particular reference point in time and place. This spatio-temporal reference is important, not only because it evokes aridity, sterility,
devastation, and futility, for we are talking about that part of the
Middle East whose only reliable sources of water are River Jordan
and the Lake of Galilee, which are uncomfortably abutted by the
Dead Sea, but also because the catastrophe that was Sodom and
Gomorrah took place there. It is thus in order that the poet should
be talking of "camphor," pest-repellent and air-seasoner; "iodine,"
antiseptic used in dressing fresh wounds; and "chloroform," a gas
which induces general anaesthesia prior to, and during, radical
surgery. Of this area Werner Keller says:

> No fish of any kind, no seaweed, no coral—no fishing boat
> had ever rocked on this sea. Here was neither a harvest from
> the sea nor from the land, for the banks were equally bare and
> desolate. Huge deposits of coagulated salt made the beach
> and the rock face above it sparkle in the sun like diamonds.
> The air was filled with sharp acrid odors, a mixture of
> petroleum and sulphur. Oily patches of asphalt—the Bible
> calls it "slime"—float on the waves. Even the bright blue sky
> and the all powerful sun could not breathe any life into this
> forbidding-looking landscape. (1956:77)

Dan is described "as the most northerly point in [this] country"
(76). And Beersheba is said to be so arid that only a particularly
sturdy and adapted species of plant could grow and survive there:

> "the first tree which Abraham planted in the soil of Beersheba
> was a tamarisk." . . . Abraham did absolutely the right thing.
> For the tamarisk is one of the few trees . . . that will flourish
> at all in the south where the annual rainfall is under 6 inches.
> . . . "And Abraham planted a tamarisk in Beersheba." (417)

So the routed pilgrims desperate for a "cure" will not only traverse unimaginable distances between Dan and Beersheba; they will also be exposed to extremely inhospitable, almost inhuman, elements. Apart from the "prophets martyrs lunatics" who again are in a special class by themselves, "On the stone steps on the marble / beyond the balcony," a vantage point, the rest of the pilgrims are the "dantini" and "dillettanti," as well as "vendors princes negritude / politicians in the tall wood . . ." Already characterized as the "rhombus" (CP: 23), the fate of the "selfish selfseekers" has already been made clear to us. Could the poet's reference to this historico-biblical impasse be for nothing, given the direction the "rhomboid" leaders of his society were driving it?

Of course, only the poet/seer/prophet can redirect such a misdirected society. But to execute such an impossible task, he needs to become one, to be consummated, with the creative essence itself, here imaged as the goddess, "O Maid." But that consummation can be achieved only after a mental, physical, and spiritual ordeal of indescribable excruciation. To begin with, the poet has to pass two tests of divination/interpretation. He first has to pass through the archway from which hangs a sign which must be decoded for the poet's direction to the next stage:

the only way to go
through the marble archway
to the catatonic ping pong
of evanescent halo . . . (CP: 73)

But before getting to this sign the poet confronts:

a triangular lintel
of solid alabaster
enclosed in a square
inscribed in a circle
with a hollow centre,
above the archway
yawning shutterless
like celestial pincers
like a vast countenance: (73)

In this stanza without verbs, the poet not only has to decode the geometric symbolism of superimposed patterns, but he has to tread cautiously, for the invitingly "shutterless" archway yawns "like celestial pincers," capable of literally/symbolically making a mincemeat of one.

Next, beyond the archway, with increasing illumination, the poet finally deciphers not simply the shape of the "immense crucifix," but its signification, as well as his own implication in divine creativity:

> after we had formed
> then only the forms were formed
> and all the forms
> were formed after our forming . . . (73)

If we tried to "understand" these lines literally we would fail, and any attempt at explication as such were futile. Even Heywood, who dismisses Anozie's structuralist play as "worse than unhelpful" (Heywood 1984: 214), despairs of explication: "I shall not attempt an explanation. These quotations suffice to demonstrate . . . not only the building up of potency through repeated usage in powerful contexts of Okigbo's motifs, but also their multivocality" (214). I would myself rather appreciate the cumulative evocativeness of these concrete and immense images:

> like pentecostal orbs
> resplendent far distant
> in the intangible void
> an immense crucifix
> of phosphorescent mantles.... (CP: 73)

But I would also point out that the "immense crucifix" refers to the successful outcome of the poet's second test, which interpretive exercise implicated the poet in that creative act with the divine; the immense crucifix also anticipates the immense burden of the poet/prophet, as well as his impending sacrifice.

This apprehension of his destiny accounts for the sober and somber mood of "Distances V," which begins dramatically with the statement of anguish and burden:

Sweat over hoof in ascending gestures
each step is the step of the mule in the abyss — (74)

The mule is the burdened beast whose labors are hardly appreciated. On account of its hairy skin it is not generally recognized that it also sweats, very much like the long-suffering ram which, even before the flashing sword, emits only a muted shriek, a silent prayer. So too is the poet/elect's destiny. His trajectory so far has been as tedious as the slow, painful steps "of the mule in the abyss," and after having endured "the archway the oval the panel oblong" he arrives at the "sanctuary" which is located at "the earth's molten bowel." Only someone who cannot apprehend what happens in that place from which volcanoes erupt can read this poem without shuddering at the poet's plight. Even the music that is invoked is "woven into funerary rose," "the water in the tunnel its effervescent laughter" (74). Most ominously important of all, and suggestive of the cosmic impossibility of the question "How does one say No in thunder?," the first stanza of "Distances V" ends with a terrible hyperbole:

the question in the inkwell the answer on the monocle
the unanswerable question in the tabernacle's silence.... (74)

So, even the tabernacle (/oracle), usually a most dependable source of answers to the poet/prophet, is *silent*. This silence rapidly spreads and envelopes time itself, enveloping also humanity, and transforming that sign and expression of human affection and bonding, the kiss, into a vampiric act which only leaves a "scar," and is associated with "two swords."

The apparent excitement of "Distances VI" is, therefore, appropriate, for the weary acolyte, in this "season" whose atmosphere is suggestive of mating, to respond with hope at the invitation of the goddess:

Come into my cavern,
Shake the mildew from your hair;
Let your ear listen:
My mouth calls from a cavern.... (75)

But it is important to note that the invitation is "into my cavern;" and that the admonition, "Lo, it is the same blood that flows," which follows, while it may, indeed, suggest consanguinity, does not fail to reverberate with vampiric implications, for we are yet to recover from the blood-chilling experience of watching the macabre performance of "Death herself / the chief celebrant" only four sections (or four pages) back. Moreover, the whole atmosphere in the cavern is redolent with the smell of death, violence, blood, fear, predation:

Shadows distances labyrinths violences,
Skeletal oblong
of my sentient being, I receive you
in my perforated
mouth of a stranger: empty of meaning
stones without juice—
the goat knows its fodder,
the leopards on its trail—
For it is the same blood
through the same orifices,
the same branches
trembling intertwined,
and the same faces
in the interspaces.
And it is the same breath, liquid, without acolyte,
like the invisible mushroom on stone surfaces. (75)

Thus even when the "consummation" is achieved, there is nothing "orgasmic" (Anozie 1972: 151) or ecstatic about it. Instead, the mood of gloom and disappointment, accentuated by the concatenation of images that build up to onanism and anticlimax, prevails in: "this chaste instant of delineated anguish," "unquenchable, yellow," "darkening homeward," "cry of wolf above crumbling houses," "bares the entrails," "feverish, solitary shores," "variegated teeth," and "putrescent laughter." The result is that the "climactic" homecoming—"darkening homeward"—becomes a solitary affair, unaccompanied by buntings and festive reception:

I am the sole witness to my homecoming. (CP: 76)

The consummation, indeed, has taken place—"I have entered your bridal/chamber" (76)—and with it came the final illumination. But it is the anguished realization that all the poet had dreamt, wished for, and sung, has come to naught; that all he foresaw, agonized over, and warned against is coming inexorably to pass, as only "the glimpse of a dream [now] lies smouldering in a cave,/together with the mortally wounded birds" (79). The poet's disappointment is almost cosmic, and he who in his optimism had earlier prayed Mother Earth to "bind me fast" (89) and rejoiced that "our dividing airs are gathered home" (89) now laments the insistence "of our dissonant airs" and "our crumbling towers" (99) and prays rather:

O mother mother Earth, unbind me; let this be
my last testament; let this be
The ram's hidden wish to the sword the sword's
secret prayer to the scabbard— . . .
Earth, unbind me; let me be the prodigal; let this be
the ram's ultimate prayer to the tether.... (99)

The poet bade sad farewell to the dream, to the people, to the world:

And the horn may now paw the air howling goodbye
So let the horn paw the air howling goodbye.... (98)

In his departure was contained the crumbling and dissipation of the dream; in the prophecy of his own exit was contained the sad prophecy, not only of the impossibility of attaining the dream/goal of Nigerian unity and nationhood, but also of the doomed cycle of repetition, whereby, the leaders of that country, having learnt nothing from history, would not only return to the condition *status quo ante bellum*, but would set in motion once again the very forces—the dance above the carrion, the dance of fireflies—which drove the country to the impasse in the first place, and which will ensure the continuation of the cycle of repetition and of doom.

Thus, as Okigbo foretold:

An old star departs, leaves us here on the shore
Gazing heavenward for a new star approaching;
The new star appears, foreshadows its going
Before a going and coming that goes on for ever.... (CP: 99)

Nigeria did not heed the warning of its most articulate and bold poet-prophet in 1966 and is still paying dearly for that heedless obduracy. Between 1970 and 1996 it has repeated multiply all the stupidities of the past, with the result that the country is still ruled by a strange but, at this time, dangerously armed "Celaeno and her harpy crew / Laden with night and their belly's excrement" (63), and there is no sign to indicate that the sad prophecy of tragic repetition, writ large on the pages of Okigbo's poetry, will be heeded now. Consequently, the dance of death continues.

BIBLIOGRAPHY

Achebe, Chinua. "African Literature as Restoration of Celebration."
　　New African (March 1990): 40-43.
———. *Christmas in Biafra & Other Poems.* New York: Doubleday,
　　1973.
———. *Hopes and Impediments: Selected Essays.* New York:
　　Doubleday, 1989.
———. *A Man of the People.* New York: Doubleday, 1966.
———. *Morning Yet On Creation Day.* London: Heinemann, 1975.
———. *Things Fall Apart.* London: Heinemann, (1958) 1986.
———. *The Trouble With Nigeria.* London: Heinemann, 1983.
——— & Dubem Okafor, eds. *Don't Let Him Die: An Anthology of
　　Memorial Poems for Christopher Okigbo 1932-1967.*
　　Enugu: Fourth Dimension Publishers, 1978.
Acholonu, Catherine. "From Rhetoric to Occultism: The Word as
　　Music in Okigbo's *Labyrinths.*" *African Literature Today
　　(ALT)* 17 (1991): 131-40.
———. "*Ogbanje*: A Motif and a Theme in the Poetry of Christopher
　　Okigbo." *ALT* 16 (1988): 103-111.
———. "Who Was Christopher Okigbo: Interview with Mr. Bob
　　Njemanze." *OKIKE* 29 (Feb. 1989): 92-102.
Acholonu, Rose C. "The Nigerian Novelist: A Victim of Identity
　　Crisis?" In Emenyonu, ed. (1986): 259-74.
Adams, J.R.R. *The Printed Word and the Common Man: Popular
　　Culture in Ulster 1700-1900.* Belfast: Queens University of
　　Belfast, 1987.
Adedeji, J.A. "A Dramatic Approach to Okigbo's *Limits.*" *Conch* 3, 1
　　(1971): 45-59; also in Nwoga, ed., (1984): 48-54.
Adisa, F.O. "The Civil War, The Economy and Nigerian Foreign
　　Policy." *ODU* 25 (Jan. 1984): 93-104.

Afigbo, A.E., E.A. Ayandele, R.J. Gavin & J.D. Omer-Cooper, eds. *The Making of Modern Africa: The Nineteenth Century.* London: Longman, (1971) 1986.

Ahmad, Aijaz. *In Theory: Classes, Nations, Literatures.* London & New York: Verso, 1992.

Ainabe, Roland, "The Futility of Forced Unity." *National Concord.* (Lagos, Nigeria, Dec. 29, 1993) 7.

Aizenberg, Edna, ed. *Borges and His Successors: The Borgesian Impact on Literature and the Arts.* Columbia: University of Missouri Press, 1990.

Ajulo, E.B. "English Language and Human Resource Development in Multilingual and Multicultural Countries: The Example of Multilingual and Multicultural Nigeria." *ODU* 35 (Jan. 1989): 53-78.

Allen, Christopher, & R.W. Johnson, eds. *African Perspectives: Papers in the History, Politics and African Literatures, 1986.* Washington, D.C.: Three Continents & African Literature Association, 1991.

Althusser, Louis. *Lenin and Philosophy and Other Essays.* Trans., Ben Brewster. New York: Monthly Press, 1971.

Amadi, Elechi. *Ethics in Nigerian Culture.* Ibadan, Nigeria: Heinemann Books (Nig.) Ltd., 1982.

———. *Sunset in Biafra.* London: Heinemann, 1973.

Amanuddin, Syed. *Creativity and Reception: Toward a Theory of Third World Criticism.* New York: Peter Lang, 1988.

Amin, Samir. *Eurocentrism.* Trans., Russell Moore. New York: Monthly Review Press, 1989.

Amoda, Moyibi. "Background to the Conflict: A Summary of Nigeria's Political History from 1914 to 1964." In Joseph Okpaku, ed. (1972): 14-75.

Amucheazi. E. "Pressure Group Politics and Public Interest in the Nigerian Political System." *ODU* 25 (Jan. 1984): 20-38.

Amuta, Chidi. *The Theory of African Literature: Implications for Practical Criticism.* London: Zed Books, 1989.

Anderson, Benedict. *Imagined Communities: Reflections on the Origins and Spread of Nationalism.* London: Verso, 1983.

Anderson, Perry. *Considerations on Western Marxism.* London: Verso, 1979.

Andrai, Charles F. *Political Change in the Third World.* Boston: Unwin Hyman, 1988.

Andreski, Stanislav. *The African Predicament: A Study in the Pathology of Modernisation*. London: Michael Joseph, 1968.

Andrzejewski, B.W., S. Pilaszwicz, & W. Tyloch, eds. *Literatures in African Languages: Theoretical Issues and Sample Surveys*. Warsaw: Wiedza P Powszechna, 1985.

Anene, Joseph C., & Godfrey N. Brown. *Africa in the Nineteenth and Twentieth Centuries*. New York: Humanities Press, (1966) 1972.

Anozie, Sunday O. *Christopher Okigbo: Creative Rhetoric*. New York: Africana Publishing Corp., 1972.

————. "Okigbo's *Heavensgate*: A Study of Art as Ritual." *Ibadan* 15 (1963): 11-13; also in Nwoga, ed. (1984): 47-54.

Anyidoho, Kofi. "Language and Development Strategy in Pan-African Literary Experience." *RAL* 23:1 (Spring 1992): 45-63.

————. "Literature and African Identity: The Example of Ayi Kwei Armah." In Breitinger & Sander, eds. (1986): 23-42.

————. Abioseh M. Porter, Daniel Racine, & Janice Spleth, eds. *Interdisciplinary Dimensions of African Literature*. Washington, D.C.: Three Continents & African Literature Association, 1985.

Appadurai, Arjun, ed. *The Social Life of Things*. Cambridge: Cambridge University Press, 1986.

Appiah, Anthony Kwame. *In My Father's House: Africa in the Philosophy of Culture*. New York: Oxford University Press, 1992.

————. "Is the Post- in Postmodernism the Post- in Postcolonial?" *Critical Inquiry* XVII (Winter 1991):336-57.

————. "Out of Africa: Topologies of Nativism." In LaCapra, ed. (1991):134-63.

————. "Racisms." In Goldberg, ed., (1990):3-17.

————. "Soyinka's Myth of an African World." In Harrow, Kenneth, et al., eds. (1991):11-24.

Armah, Ayi Kwei. *Two Thousand Seasons*. London: Heinemann, 1973.

Arnold, Stephen, ed. *African Literature Studies: The Present State*. Washington, D.C.: Three Continents & African Literature Association, 1985.

Ashcroft, Bill "Intersecting Marginalities: Postcolonialism and Feminism." *Kunapipi* VI:2 (1989): 23-35.

————, Gareth Griffiths, & Helen Tiffin. *The Empire Writes Back:*

Theory and Practice in Post-Colonial Literature. London &
New York: Routledge, 1989.

Attridge, Derek, Geoff Bennington, & Robert Young, eds. *Post-structuralism and the Question of History.* Cambridge: Cambridge
University Press, (1987) 1989.

Austin, Dennis. *Africa Repartitioned?* London: Centre for Security
and Conflict Studies, 1986.

Avineri, Shlomo, ed. *Karl Marx on Colonialism and Modernization.*
Garden City, NY: Doubleday, 1968.

Awolowo, Obafemi. *Paths to Nigerian Freedom.* London: Faber,
1947.

Awoonor, Kofi. *The Breast of the Earth: A Survey of the History,
Culture and Literature of Africa South of the Sahara.* New
York: Anchor Press / Doubleday, 1974 / 75.

———. *This Earth, My Brother.* London: Heinemann, 1972.

Azuonye, Chukwuma. "Christopher Okigbo and the Psychological
Theories of Carl Gustav Jung." *Journal of African &
Comparative Literature* I:1 (March 1981): 30-51.

Azvedo, Warren, ed. *The Traditional Artist in African Societies.*
Bloomington & Indianapolis: Indiana University Press, 1989.

Baker, Houston A., Jr. "Caliban's Triple Play," In Gates, Jr., ed.
(1986): 381-95.

———, ed. *Reading Black: Essays in the Criticism of African,
Caribbean, and Black American Literature.* Ithaca, NY:
Cornell University African Studies & Research Center, 1976.

———. *The Journey Back: Issues in Black Literature and Criticism.*
Chicago & London: The University of Chicago Press, (1980)
1983.

———. *Blues, Ideology, and Afro-American Literature: A
Vernacular Theory.* Chicago & London: the University of
Chicago Press, (1984) 1987.

Balakian, Anna. *The Symbolist Movement: A Critical Appraisal.*
New York: NYU Press, 1977.

Balibar, Etienne. "Paradoxes of Universality." In Goldberg, ed. (1990):
283-94.

——- & Immanuel Wallerstein. *Race, Nation, Class: Ambiguous
Identities.* London & New York: Verso, 1991.

Bamgbose, Ayo. *Language and the Nation: The Language Question
in Sub-Saharan Africa.* Edinburgh: Edinburgh University Press,
1991.

Bamikunle, Aderemi. "Problems of Language in Understanding Soyinka's *A Shuttle in the Crypt.*" *ALT* 16 (1988): 77-90.

Barbag-Stoll, Ann. *Social and Linguistic History of Nigerian Pidgin English.* Tubingen: Staffenberg-Verlag, 1983.

Barkan, Sandra, with Dennis Brutus, Hans Panofsky, & Angelita Reyes, eds. *African Literatures: Retrospectives and Perspectives.* Washington, D.C.: Three Continents & African Literature Association, 1990.

Barker, Francis, et al., eds. *Literature, Politics and Theory: Papers From the Essex Conference, 1976-84.* London: Metheun, 1986.

Baugh, Edward. "Yes, But ... Some Issues Concerning the Study of New Literatures in English."In Riemenschneider, ed. (1989):52-61.

Baumgarten, Murray. "The Mind Is a Muscle: Carlyle, Literary Revolution and Linguistic Nationalism." In Drescher & Volkel, eds. (1989):43-105.

Becker, John E. "The Law, the Prophets, and Wisdom: On the Functions of Literature." *College English* 37 (1975):254-64.

Beier, Ulli, ed. *Introduction to African Literature.* Evanston: Northwestern University, 1970.

———, ed. *Introduction to African Literature: An Anthology of Critical Writing from "Black Orpheus."* London: Longman, 1967.

———. "Three Mbari Poets." *Black Orpheus* 12 (1962): 46-50.

Benjamin, Walter. *Illuminations.* Hannah Arendt, ed. Trans., Harry Zohn. New York: Schocken Books, 1969.

Bennett, Tony. *Formalism and Marxism.* London & New York: Methuen, 1979.

———. *Outside Literature.* London & New York: Routledge, 1990.

———. *Popular Fiction: Technology, Ideology, Production, Reading.* London: Routledge, 1990.

———. "Texts, Readers, Reading Formations." *Bulletin of the Midwest MLA*, XVI (1983): 3-17.

———, et al., eds. *Culture, Ideology and Social Process: A Reader.* London: Open University, 1981.

Berger, Peter & Thomas Luckmann. *The Social Construction of Reality.* New York: Doubleday, 1966.

Berlant, Lauren. "National Brands/National Body: Imitations of Life." In Spillers, ed. (1991):110-40.

Bhabha, Homi K. "Articulating the Archaic: Notes on Colonial Nonsense." In Peter Collier & Helga Ryan, eds. (1990): 203-18.

———. "Interrogating Identity: The Postcolonial Prerogative." In Goldberg, ed. (1990):183-209.

———, ed. Nation and Narration. London & New York: Routledge, 1990.

———. "Of Mimicry and Man: The Ambivalence of Colonial Discourse." October XXVIII (Spring 1984): 125-33.

———. "The Other Question: Difference, Discrimination and the Discourse of Colonialism." In Francis Barker, et al., eds.(1986):148-72.

———. "'Race,' Time and the Revision of Modernity." Oxford Literary Review XIII:1-2 (1991): 193-219.

———. "Signs Taken for Wonders: Questions of Ambivalence and Authority Under a Tree Outside Delhi, May 1817." Critical Inquiry XII (Fall 1985): 144-65.

Bishop, Rand. African Literature, African Critics: The Formation of Critical Standards, 1947-1966. New York / Westport, CT: Greenwood Press, 1988.

Blake, William. Complete Writings. G. Keynes, ed. London: Oxford University Press, 1974.

Bloom, Harold. The Visionary Company: A Reading of English Romantic Poetry. New York: Anchor Books, 1963.

Bodunle, Charles A. "Oral Traditions and Modern Poetry: Okot p'Bitek's Song of Lawino and Okigbo's Labyrinths." ALT 18 (1992): 24-34.

Booth, James. Writers and Politics in Nigeria. London: Hodder & Stoughton, 1981.

Bouyssou, Roland. "Labyrinths, or the Initiation Quest of Christopher Okigbo." In Nwoga, ed. (1984): 226-34.

Bown, Lalage J. Two Centuries of African English: A Survey and Anthology of Non-Fictional English Prose by African Writers since 1769. London: Heinemann, 1973.

Boyce-Davies, Carole. "Private Selves and Public Spaces: Autobiography and the African Woman Writer." In Harrow, Kenneth, et al., eds. (1991):109-27.

Bradbury, Malcolm. The Social Context of Modern English Literature. Oxford: Basil Blackwell, 1972.

Brantlinger, Patrick. "Victorians and Africans: The Genealogy of the

Myth of the Dark Continent." In Gates, Jr., ed. (1986): 185-222.

Breitinger, Eckhard & Reinhard Sander, eds. *Literature and African Identity*. Bayreuth: German Research Council & University of Bayreuth, 1986.

Brenkman, John. *Culture and Domination*. Ithaca, NY: Cornell University Press, 1987.

Bromley, Roger. *Lost Narratives: Popular Fictions, Politics, and Recent History*. London & New York: Routledge, 1988.

Burger, Peter. *Theory of the Avant-Garde*. Trans., Michael Shaw. Minneapolis: University of Minnesota Press, 1984.

——— & Christa Burger. *The Institutions of Art*. Trans. Loren Kruger. Lincoln, NE: University of Nebraska Press, 1992.

Busia, Abena P.A. "But Caliban and Ariel Are Still Both Male: On African Colonial Discourse and the Unvoiced Female." In Harrow, Kenneth, et al., eds. (1991):129-40.

———. "Imagined Communities and Fixed Boundaries." *ALA Bulletin* XIX:3 (Summer 1993):7-13.

Cartey, Wilfred. *Whispers from a Continent: The Literature of Contemporary Black Africa*. New York: Random House, 1970.

Cartey, Wilfred & Martin Kilson, eds. *The African Reader: Colonial Africa*. New York: Random House, 1970.

——— & Martin Kilson, eds. *The African Reader: Independent Africa*. New York: Random House, 1970.

Certeau, Michel de. *Heterologies: Discourse on the Other*. Trans., Brian Massumi. Minneapolis: University of Minnesota Press, 1986.

———. *The Practice of Everyday Life*. Trans., Steven Rendall. Berkeley: University of California, 1984.

———. *The Writing of History*. Trans., Tom Conley. New York: Columbia University Press, 1988.

Cervenka, Zdenek. *The Nigerian War 1967-1970: History of the War, Selected Bibliography and Documents*. Frankfurt: Bernard & Verlag, 1971.

Chatterjee, Partha. *The Nation and Its Fragments: Studies in Colonial and Post-Colonial Histories*. Calcutta, India: Centre for Studies in Social Sciences, 1992.

———. *Nationalist Thought and the Colonial World: A Derivative Discourse*. London: Zed Books, 1986.

Chinweizu, & Onwuchekwa Jemie. "African Literary Criticism Today."
    OKIKE 9 (1975): 9-105.
—— & ——. *Decolonizing the African Mind*. Lagos: Pero Press,
    1987.
—— & ——. "Prodigals Come Home." In Nwoga, ed. (1984):
    177-83.
—— & ——. *The West and the Rest of Us*. New York: Random
    House, 1975.
——, ——, & Ihechukwu Madubuike. *Toward the Decolonization of
    African Literature*. Enugu, Nigeria: Fourth Dimension
    Publishers, 1980.
——, ——, *et al.* "Towards the Decolonization of African
    Literature—I." *Transition* 48 (1975): 11-27.
——, ——, *et al.* "Towards the Decolonization of African
    Literature—II: The Critics." *OKIKE* 7 (1975): 65-81.
Christopher, A.J. *Colonial Africa*. London & NH: Croon Helm and
    Barnes & Nobel, 1984.
Chukwukere, B.I. "The Problem of Language in African Creative
    Writing." *ALT* 3 (1969): 15-26.
Clark, John Pepper (Bekederemu). *The Example of Shakespeare*.
    London: Longman, 1970.
——. "Poetry in Africa Today." *Transition* 18 (1965): 20-26.
——. *Casualties*. London: Longman, 1971.
Clarke, John D. *Yakubu Gowon: Faith in a United Nigeria*. London:
    Frank Cass, 1987.
Cole, Herbert M. *Mbari: Art and Life Among the Owerri Igbo*.
    Bloomington: Indiana University Press, 1982.
Coleman, James S. *Nigeria: Background to Nationalism*. Berkeley &
    Los Angeles: University of California Press, 1958.
Collier, Gordon, ed. *Us / Them: Translation, Transcription and
    Identity in Post-colonial Literary Cultures*. Amsterdam /
    Atlanta, GA: Rodopi, 1992.
Collier, Peter & Helga Geyer-Ryan, eds. *Literary Theory Today*.
    Ithaca, NY: Cornell University Press, 1990.
Collins, Robert O., ed. *Problems in the History of Colonial Africa:
    1860-1960*. New Jersey: Prentice-Hall, 1970.
Collis, Robert. *Nigeria in Conflict*. London: Secker & Warburg,
    1970.
Cooke, Michael G. "Christopher Okigbo and Robert Hayden: From
    Mould to Stars." *World Literatures Written in English* 30:2

(1990): 131-44.

Craige, Betty Jean, ed. *Literature, Language, and Politics*. Athens & London: The University of Georgia Press, 1988.

Crowder, Michael. *The Story of Nigeria*. London: Faber & Faber, 1962.

Culler, Jonathan. "Political Criticism." In David Wood, ed. (1990):192-204.

Daiches, David. *Critical Approaches to Literature*. London: Longman, (1956) 1971.

Dathorne, O.R. "African Literature IV: Ritual and Ceremony in Okigbo's Poetry." *Journal of Commonwealth Literature* 5 (1968): 79-91; also in Nwoga, ed. (1984): 261-73.

———. *African Literature in the Twentieth Century*. Minneapolis: University of Minnesota, (1974) 1975.

———. *The Black Mind: A History of African Literature*. Minneapolis: University of Minnesota, 1974.

———. "Okigbo Understood: A Study of Two Poems." *ALT* 1 (1968): 19-23.

———. "Tradition and the African Poet." *Presence Africaine* 63 (1967): 202-06.

Davidson, Basil. *Africa in History: Themes and Outlines*. New York: Collier Books, 1974.

———. *The African Past: Chronicles from Antiquity to Modern Times*. Boston: Atlantic Monthly Press, 1964.

———. *The Black Man's Burden: Africa and the Curse of the Nation-State*. New York: Times Books (Random House), 1992.

Davies, Carol Boyce & Anne Adams Graves, eds. *Ngambika: Studies of Women in African Literature*. Trenton, NJ: Africa World Press, 1986.

Davis, Geoffrey & Hena Maes-Jelinek, eds. *Crisis and Creativity in the New Literatures in English*. Amsterdam / Atlanta, GA: Rodopi, 1990.

Deleuze, Gilles & Felix Guattari. *A Thousand Plateaus: Capitalism and Schizophrenia*. Minneapolis & London: University of Minnesota Press, 1987.

—— & ———. "What Is a Minor Literature?" In Richter, ed. (1994):166-72.

Derrida, Jacques. *The Other Heading: Reflections on Today's Europe*. Trans., Pascale-Anne Brault & Michael B. Naas.

Bloomington: Indiana University Press, 1992.
———. *Writing and Difference*. Trans., Alan Bass. Chicago: Chicago University Press, 1978.

Diawara, Manthia. "Reading Africa Through Foucault: V.Y. Mudimbe's Reaffirmation of the Subject." *October* 55 (Winter 1990): 79-92.

Dieke, Ikenna. *The Primordial Image: African, Afro-American and Caribbean Mythopoetic Text*. New York: Peter Lang, 1993.

Dike, Kenneth O. *Trade and Politics in the Niger Delta*. London: Oxford University Press, 1962.
———. *A Hundred Years of British Rule in Nigeria, 1857–1957*. Lagos: Federal Ministry of Information, 1957.

Divine, Donna Robinson. "The Dialectics of Palestinian Politics." In Migdal, ed. 211-29.

Dorsey, David. "Critical Perception of African Poetry." *ALT* 16 (1988): 26-38.

Dorsey, David F., Phanuel Egejuru, & Stephen H. Arnolds, eds. *Design and Intent in African Literature*. Washington, D.C.: Three Continents & African Literature Association, 1982.

Douglas, Mary. *Purity and Danger*. New York: Frederick A. Praeger, 1966.

Drescher, Horst W. & Herman Volkel, eds. *Nationalism in Literature: Literature, Language and National Identity*. Frankfurt: Peter Lang, 1989.

Duerden, Dennis. *The Invisible Present: African Art and Literature*. New York: Harper & Row, 1975.
——— & Cosmo Pieterse, eds. *African Writers Talking: A Collection of Interviews*. London: Heinemann, 1972.

Dunne, Tom. "Fiction as 'the best history of nations': Lady Morgan's Irish Novels." In Dunne, ed. (1987):133-59.

Dunne, Tom, ed. *The Writer as Witness: Literature as Historical Evidence*. Cork, Ireland:Cork University Press, 1987.

Durix, Jean-Pierre. *The Writer Written: The Artist and Creation in the New Literatures in English*. Westport, Conn: Greenwood Press, 1987.

Eagleton, Terry. *Criticism and Ideology: A Study in Marxist Literary Theory*. London & New York: Verso, 1978.
———. *Literary Theory: An Introduction*. Minneapolis: University of Minnesota Press, 1983.
———. *Marxism and Literary Criticism*. Berkeley & Los Angeles:

University of California Press, 1976.

———. "The Rise of English." In Richter, ed. (1994):44-54.

———. *The Significance of Theory.* Oxford, UK / Cambridge, MA: Blackwell, 1990.

———, Frederic Jameson & Edward Said. *Nationalism, Colonialism, and Literature.* Minneapolis: University of Minnesota Press, 1990.

Ebong, Inih Akpan. "Towards the Revolutionary Consciousness: The Writer in Contemporary Africa." In Emenyonu, ed. (1986):71-83.

Echeruo, M.J.C. *A Matter of Identity: "Afamefula."* 1979 Ahiajoku Lecture. Owerri, Nigeria: Imo Newspapers Ltd., 1979.

———. "Traditional and Borrowed Elements in Nigerian Poetry." *Nigerian Magazine* 89 (June 1966): 141-55.

———. *Victorian Lagos: Aspects of Nineteenth Century Lagos Life.* New York: Holmes & Meier, 1977.

Egejuru, Phanuel A. *Towards African Literary Independence: A Dialogue with Contemporary African Writers.* Westport, CT: Greenwood Press, 1980.

Egudu, Romanus N. "African Literature and Social Problems." *Canadian Journal of African Studies* 9:3 (1975): 421-27.

———. "African Poetry and the Paradox of African Independence." *BA SHIRU* VI:1 (1974): 25-53.

———. "Anglophone African Poetry and Vernacular Rhetoric: The Example of Okigbo." *Lagos Review of English Studies* I:1 (1979): 104-13.

———. "Defence of Culture in the Poetry of Christopher Okigbo." *ALT* 6 (1973): 14-25.

———. "Ezra Pound in African Poetry: Christopher Okigbo." *Comparative Literature Studies* 8:2 (1971): 143-54; also in Nwoga, ed. (1984): 337-48.

———. *Four Modern West African Poets.* New York: Nok Publishers International Ltd., 1977.

———. *Modern African Poetry and the African Predicament.* New York: Barnes & Nobel, 1978.

———. "Modern African Poetry and Post-Colonial Politics." *BA SHIRU* V:2 (1974): 45-53.

———. "Nigerian Poets and Nigerian Traditional Religion." *West African Religion* 16:1 (1975): 1-7.

———. "Okigbo Misrepresented: Edwin Thumbo On 'Love Apart'."

Presence Africaine 76 (1970): 187-93.

———. "Okigbo's 'Distances': A Retreat from Christ to Idoto." *Conch* 5:1&2 (1973): 29-42; also in Nwoga, ed., 1984: 153-66.

——— & Donatus Nwoga, Comp. & Trans. *Poetic Heritage: Igbo Traditional Verse.* Enugu, Nigeria: Nwankwo-Ifejika & Co., 1971.

———. "The Nigerian Literary Artist and His Society." Unpublished Lecture Delivered at the University of Nigeria, Nsukka, Nigeria, December 15, 1972.

Ekeh, Peter P. "Citizenship and Political Conflict: A Sociological Interpretation of the Nigerian Crisis." In Okpaku, ed., 76-117.

Ekwe-Ekwe, Herbert. *The Biafran War: Nigeria and the Aftermath.* Lewiston, NY: The Edwin Mellen Press, 1990.

Ekwe-Ekwe, Herbert. *Conflict and Intervention in Africa: Nigeria, Angola, Zaire.* New York: St. Martin's Press, 1990.

Eliade, Mircea. *The Sacred and the Profane.* New York: Harcourt, Brace & World, Inc., 1959.

Elimimian, Isaac. "Poetry as a Vehicle for Promoting National Consciousness and Development: The Example of Four Nigerian Poets." *ALT* 16 (1988): 112-23.

———. *Theme and Style in African Poetry.* Lewiston, NY: The Edwin Mellen Press, 1991.

Emenyonu, Ernest, ed. *Ekwensi, Okara, Amadi and Anyidoho.* Enugu, Nigeria: New Generation Books, 1992.

———., ed. *Literature and Society: Selected Essays on African Literature.* Oguta, Nigeria: Zim Pan African Publishers, 1986.

———. *The Rise of the Igbo Novel.* Ibadan: Oxford University Press, 1978.

Eriksen, Thomas Hylland. *Us and Them in Modern Societies: Ethnicity and Nationalism in Mauritius, Trinidad, and Beyond.* Oslo, Norway: Scandinavian University Press, 1992.

Etherton, N.J. "Christopher Okigbo and African Tradition: A Reply to Professor Ali Mazrui." *Zuka* 2 (1968): 48-52.

Even-Zohar, Itamar. "Polysystem Theory." *Poetics Today* I (1979): 287-310.

Eysteinsson, Astradur. *The Concept of Modernism.* Ithaca & London: Cornell University Press, 1990.

Ezenwa-Ohaeto. "Dimensions of Language in New Nigerian Poetry." *ALT* 17 (1991): 155-64.

Fabian, Johannes. *Language and Colonial Power: The*

Appropriation of Swahili in the Former Belgian Congo
1880-1938. Berkeley: University of California Press, 1986.
————. *Time and the Other: How Anthropology Makes Its Object.*
New York: Columbia University Press, 1983.
Falola, Toyin & Julius Ihonvbere. *The Rise and Fall of Nigeria's*
Second Republic, 1979-84. London: Zed Books, 1985.
Fanon, Frantz. *Black Skin, White Masks.* Trans., Charles Lam
Markmann. New York: Grove Press, [1967] 1982.
————. *A Dying Colonialism.* Trans., Haakon Chevalier. New York:
Grove Weidenfeld, 1965.
————. "The Fact of Blackness." In Goldberg, ed. [1990]: 108-26.
————. *Toward the African Revolution: Political Essays.* Trans.,
Haakon Chevalier. New York: Grove Press, [1969] 1988.
————. *The Wretched of the Earth.* Trans., Constance Farrington.
London: Macgibbon & Mckee, 1963.
Featherstone, Mike, ed. *Global Culture: Nationalism, Globalization*
and Modernity. London: Sage Publications, 1990.
Fido, Elaine Savory. "Okigbo's *Labyrinths* and the Context of Igbo
Attitudes to the Female Principle." In Davies & Graves, eds.
(1986): 223-39.
Finnegan, Ruth. *Literacy and Orality: Studies in the Technology of*
Communication. Oxford: Basil Blackwell, 1988.
————. *Oral Literature in Africa.* Oxford: Oxford University Press,
1970.
First, Ruth. *The Barrel of a Gun.* London: Penguin, 1970.
Fiske, John. *Reading the Popular.* Boston: Unwin Hyman, 1989.
————. *Understanding Popular Culture.* Boston: Unwin Hyman,
1989.
Flint, John E. *Sir George Goldie and the Making of Nigeria.*
London: Oxford University Press, 1960.
Fraser, Robert. *West African Poetry: A Critical History.* Cambridge:
Cambridge University Press, 1986.
Frow, John. *Marxism and Literary History.* Oxford: Basil Blackwell,
1986.
Gaitet, Pascale. *Political Stylistics: Popular Language as Literary*
Artifact. New York: Routledge, 1992.
Gakwandi, Shatto Arthur. *The Novel and Contemporary Experience*
in Africa. London: Heinemann, 1977.
Gates Jr., Henry Louis, ed. *Black Literature and Literary Theory.*
New York & London: Methuen, 1984.

————. *Figures in Black: Words, Signs, and the Racial Self.* New York: Oxford University Press, 1987.

————. "Literature, Theory and Commitment: I." In Harrow, Kenneth, et al., eds. (1991):59-64.

————, ed. *"Race," Writing, and Difference.* Chicago & London: University of Chicago Press, (1985) 1986.

————. *The Signifying Monkey: A Theory of African-American Literary Criticism.* New York: Oxford University Press, 1988.

————. *Loose Canons: Notes on the Culture Wars.* New York & Oxford: Oxford University Press, 1992.

Geary, William Nevill M. *Nigeria Under British Rule.* London: Methuen, 1927.

Geertz, Clifford. "The Integrative Revolution: Primordial Sentiments and Civil Politics in the New States." In ed. *Old Societies and New States: The Quest for Modernity in Asia and Africa.* New York: Free Press of Glencoe, 1963. 105-57.

Gerard, Albert S. *African Language Literatures.* Washington, D.C.: Three Continents Press, 1981.

————. *African Language Literatures: An Introduction to the Literary History of Sub-Saharan Africa.* Washington, D.C.: Three Continents Press, 1981.

————. *Contexts of African Literature.* Amsterdam / Atlanta, GA: Editions Rodopi, 1990.

————., ed. *European-Language Writing in Sub-Saharan Africa,* 2 vols. Budapest: Academia Kiado, 1986.

————. "Historiography of Black Africa: A Personal Testimony." *ALA Bulletin* XIX:3 (Summer 1993): 24-32.

————. "Literary Tradition and Literary Change in Black Africa."*Journal of Commonwealth Literature* XXIX:1 (1984): 44-51.

————. "Literature, Language, Nation and Commonwealth." In Davis & Maes-Jelinek, eds. (1990): 93-102.

Gibbs, James, ed. *A Critical Perspective on Wole Soyinka.* London: Heinemann, 1980.

Giddens, Anthony. *The Consequences of Modernity.* Palo Alto, Calif.: Stanford University Press, 1990.

Giddings, Robert. *Literature and Imperialism.* New York: St. Martin's Press, 1991.

Gifford, Posser & Wm. Roger Louis, eds. *Decolonization and African Independence: The Transfers of Power, 1960-1980.* New

Haven: Yale University Press, 1988.

Gikandi, Simon. "Ngugi's Conversion: Writings and the Politics of Language." *RAL* 23:1 (Spring 1992): 130-44.

Ginzburg, Carlo. *The Cheese and the Worms*. Trans., John & Anne Tedeschi. New York: Penguin, 1982.

Goldberg, David Theo, ed. *Anatomy of Racism*. Minneapolis & Oxford: University of Minnesota Press, 1990.

Gomwalk, Philemon Victor. "The Stages of Style and Thematic Preoccupation in Okigbo's Poetry of *Labyrinths*." In Nwoga, ed., (1984): 201-006.

Goody, Jack. *The Domestication of the Savage Mind*. Cambridge & New York:Cambridge University Press, 1977.

————. *The Interfaces Between the Written and the Oral*. Cambridge & New York: Cambridge University Press, 1987.

Goonetilleke, D.C.R.A. "Sri Lanka's 'Ethnic' Conflict in Its Literature in English." In Davis & Maes-Jelinek, eds. (1990): 333-44.

Gorlach, Manfred. "The Sociolinguistics of English as a World Language." In Riemenschneider, ed., 116-30.

Gowda, H.H. Anniah, ed. *The Colonial and Neo-Colonial Encounters in Commonwealth Literature*. Mysore, India: University of Mysore, 1983.

Gramsci, Antonio. *Selections From Cultural Writings*. Forgacs, David & Geoffrey Nowell-Smith, eds. Trans., William Boelhower. Cambridge, Mass.: Harvard University Press, 1985.

Granqvist, Raoul, ed. *Canonization and Teaching of African Literatures*. Amsterdam / Atlanta, GA: Rodopi, 1990.

———— & John Stotesbury, Interviewers. *African Voices: Interviews with Thirteen African Writers*. Sydney, Australia: Dangoro Press, 1989.

Greenblatt, Stephen J. "Learning to Curse: Aspects of Linguistic Colonialism in the Sixteenth Century." In Fredi Chiapelli, ed. *First Images of America: The Impact of the New World on the Old*. Los Angeles: University of California Press, 1976.

————. "The Politics of Culture." In Richter, ed. (1994): 288-90.

Griaule, Marcel. *Conversations with Ogotemmeli: An Introduction to Dogon Religious Ideas*. London: Oxford University Press (for International African Institute), 1965.

Gudykunst, William B., ed. *Language and Ethnic Identity*. Clevedon, PA: Multilingual Matters, 1988.

Gugelberger, Georg M., ed. *Marxism and African Literature.*
Trenton, NJ: Africa World Press, 1985.

Gurr, Andrew & Pio Zirimu, eds. *Black Aesthetics: Papers from a
Colloquium Held at the University of Nairobi, June 1971.*
Nairobi: EALB, 1973.

Haarmann, Harold. *Language in Ethnicity: A View of Basic
Ecological Relations.* Berlin: Mouton de Gruyter, 1986.

Hammond, Nicholas. "Birago Diop: The 'Conteur' as Nation Builder."
In Ngara & Morrison, eds. (1989):104-12.

Harbeson, John W., ed. *The Military in African Politics.* New York:
Praeger, 1987.

———. & Ronald Rothchild, eds. *Africa in World Politics.* Boulder,
Colo.: Westview Press, 1991.

Hargreaves, John D. *Decolonization in Africa.* London: Longman,
1988.

———. *The End of Colonial Rule in Africa: Essays in
Contemporary History.* New York: Barnes & Nobel, 1979.

Harrow, Kenneth, Jonathan Ngathe & Clarisse Zimra, eds. *Crossing
Boundaries in African Literatures, 1986.* Washington, D.C.:
Three Continents & American Literature Association, 1991.

Hartog, Francois. *The Mirror of Herodotus; The Representation of
the Other in the Writing of History.* Trans. Janet Lloyd.
Berkeley & Los Angeles: University of California Press, 1988.

Harvey, Arnold D. *Literature Into History.* New York: St. Martin's
Press, 1988.

Heinemann, Margot & Willie Thompson, eds. *History and the
Imagination: Selected Writings of A.L. Morton.* London:
Lawrence & Wishart, 1990.

Heywood, Annemarie. "The Ritual and the Plot: The Critic and
Okigbo's *Labyrinths.*" In Nwoga, ed. (1984): 207-25.

Heywood, Christopher, ed. *Perspectives on African Literature.* New
York: Africana; London: Heinemann, 1971.

Hicks, D. Emily. *Border Writing: The Multidimensional Text.*
Minneapolis & Oxford: University of Minnesota Press, 1991.

Hitchcock, Peter. *Dialogics of the Oppressed.* Minneapolis &
London: University of Minnesota Press, 1993.

Hobsbawn, E.J. *Nations and Nationalism Since 1780.* Cambridge:
Cambridge University Press, 1990.

Hodgkin, Thomas. *Nationalism in Colonial Africa.* London:
Frederick Muller Ltd., 1956.

Hohendahl, Peter Uwe. *The Institution of Criticism.* Ithaca, NY: Cornell University Press, 1982.

————. *Building a National Literature: The Case of Germany 1830-1870.* Trans., Renate Baron Fransicono. Ithaca & London: Cornell University Press, 1989.

Hoskins, Halford Lancaster. *European Imperialism in Africa.* New York: Henry Holt & Co., 1930.

Igiehon, Noser. *To Build a Nigerian Nation.* Devon: Arthur Stockwell, 1975.

Ikiddeh, Ime. "Dathorne on Okigbo: A Comment." *ALT* 2 (1969): 55-56.

————. "Iron, Thunder and Elephants: A Study of Okigbo's *Path of Thunder.*" *New Horn* 1:2 (1974): 46-67; also in Nwoga, ed., 1984: 184-95.

————. "Literature and the Nigerian Civil War." *Presence Africaine* 98 (1960): 162-74.

Ikoku, S.G. *Nigeria's Fourth Coup D'etat: (Options for Modern Statehood).* Enugu, Nigeria: Fourth Dimension Publishers, 1985.

Irele, Abiola. *The African Experience in Literature and Ideology.* London & Ibadan: Heinemann, 1981.

————. "African Poetry of English Expression." *Presence Africaine* 57 (1966): 263-65.

Iser, Wolfgang, ed. *The Act of Reading: A Theory of Aesthetic Response.* Baltimore: Johns Hopkins University Press, 1978.

————. "The Reading Process: A Phenomenological Approach." In Jane P. Tompkins, ed. (1980):50-59.

Isichei, Elizabeth. *A History of Nigeria* (With a Contribution by Dr. Peter Uche Isichei). London: Longman, 1983.

Isola, Akinwumi. "The African Writer's Tongue." *RAL* 23:1 (Spring 1992): 17-26.

Iyasere, Solomon. "Oral Tradition in the Criticism of African Literature." *Journal of Modern African Studies* 13 (1975): 107-19.

Iyayi, Festus. *Heroes.* Essex, England: Longman, 1986.

Iyengar, K.R. Srinivasa. "Commonwealth Literature: National Identity." In ed. (1970): 44-67.

————, ed. *Two Cheers for the Commonwealth: Talks on Literature and Education.* New York: Asia Publishing House, 1970.

Izevbaye, Dan S. "From Reality to Dream: The Poetry of Christopher

Okigbo." In Nwoga, ed. (1984): 300-27.
———. "Okigbo's Portrait of the Artist as a Sunbird: A Reading of 'Heavensgate' (1962)." In Nwoga, ed., 1984: 65-77.
———. "Nigeria." In Bruce King, ed., 1974: 136-53.
———. "The Poetry of Christopher Okigbo." In Heywood, ed. 121-48.
———. "Politics in Nigerian Poetry." *Presence Africaine* 78 (1971): 143-67.
———. "The State of Criticism in African Literature." *ALT* 7:1 (1975): 1-19.
Jahn, Janheniz. *Muntu: African Culture and the Western World.* Trans. Marjorie Grene. New York: Grove Weidenfeld, 1990.
James, Adeola, ed. *In Their Own Voices: African Women Writers Talk.* London: James Currey/Portsmouth, NH: Heinemann, 1990.
James, I. "The Challenges of Readjustment in a Rapidly Changing Multi-Religious Society of Nigeria: Conflict or Compromise?" *ODU* 37 (Jan./July 1990): 180-91.
JanMohamed, Abdul R. "The Economy of Manichean Allegory: The Function of Racial Difference in Colonialist Literature." In Gates, Jr., ed. (1986): 78-106.
———. *Manichean Aesthetics: The Politics of Literature in Colonial Africa.* Amherst: The University of Massachusetts Press, 1983.
———. & David Lloyd, eds. *The Nature and Context of Minority Discourse.* New York & Oxford: Oxford University Press, 1990.
Johnson, Lemuel A. et al., eds. *Toward Defining the African Aesthetic.* Washington, D.C.: A.L.A./Three Continents Press, 1982.
Johnson, Paul. *The Birth of the Modern: World Society 1815-1830.* New York: HarperCollins, 1991.
Johnson, Richard, et al., eds. *Making Histories: Studies in History Writing and Politics.* Minneapolis: University of Minnesota Press, 1982.
Jones, Eldred D. "The Decolonization of African Literature." In Wastberg, ed. (1967): 71-78.
———. "Jungle Drums and Wailing Pianos: West African Fiction and Poetry in English." *African Forum* I:4 (1966): 93-106.
———, 'Nationalism and the Writer." In John Press, ed. (1965): 151-56.

————, ed. *Women in African Literature Today*. London & Trenton, New Jersey: James Currey & Africa World Press, 1987.

————, Eustace Palmer & Marjorie Jones, eds. *Oral and Written Poetry in African Literature Today #16*. London & Trenton, New Jersey: James Curry & Africa World Press, 1988.

Kaarsholm, Preben. "Culture, Democratisation and Nation Building in Scandinavia and Africa." In Ngara & Morrison, eds. (1989):140-49.

Kane, Paul. "Postcolonial / Postmodern: Australian Literature and Peter Carey." *WLT* 67:3 (1993): 519-22.

Kedourie, Elie, ed. *Nationalism in Asia and Africa*. New York: World Publishing, 1970.

Keller, Werner. *The Bible as History*. Trans., William Neil. New York: William Morrow & Co., (1956) 1981.

Khatibi, Abdelkebir. "Literary Nationalism and Internationalism." In Harrow, Kenneth, et al., eds. (1991): 3-10.

Kiiru, Muchugu. "The Colonial Impact." *Busara* 5:1 (1973): 56-60.

Killam G.D., ed. *African Writers on African Writing*. London: Heinemann; New York: Africana Publishing Corporation, 1973.

King, Bruce, ed. *Introduction to Nigerian Literature*. Lagos & London: University of Lagos / Evans Brothers Ltd., 1971.

————. "Is There a Nigerian Literature? In Breitinger & Sander, eds. 43-73.

————, ed. *Literatures of the World in English*. London & Boston: Routledge & Kegan Paul, 1974.

————. *The New English Literatures: Cultural Nationalism in a Changing World*. London: Macmillan, 1980.

———— & Kolawole Ogungbesan, eds. *A Celebration of Black and African Writing*. Zaria, Nigeria: Ahmadu Bello University Press, 1975.

King, Thomas. "Godzilla vs. Post-Colonial." *WLWE* 30:2 (1990): 10-16.

Kirk-Greene, A.H.M. (Compiler). *Lugard and the Amalgamation of Nigeria: A Documentary Record. Being a Reprint of The Report by Sir F.D. Lugard on the Amalgamation of Northern and Southern Nigeria and Administration, 1912-1919*. London: Frank Cass & Co. Ltd., 1968.

————. *Crisis and Conflict in Nigeria: A Documentary Sourcebook*

1966-1970. 2 Vols. London: Oxford University Press, 1971.

Klima, Vladimir. *Black Africa: Literature and Language*. Dordrecht, Netherlands & Boston: Reidel, 1975.

Knipp. Thomas. "Poets and Politics: Speculations on Political Roles and Attitudes in West African Poetry." *African Studies Review* 18: 1 (1975): 39-49.

———. "Politics and Aesthetics: The Theory of Literature and the Practice of Poetry in West Africa." In Harrow, Kenneth, *et al.*, eds. (1991): 171-80.

Kristeva, Julia. *Strangers to Ourselves*. Trans., Leon S. Roudiez. New York: Columbia University, 1991.

Kroller, Eva-Marie. "The Cultural Contribution of the 'Other' Ethnic Groups: A New Challenge to Comparative Canadian Literature." In Riemenschneider, ed. (1989): 83-90.

Kunene, Daniel P. "African Literature: Tragedy and Hope." *RAL* 23:1 (Spring 1992): 7-15.

Kunene, Mazisi. "Problems in African Literature." *RAL* 23:1 (Spring 1992): 27-44.

Kuper Leo & M.G. Smith, eds. *Pluralism in Africa*. Berkeley: University of California Press, 1969.

Lacan, Jacques. "The Subject and the Other: Alienation." *The Four Fundamental Concepts of Psychoanalysis*. Trans., Alan Sheridan. London: Hogarth Press, 1977, ch. 16.

LaCapra, Dominick, ed. *The Bounds of Race: Perspectives on Hegemony and Resistance*. Ithaca: Cornell University Press, 1991.

Lamming, George. "The Negro Writer and His World." *Presence Africaine* VIII-X (1956): 318-25.

Landy, Rev. Fr. Joseph W. "Is There Anything as a National Literature?" *The Muse* 7 (Nsukka: University of Nigeria, 1975): 47-54.

Langley, J. Ayodele. *Pan-Africanism and Nationalism in West Africa: 1900-1945*. Oxford: Clarendon Press, 1973.

Larrain, Jorge. *Theories of Development: Capitalism, Colonialism and Dependency*. Cambridge: Polity Press, 1989.

Larson, Charles R. "Long Shadows of the Biafran War." *Nation* Number 3 (December 1973): 598-602.

Laurence, Margaret. *Long Drums and Cannons*. London: Macmillan, 1968.

Lazarus, Neil. *Resistance in Postcolonial African Fiction*. New Haven: Yale University Press, 1990.

Levinas, Emmanuel. *Time and the Other and Additional Essays.* Trans., Richard Cohen. Pittsburgh: Duquesne University Press, 1987.

Liddle, R. William. *Ethnicity, Party, and National Integration.* New Haven: Yale University Press, 1970.

Lindfors, Bernth. "Are There Any National Literatures in Sub-Saharan Black Africa Yet?" *English in Africa* II:2 (1975): 1-9.

————. *Black African Literature in English, 1977-1981 Supplement.* New York: Africana, 1986.

————, ed. *Critical Perspectives on Nigerian Literatures.* Washington, D.C.: Three Continents Press, 1976.

————. "Okigbo As Jock." *English in Africa* VI:1 (1979): 52-59.

————. *Long Drums and Canons: Teaching and Researching African Literatures.* Trenton, New Jersey: Africa World Press, 1995.

Lloyd, David. *Nationalism and Minor Literature: James Clarence Mangan and the Emergence of Irish Cultural Nationalism.* Berkeley & Los Angeles: University of California Press, 1987.

Loomba, Ania. "Overworlding the 'Third World'." *Oxford Literary Review* XIII:1-2 (1991): 164-91.

Lubbers, Klaus. "Literature and National Identity: The Irish Example." In Drescher & Volkel, eds. (1989): 269-79.

Luckham, Robin. *The Nigerian Military.* Cambridge: Cambridge University Press, 1971.

Luhmann, Niklas. *The Differentiation of Society.* Trans., Stephen Holmes & Charles Larmore. New York: Columbia University Press, 1982.

Luvai, Arthur. "For Whom Does the African Poet Write?: An Examination of (Form / Content in) the Poetry of Okigbo and Soyinka." *Busara* 8:2 (1976): 38-52.

————. "Negritude: A Redefinition." *Busara* VI:2 (1974): 79-90.

————. "The Poetry of Wole Soyinka and Christopher Okigbo." In Wanjala, ed. (1973): 284-301.

Lyotard, Jean-Francois. *The Postmodern Condition: A Report on Knowledge.* Trans., Geoff Bennington & Brian Massumi. Minneapolis: University of Minnesota Press, 1984.

Macebuh, Stanley. "Politics and the Mythic Imagination." *Transition* 50 (1975): 79-84.

Madiebo, Alexander A. *The Nigerian Revolution and the Biafran War.* Enugu: Fourth Dimension Publishers, 1980.

Maes-Jelinek, Hena, ed. *Commonwealth Literature and the Modern World*. Brussels: Didier, 1975.

Manaka, Matsemela. "Challenges of African Artists." *Matatu* II:3&4 (1988): 101-05.

Maquet, Jacques. *Africanity: The Cultural Unity of Black Africa*. Trans., Joan R. Rayfield. London / New York: Oxford University Press, 1972.

Marglin, Frederique Apffel & Stephen A. Marglin, eds. *Dominating Knowledge: Development, Culture, and Resistance*. Oxford: Clarendon Press, 1990.

Mazuri, Ali A. "Abstract Verse and African Tradition." *Zuka* 1 (1968): 47-49.

———. "Meaning Versus Imagery in African Poetry." *Presence Africaine* 66 (1968): 49-59.

———. *The Trial of Christopher Okigbo*. New York: The Third Press, 1971.

———. & Michael Tidy. *Nationalism and New States in Africa: From about 1935 to the Present*. London: Heinemann, 1984.

Mazrui, Alamin. "Relativism, Universalism, and the Language of African Literature." *RAL* 23:1 (Spring 1992): 65-72.

Mbadiwe, Kingsley O. *Rebirth of a Nation (Autobiography)*. Ed. Luke I. Agusiegbe. Enugu: Fourth Dimension Publishers, 1991.

Mbele, Joseph. "Language in African Literature: An Aside to Ngugi." *RAL* 23:1 (Spring 1992): 145-51.

McGuire, James. "Forked Tongues, Marginal Bodies: Writing as Translation in Khatibi." *RAL* 23:1 (Spring 1992): 107-16.

McLeod, A.L., ed. *African Literature in English: Development and Identity*. Philadelphia: African Studies Association (23rd Meeting, 1980), 1981.

McLuckie, Craig W. *Nigerian Civil War Literature: Seeking an "Imagined Community."* Lewiston, New York: The Edwin Mellen Press, 1990.

Memmi, Albert. *The Colonizer and the Colonized*. Boston: Beacon Press, 1991.

Mezu, S. Okechukwu. *The Black Dawn*. Buffalo, NY: Black Academy Press, 1970.

———. "The Origins of African Poetry." In Okapku, ed. (1970): 52-63.

Midiohouan, Guy Ossito. "The Nation-Specific Approach to African Literature." In Harrow, Kenneth, *et al.*, eds. (1991): 35-38.

Migdal, Joel S., ed. *Palestinian Society and Politics*. Princeton: Princeton University Press, 1980.

Miller, Christopher L. "Ethnicity and Ethics in the Criticism of Black South African Literature." *South Atlantic Quarterly* 87:1 (1988): 75-108.

———. *Theories of Africans: Francophone Literature and Anthropology in Africa*. Chicago: University of Chicago Press, 1990.

———. "Theories of Africans: The Question of Literary Anthropology." In Gates, Jr., ed. (1986): 262-80.

Minh-ha, Trinh T. *Woman, Native, Other: Writing Postcoloniality and Feminism*. Bloomington & Indianapolis: Indiana University Press, 1989.

Miyoshi, Masao. "A Borderless World? From Colonialism to Transnationalism and the Decline of the Nation-State." *Critical Inquiry* XIX:4 (Summer 1993): 726-51.

Molloy, Sylvia. "The Unquiet Self: Spanish American Autobiography and the Question of National Identity." In Spillers, ed. 26-39.

Moore, Gerald H., ed. *African Literature and the Universities*. Ibadan: Ibadan University Press (for The Congress for Cultural Freedom), 1965 [a].

———. "The Arts in the New Africa." *Nigeria Magazine* 92 (1967[a]): 92-97.

———. "The Debate on Existence in African Literature." *Presence Africaine* 81 (1972): 18-48.

———. "The Imagery of Death in African Poetry." *Africa* 38 (1968[a]): 57-70.

———. "The Language of Poetry." In G.H.Moore, ed. (1965[b]): 96-114.

———. "Modern African Literature and Tradition." *African Affairs* 66 (1967[b]): 246-47.

———. "Poetry and the Nigerian Crisis." *Black Orpheus* II:3 (1968[b]): 10-13.

———. "Reintegration With the Lost Self: A Theme in Contemporary African Literature." *AFRAS* I:4 (1973): 7-12.

———. "Poetry and the Nigerian Crisis." *Black Orpheus* 2,3 (1969[a]): 10-13.

———. "The Imagery of Death in African Poetry." *Africa* 38 (1968[c]): 57-70.

———. "Surrealism on the Congo River." In G.H. Moore, ed.

(1965[c]): 41-50.

———. *Twelve African Writers.* London: Hutchinson, 1980.

———. "Vision and Fulfillment." In Nwoga, ed. (1984): 274-87.

———. *The Chosen Tongue: English Writing in the Tropical World.* London: Longmans, 1969[b].

Mordi, A.A. "A Socio-Historical Reconstruction of Ethnicism in Nigeria." *ODU* 25 (Jan. 1984): 83-92.

Morse, Peckham. "Literature and the State." Minneapolis: University of Minnesota Center for Humanistic Studies Occasional Papers Number 20, 1987.

Mowitt, John. *Text: The Genealogy of an Antidisciplinary Object.* Durham & London: Duke University Press, 1992.

Mphahlele, Ezekiel. "African Literature and the Universities." *Transition* IV:10 (1963): 16-18.

———. "The Function of Literature at the Present Time: The Ethnic Imperative." *Transition* 45 (1974): 47-53.

———. "The New Mood in African Literature." *Africa Today* 19:4 (1972): 53-70.

———. "The Voice of Prophecy in African Poetry." *UMOJA* I:2 (1973): 10-14.

Mudimbe, V.Y. "Which Idea of Africa? Herskovits's Cultural Relativism." *October* 55 (Winter 1990): 93-104.

———. *The Invention of Africa: Gnosis, Philosophy, and the Order of Knowledge.* Bloomington: Indiana University Press, 1988.

Muir, Edwin. *Essays on Literature and Society.* London: Hogarth Press, 1965.

Mukherjee, Arun P. "Whose Postcolonialism and Whose Postmodernism?" *WLWE* 30:2 (1990): 1-9.

Narogin, Mudrooroo. "Celebration of a Nation." In Davis & Maes-Jelinek, eds. (1990): 3-8.

Nazareth, Peter. *Literature and Society in Modern Africa: Essays on Literature.* Nairobi: EALB, 1972.

———. "The Social Responsibility of the East African Writer." *Iowa Review* VII: 2-3 (1976): 249-63.

———. "The Trial of a Juggler." In Wanjala, ed. (1973): 147-57.

———. *In the Trickster Tradition: The Novels of Salkey, Ebejar and Reed.* London: Bogle-L'Ouverture, 1994.

Nazombe, Anthony. "Meaning in Okigbo's Poetry." In Nwoga, ed. (1984): 328-36.

Ndu, Pol. "Mytho-Religious Roots of Modern Nigerian Poetry:

Christopher Okigbo —*Heavensgate*." *Greenfield Review* V: 3-4 (1976/77): 7-12.

Nelson, Cary & Lawrence Grossberg, eds. *Marxism and the Interpretation of Culture*. Urbana & Chicago: University of Illinois Press, 1988.

Nethersole, Reingard, ed. *Emerging Literatures*. Bern: Peter Lang, 1990.

Ngara, Emmanuel. *Ideology and Form in African Poetry: Implications for Communication*. Portsmouth, NH: Heinemann, 1990.

—— & Andrew Morrison, eds. *Literature, Language and the Nation: Proceedings of the Second General Conference of the Association of University Teachers of Literature and Language (ATOLL) Held at the University of Zimbabwe 24-28 August, 1987*. Harare: ATOLL / Baobab Books, 1989.

Ngugi, wa Thiong'o. *Decolonizing the Mind: The Politics of Language in African Literature*. London: James Currey, 1986.

——. *Homecoming: Essays on African and Caribbean Literature, Culture and Politics*. London: Heinemann, 1972.

——. "Language and Literature." In Emenyonu, ed. (1986): 84-95.

——. *Moving the Centre: The Struggle for Cultural Freedoms*. London: Heinemann, 1993.

——. *Writers in Politics: Essays*. London: Heinemann, 1981.

——. *Writing Against Neocolonialism*. Middlesex, England: Vita Books, 1986.

Ngwube, Anerobi. "Nigerian War Literature." *Indigo* 2 (1974): 3-4, 6-7.

Nichols, Lee. *African Writers at the Microphone*. Washington, D.C.: Three Continents Press, 1984.

——. *Conversations with African Writers*. Washington, D.C.: Voices of America, 1981.

Niebuhr, Reinhold. *The Structure of Nations and Empires*. New York: Scribner, (1959) 1977.

Nkosi, Lewis. *Home and Exile*. London: Longman, 1965.

——. "A Release of Energy: Nigeria, the Arts and Mbari." *New African* I:11 (1962): 10-11.

——. *Tasks and Masks: Themes and Styles of African Literature*. Essex, U.K.: Longman Group, 1981.

Nnoli, Okwudiba. *Ethnic Politics in Nigeria*. Enugu: Fourth

Dimension Publishers, 1978.

———. "The Nigeria-Biafra Conflict — A Political Analysis." In Okpaku, ed. (1972): 118-51.

Noble, R.W. "From Cary to Okigbo: The Critical Task." *West Africa* (4 July 1970): 734-35.

Nwabara, S.N. *Iboland: A Century of Contact with Britain: 1860-1960.* Atlantic Highlands, NJ: Humanities Press, 1978.

Nwachukwu, Richard O. *The Dark and Bright Continent: Africa in the Changing World.* Dallas, TX: Good Hope Enterprises, Inc., 1989.

Nwachukwu-Agbada, J.O.J. "The Language of Post-war Nigerian Poetry." *ALT* 17 (1991): 165-75.

Nwamuo, Chris. "Young Nigerian Poets and Dedication." In Emenyonu, ed. (1986): 227-45.

Nwankwo, Arthur. Nigeria: *The Challenge of Biafra.* London: Rex Collings, 1972.

—— & Samuel Ifejika. *Biafra: The Making of a Nation.* New York: Praeger Publishers, 1970.

Nwoga, Donatus I. "The Changing Identity of the Igbo in Literature." In Breitinberg & Sander, eds. (1986):75-103.

———, ed. *Critical Perspectives on Christopher Okigbo.* Washington, D.C.: Three Continents, 1984.

———, "The Emergence of the Poet of Destiny: A Study of Okigbo's 'Lament of the Silent Sisters'." In Nwoga, ed. (1984): 117-30.

———, "The Limitations of Universal Literary Criteria." *UFAHAMU* IV:1 (1973): 10-33.

———, "Obscurity and Commitment in Modern African Poetry." *ALT* 6 (1973): 26-43.

———, "Okigbo's Limits: An Approach to Meaning." In Nwoga, ed. (1984): 95-104.

———, "Plagiarism and Authentic Creativity in West Africa." In Lindfors, ed. *Critical Perspectives on Nigerian Literatures.* 159-67; *RAL* 6 (Spring 1975): 32-39.

———, ed. *West African Verse: An Anthology.* London: Longman Group Ltd., 1967.

Obichere, Boniface I. "African Literature and Its Role in Postcolonial Africa: An Introduction." *Journal of African Studies* XII:2 (Summer 1985): 52.

Obiechina, Emmanuel N. *Christopher Okigbo: The Poet of Destiny.* Enugu, Nigeria: Fourth Dimension Publishers, 1980.

———. "Cultural Nationalism in Modern African Creative Literature." *ALT* 1 (1968): 24-35.

———. "Growth of Written Literature in English-Speaking West Africa." *Presence Africaine* 66 (1968): 58-78.

———. *Language and Theme: Essays on African Literature.* Washington, D.C.: Howard University Press, 1990.

———. *"Nchetaka": The Story, Memory and Continuity of Igbo Culture.* (Ahiajoku Lecture).Owerri, Nigeria: Ministry of Information & Social Development, 1994.

———. "Perceptions of Colonialism in West African Literature." *UFAHAMU* V:1 (1974): 45-70.

———. "The Writer and His Commitment in Contemporary Nigeria." *OKIKE* 27/28 (March 1988): 1-9.

Obumselu, Ben. "The Background of Modern African Literature." *Ibadan* 22 (1966): 46-59.

Odetola, Theophilus O. *Military Politics in Nigeria.* New Brunswick, NJ: Transaction Books, 1978.

Ogbemudia, Samuel O. *Years of Challenge.* Ibadan: Heinemann Educational Books Nig. PLC, 1991.

Ogundipe-Leslie, Molara. "Christopher Okigbo: The Development of a Poet." *New Horn* 1:2 (1974): 17-32.

———. "The Poetry of Christopher Okigbo: Its Evolution and Significance." In Nwoga, ed. (1984): 288-99.

Ogungbesan, Kolawole. "Literature and Cultural Values in Nigeria." *West African Journal of Modern Languages* 2 (1976): 87-94.

———, ed. *New West African Literature.* London: Heinemann, 1979.

Ohaegbulam, Festus U. *Towards an Understanding of the African Experience from Historical and Contemporary Perspectives.* Lanham, MD: University Press of America, Inc., 1990.

Ohaeto, Ezenwa. *"Ekwensi, Okara, Amadi and Anyidoho."* Ernest Emenyonu, ed. *World Literature Today* 67:3 (1993): 654-55.

Okafor, Dubem. *My Testaments.* Onitsha, Nigeria: University Publishing Co., 1981.

———. *Nationalism in Okigbo's Poetry.* Enugu: Fourth Dimension Publishers, 1980.

——— & Chinua Achebe, eds. *Don't Let him Die: An Anthology of Memorial Poems for Christopher Okigbo 1932-1967.* Enugu: Fourth Dimension Publishers, 1978.

———. *Garlands of Anguish.* Rockville, MD: Eagle & Palm Publishers, 1997.

Okara, Gabriel. "African Speech ... English Words." *Transition* IV:10 (September 1963): 15-16.

Okeke-Ezigbo, Emeka. "The Role of the Nigerian Writer in a Carthaginian Society." *OKIKE* XXI (July 1982): 28-37.

―――. "The Strangling Hold of Zurrjir: Nigerian Writers and the Burden of the 'Half-Bodied Baby'." *Ariel* XV:4 (Oct. 1984): 5-18.

―――. "What Is a National Literature?" *Nigeria Magazine* #149 (1984): 1-13.

Okigbo, Christopher. *Collected Poems*. Introduction by Adewale Maja-Pearce. London: Heinemann, 1986.

―――. *Labyrinths With "Path of Thunder"*. London: Heinemann, 1971.

―――. *Path of Thunder: Poems Prophesying War*. Black Orpheus, 1968.

―――. *Distances.* (*Transition*) 1964.

―――. *Silences.* (*Transition*) 1963.

―――. *Limits.* Ibadan, Nigeria: Mbari, 1964.

―――. *Heavensgate.* Ibadan, Nigeria: Mbari, 1962

Okokunefor, Henrietta & Obiageli Nwodo, eds. *Nigerian Female Writers: A Critical Perspective*. Lagos: Malthouse Press Ltd., 1989.

Okonta, Ike. "Preparing for the Worst." *The News* (Lagos, Nigeria 14 February, 1994): 22+.

Okoth, Assa. *A History of Africa, 1855-1914*. Nairobi: Heinemann, 1979.

Okpaku, Joseph O., ed. *New African Literature and the Arts, Vol. I*. New York: Crowell & Third Press, 1970.

―――, ed. *Nigeria: Dilemma of Nationhood*. New York: The Third Press, 1972.

―――. "The Writer in Politics: Christopher Okigbo, Wole Soyinka, and the Nigerian Crisis." *Journal of the New African Literature and the Arts* IV (Fall 1967): 1-13.

Okpewho, Isidore. *African Oral Literature*. Bloomington & Indianapolis: Indiana University Press, 1992.

―――. "African Poetry: The Modern Writer and the Oral Tradition." *ALT* 16 (1988): 3-25.

―――. *The Epic in Africa: Towards a Poetics of the Oral Performance*. New York: Columbia University Press, 1979.

Okpu, Ugbana. *Ethnic Minority Problems in Nigerian Politics 1960-*

1965. Uppsala: ACTA Univ. / Almqvist & Wiksell Int., 1977.

Oladitan, Olalere. "The Nigerian Crisis in the Nigerian Novel." In Ogungbesan, ed. 10-20.

Olafioye, Ebun Tayo Peter. "The Poet as Elegist: The Poet as Prophet." *Black Images* III:2 (1974): 40-62.

Olajuyin, L.O. "An Appraisal of the Theoretical and Empirical Analysis of the Core-Periphery Model as Applied to the Nigerian Case." *ODU* 37 (Jan. / July 1990): 161-69.

Olaogun, Modupe. "Graphology and Meaning in the Poetry of Christopher Okigbo." *ALT* 17 (1991): 108-30.

Oluleye, James J. *Military Leadership in Nigeria, 1966-1979*. Ibadan: University of Ibadan Press, 1985.

Omotoso, Kole. "Christopher Okigbo: A Personal Portrait, 1932-1967." *New Horn* 1:2 (1974): 4-15.

———. *Just Before Dawn*. Ibadan, Nigeria: Spectrum Books, 1988.

Ong, Walter J. *Interfaces of the Word*. Ithaca & London: Cornell University Press, 1977.

———. *The Presence of the Word*. New Haven & London: Yale University Press, 1967.

Onwueme, Tess Akaeke. *Three Plays*. Detroit, MI: Wayne State University Press, 1993.

Onwuka, Ralph I. & Timothy M. Shaw, eds. *Africa in World Politics: Into the 1990s*. New York: St. Martin's Press, 1989.

Osae, T.A., S.N. Nwabara & A.T.O. Odunsi. *A Short History of West Africa: A.D. 1000 to the Present*. New York: Hill & Wang, 1973.

Osofisan, Femi. "Anubis Resurgent: Chaos and Political Vision in Recent Literature." *CH'INDABA* 2 (1976): 44-49.

———. "Enter the Carthaginian Critic...? — a comment on Okeke-Ezibgo's 'The Role of the Writer in a Carthaginian Society'." *OKIKE* XXI (July 1982): 38-44.

———. "The Quality of Hurt: A Survey of Recent Nigerian Poetry." *Afriscope* IV:7 (1974): 45-48, 52-53; VI:9 (1974):P 46-49, 51, 53-55.

Owomoyela, Oyekan, ed. *A History of Twentieth-Century African Literatures*. Lincoln & London: University of Nebraska Press, 1993.

———. "Language, Identity, and Social Construction in African Literatures." *RAL* 32:1 (Spring 1992): 83-94.

———. *Visions and Revisions: Essays on African Literatures and*

Criticism. New York: Peter Lang, 1991.

Oyediran, Oyeleye, ed. *Nigerian Government and Politics Under Military Rule, 1966-79.* London: MacMillan Press, 1979.

Oyeneye, O.Y. "Indigenous Cultural Forms as Basis for Nigeria's Development." *ODU* 25 (Jan. 1984): 59-69.

Pagnini, Marcello. *The Pragmatics of Literature.* Trans., Nancy Jones-Henry. Bloomington: Indiana University Press, 1987.

Paolucci, Anne, ed. *Review of National Literatures: Black Africa.* Jamaica, NY: St. John's University Press, 1972.

Parini, Jay. "The Theory and Practice of Literature: a New Dialogue?" *The Chronicle of Higher Education* (September 9, 1992): B1-B2.

Parry, Benita. "Problems in Current Theories of Colonial Discourse." *Oxford Literary Review* IX: 1-2 (1987): 27-58.

Pechey, Graham. "On the Borders of Bakhtin." *Oxford Literary Review* IX: 1-2 (1987): 59-84.

Pedler, Frederick. *Main Currents of West African History, 1940-1978.* London: MacMillan Press, 1979.

Peters, Jonathan A., Mildred P. Motimer, & Russell V. Linnemann, eds. *Literature of Africa and the African Continuum.* Washington, D.C.: Three Continents Press & African Literature Association, 1989.

Petersen, Kirsten & Anna Rutherford, eds. *Chinua Achebe: A Celebration.* Oxford and Portsmouth, NH: Heinemann / Sydney, Australia: Dangaroo Press, 1990.

Philipson, Robert. "The Persistence of Orality in the Post-Literate Narrative: A Swahili Example." In Harrow, Kenneth, et al., eds. (1991):159-69.

Pieterse, Cosmo & Dennis Duerden, eds. *African Writers Talking: A Collection of Radio Interviews.* New York: Africana Publishing Corporation, 1972.

—— & Donald Munro, eds. *Protest and Conflict in African Literature.* New York: Africana Publishing Corp., 1969.

Pinto, Vivian de S. *Crisis in English Poetry 1880-1940.* London: Hutchinson, 1972.

Porter, Bernard. *Critics of Empire: British Radical Attitudes to Colonialism in Africa.* London: MacMillan; New York: St. Martin's Press, 1968.

Post, Ken. *The New States of West Africa.* Harmondsworth, England: Penguin, 1968.

———— & George D. Jenkins. *The Price of Liberty: Personality and Politics in Colonial Nigeria.* Cambridge: The University Press, 1973.

———— & Michael Vickers. *Structure and Conflict in Nigeria 1960-1966.* London: Heinemann, 1973.

Povey, John. "The Nigerian War: The Writer's Eye." *Journal of African Studies* 1, 3 (Fall 1974): 345-60.

Priebe, Richard M. *Myth, Realism and the West African Writer.* Trenton, NJ: Africa World Press, 1988.

Ransom, John Crowe. *The New Criticism.* Westport, Conn.: Greenwood Press, 1979.

Ravenscroft, Arthur. "The Nigerian Civil War in Nigerian Literature." In Maes-Jelinek, ed. (1975): 105-13.

————. *Nigerian Writers and the African Past.* Dharwad, India: Karnatak University, 1978.

Richardson, Thomas C. "Reinventing Identity: Nationalism in Modern Scottish Literature." In Drescher & Volkel, eds. (1989):117-29.

Richter, David H., ed. *Falling Into Theory: Conflicting Views on Reading Literature.* Boston, MA: St. Martin's Press, 1994.

Riemenschneider, Dieter, ed. *Critical Approaches to the New Literatures in English. (10th Annual Commonwealth Literature & Language Studies Conference Papers, Koenigstein, Germany, 1987).* Essen: Verlag Die Blaue Eule, 1989.

————, ed. *The History and Historiography of Commonwealth Literature.* Tubingen, Germany: Narr, 1983.

———— & Frank Schulze-Engler, eds. *African Literatures in the Eighties.* Amsterdam / Atlanta, Ga.: Rodopi, 1993.

Rodney, Walter. *How Europe Underdeveloped Africa.* Washington, D.C.: Howard University Press, (1972) 1982.

Rohr, Janelle, ed. *Problems of Africa: Opposing Viewpoints.* St. Paul, MN.: Greenhaven Press, 1986.

Ronning, Helge. "Literature, Language, Modernisation and National Consciousness." In Ngara & Morrison, eds. (1989):150-64.

Ross, Kristin. "The World Literature and Cultural Studies Program." *Critical Inquiry* XIX:4 (Summer 1993): 666-76.

Rotberg, Robert I. "African Nationalism: Concept or Confusion?" *Journal of Modern African Studies* IV (1966): 33-46.

Rotimi, Ola. *Our Husband Has Gone Mad Again.* Ibadan: Oxford University Press Nigeria, 1977.

Rowe, William. *Memory and Modernity: Popular Culture in Latin America.* New York & London: Verso, 1991.

Rutherford, Anna, ed. *From Commonwealth to Post-Colonial.* Sydney: Dangaroo, 1993.

———, ed. *Common Wealth.* Aarhus: Akademisk Boghandel, 1972.

Said, Edward W. *Culture and Imperialism.* New York: Alfred A. Knopf, 1993.

———. "Literature, Theory and Commitment: II." In Harrow, Kenneth, et al., eds. 65-70.

———. "An Ideology of Difference." In Gates, Jr., ed. (1986): 38-58.

———. "Intellectuals in the Post-Colonial World." *SALMAGUNDI* Vol. 70-71 (Spring / Summer 1986): 44-64.

———. *Orientalism.* New York: Vintage Books, 1979.

———. "Orientalism Reconsidered." In Barker, et al., eds. (1986): 210-29.

———. "The Politics of Knowledge." In Richter, ed. (1994):193-203.

———. "Representing the Colonized: Anthropology's Interlocutors." *Critical Inquiry* XV (Winter 1989): 205-25.

Salkey, Andrew, ed. *Caribbean Essays.* London: Evans, 1973.

Sampson, G. *The Concise History of English Literature.* Cambridge: University Press, 1973.

Saro-Wiwa, Ken. *Basi and Company.* Port Harcourt, Nigeria: Saros Int. Publishers, 1987.

———. "The Language of African Literature: A Writer's Testimony." *RAL* 23:1 (Spring 1992): 153-57.

———. *Sozaboy: a Novel in Rotten English.* Port Harcourt: Saros Int. Publishers, 1985.

Sartre, Jean-Paul. *What Is Literature?* Trans., Bernard Frechtman. New York: Philosophical Library, 1949.

Sathyamurthy, T.V. *Nationalism in the Contemporary World: Politics and Sociological Perspectives.* London: F. Pinter, 1983.

Saxena, S.C. *Political Conflicts and Power in Africa.* Dehli, India: UDH Publishers, 1985.

Sayer, Derek. *Capitalism and Modernity: An Excursus on Marx and Weber.* London & New York: Routledge, 1991.

Schipper, Mineke. *Beyond the Boundaries: African Literature and Literary Theory.* London: W.H. Allen & Co., 1989.

Schulze, Frank. "Uses and Misuses of Marxism as a Comparative Paradigm in the Study of African Literature." In

Riemenschneider, ed. (1989): 62-67.

Shelton, Austin J. "Relativism, Pragmatism and Reciprocity in Igbo Proverbs." *Conch: Igbo Traditional Life, Culture & Literature* III: 2 (Sept. 1971): 46-62

Shohat, Ella. "Notes on the 'Post-Colonial'." *Social Text* X:2 & 3 (1992): 99-113.

Simms, Catherine. "Bardic Poetry as a Historical Source." In Dunne, ed. (1987): 58-75.

Slemon, Stephen. "Unsettling the Empire: Resistance Theory for the Second World." *World Literatures Written in English* 30:2 (1990):30-41.

Smith, Sidonie & Julia Watson, eds. *De / Colonizing the Subject: The Politics of Gender in Women's Autobiography.* Minneapolis: University of Minnesota Press, 1992.

Smith, Steven B. *Reading Althusser: An Essay on Structural Marxism.* Ithaca & London: Cornell University Press, 1984.

Snyder, Louis Leo. *Encyclopedia of Nationalism.* New York: Paragon House, 1990.

———. *The Meaning of Nationalism.* New Brunswick, NJ: Rutgers University Press, 1954.

Society of African Culture. *Colloquium On Negro Art. (First World Festival of Negro Arts, Dakar, April 1-24, 1966).* Paris: Editions Presence Africaine, 1968.

Sofola, Zulu. "The Bogey of African Writers' Language Limitation On The Creative Process: The Core of the Matter." In Emenyonu, ed. (1986): 259-74.

Southall, Aidan, ed. *Social Change in Modern Africa.* London: Oxford University Press, 1963.

Soyinka, Wole. "Aesthetic Illusions." In Baker, ed. (1976): 1-12.

———. "And After the Narcissist?" *African Forum* I:4 (1966): 53-64.

———. *Art, Dialogue, and Outrage.* Ibadan, Nigeria: New Horn Press, 1988.

———. *Collected Plays I & II.* London: Oxford University Press, 1973/74.

———. *Idanre and Other Poems.* London: Methuen, 1967.

———. *The Interpreters.* London: Heinemann, (1965) 1970.

———. *The Jero Plays: The Trials of Brother Jero & Jero's Metamorphosis.* London: Eyre Methuen, 1973.

———. *The Man Died.* New York: Harper & Row, 1972.

———. "Neo-Tarzanism: The Poetics of Pseudo-Tradition."

Transition 48 (1975): 38-44.

———. *Seasons of Anomy.* London: Rex Collings, 1973.

———. *A Shuttle in the Crypt.* London: Rex Collings, 1972.

———. *Myth, Literature and the African World.* Cambridge: Cambridge University Press, 1976.

Spillers, Hortense J., ed. *Comparative American Identities: Race, Sex, and Nationality in the Modern Text.* New York: Routledge, 1991.

Spivak, Gayatri. "Can the Subaltern Speak?" Cary Nelson & Lawrence Grossberg, eds. (1988): 271-313.

———. *In Other Worlds: Essays in Cultural Politics.* New York: Routledge, 1988.

———. "Literature, Theory and Commitment: III." Harrow, Kenneth, et al., eds. (1991): 71-75.

———. "Neocolonialism and the Secret Agent of Knowledge: Interview by Robert Young." *Oxford Literary Review* XIII:1&2 (1991): 220-51.

———. *The Post-Colonial Critic: Interviews, Strategies, Dialogues.* Ed. Sarah Harasym. New York: Routledge, 1990.

———. "Poststructuralism, Marginality, Postcoloniality and Value." Collier & Ryan, eds. (1990): 218-44.

———. "Three Women's Texts and a Critique of Imperialism." Gates, Jr., ed. (1986): 262-80.

———. "Woman in Difference: Mahasweta Devi's 'Douloti the Beautiful'." *Cultural Critique* (Winter 1989-90): 105-28.

———. Imperialism and Sexual Difference." *Oxford Literary Review* VII: 1, 2 (1986): 225-40.

Sprinker, Michael. *Imaginary Relations: Aesthetics and Ideology in the History of Historical Materialism.* London: Verso, 1987.

Stanton, Robert J. "Poet as Martyr: West Africa's Christopher Okigbo, and His *Labyrinths with Path of Thunder.*" *Studies in Black Literature* 7:1 (Winter 1976): 10-14.

St. Jorre, John de. *The Nigerian Civil War.* London: Hodder & Stoughton, 1972.

Taiwo, Oladele. *Female Novelists of Modern Africa.* New York: St. Martin's Press, 1984.

Tejani, B. "Creative Freedom and Critical Function in African Literature." In Wanjala, ed. (1973): 3-38.

Theroux, Paul. "Christopher Okigbo." In Bruce King, ed. (1971): 135-51.

———. "Christopher Okigbo." In Nwoga, ed. (1984): 254-60.

———. "Voices Out of the Skull: A Study of Six African Poets." *Black Orpheus* 20 (1966): 41-58.

Thomas, Peter. "Great Plenty to Come: A Personal Reminiscence of the First Generation of Nsukka Poets." *The Muse* 4 (1972): 5-8.

———. "An Image Insists." *Greenfield Review* VIII:1-2 (1980): 122-26.

———. "Ride Me Memories: A Memorial Tribute to Christopher Okigbo." *African Arts* 1:4 (1968): 68-70.

———. "Voices from Nsukka: Students and the Art of Poetry." *New African* V:7 (1966): 144-45.

———. "The Water Maid and the Dancer: Figures of the Nigerian Muse." *Literature East and West* 12 (1968): 85-93.

Thomas, Rosalind. *Oral Tradition and Written Record in Classical Athens.* Cambridge & New York: Cambridge University Press, 1989.

Thompson, Richard H. *Theories of Ethnicity: A Critical Appraisal.* Westport, Conn.: Greenwood Press, 1989.

Thumbo, Edwin. "Dathorne's Okigbo: A Dissenting View." *ALT* 3 (1969): 44-49.

Tiffin, Helen. "Post-Colonial Literatures and Counter-Discourse." In Riemenschneider, ed. (1989): 32-51.

Tindall, William York. *Forces in Modern British Literature 1885-1956.* New York: Vintage Books, 1956.

Todorov, Tzvetan. *The Conquest of America: The Question of the Other.* Trans., Richard Howard. New York: Harper & Row, 1984.

Tompkins, Jane P. ed. *Reader-Response Criticism: From Formalism to Post-Structuralism.* Baltimore, MD: Johns Hopkins University Press, 1980.

Tucker, Martin. *Africa in Modern Literature: A Survey of Contemporary Writing in English.* New York: Frederick Ungar, 1967.

Turner, Victor. *The Anthropology of Performance.* New York: PAJ Publications, 1987.

———. *From Ritual to Theatre.* New York: PAJ Publications, 1982.

Udechukwu, Obiora. "Aesthetics and the Mythic Imagination: Notes on Christopher Okigbo's *Heavensgate* and Uche Okeke's *Drawings.*" In Nwoga, ed. (1984): 78-85.

————. *Homage to Christopher Okigbo: Catalogue.* Nsukka, Nigeria: Odunke Publications, 1975.

————. "Functionality, Symbolism and Decoration: Some Aspects of Traditional Igbo Art." *Conch* III: 2 (September 1971): 89-96.

Udoeyop, Nyong J. *Three Nigerian Poets.* Ibadan: University Press, 1973.

Ugah, Ada. *Naked Hearts: Preceded by Anatomy of Nigerian Poetics.* Devon, UK: Merlin Press, 1982.

Ungar, Sanford J. *The People and Politics of an Emerging Continent.* New York: Simon & Schuster, Inc., 1989.

Uwatt, Effiok B. "Poetry and Pan-Africanism: Chinweizu's 'Admonition to the Black World'." *ODU* 37 (Jan./July 1990): 126-46.

Valery, Paul. *The Art of Poetry.* Trans., Denise Folliot. New York: Random House (1958) 1961.

Vincent, Theophilus. "Okigbo's Labyrinths." In Nwoga, ed. (1984): 196-200.

————. "Two Decades of Modern Nigerian Literature." *ODUMA* 2:2 (1975): 56-67.

Vinson, James & D.L. Kirkpatrick, eds. *Contemporary Poets.* London: St. James Press; New York: St. Martin's Press, 1975.

Viswanathan, Gauri. *Masks of Conquest. Literary Study and British Rule in India.* New York: Columbia University Press, 1989.

Wake, Clive H. "Nigeria, African and the Caribbean: A Bird's Eye View." In Bruce King, ed. (1971): 193-208.

Wali, Obiajunwa. "The Dead End of African Literature?" *Transition* IV:10 (September 1963): 13-15.

Wallerstein, Immanuel. *The Modern World-System I: Capitalist Agriculture and the Origins of European World-Economy in the Sixteenth Century.* San Diego, Calif: Academic Press, 1974.

Walsh, William. *Readings in Commonwealth Literature.* Oxford: Clarendon Press, 1973.

Wanjala, Chris, ed. *Standpoints on African Literature: A Critical Anthology.* Nairobi: East African Literature Bureau, 1973.

Ward, Barbara. *Nationalism and Ideology.* New York: Norton, 1966.

Wastberg, Per, ed. *The Writer in Modern Africa.* New York: Africana, 1967.

Wauthier, Claude. *The Literature and Thought of Modern Africa: A Survey.* Trans., Shirley Kay. Washington, D.C.: Three

Continents Press, (1966) 1979.

Weingand, Darlene E. *Connections: Literacy and Cultural Heritage: Lessons from Iceland.* Metuchen, NJ: Scarecrow Press, 1992.

White, Hayden. *Tropics of Discourse: Essays in Cultural Criticism.* Baltimore: Johns Hopkins University Press, 1978.

White, Jack E. "Nigeria: Shamed by their Nation." *Time Magazine* (September 6, 1993): 36, 41.

White, Jeremy. *Central Administration in Nigeria, 1914-1948: The Problem of Polarity.* Dublin & London: Irish Academy Press & Frank Cass, 1981.

Wilkinson, Jane, ed. *Talking with African Writers: Interviews with African Poets, Playwrights and Novelists.* London: James Currey, (1990) 1992.

Will, George. "Literary Politics." In Richter, ed. (1994): 286-88.

Williams, Denis. "The Mbari Publications." *Nigeria Magazine* 75 (1962): 69-74.

Williams, Raymond. *Marxism and Literature.* Oxford & New York: Oxford University Press, 1977.

———. *The Politics of Modernism: Against the New Conformists.* Edited & Introduced by Tony Pinkney. London & New York: Verso, 1989.

Wojcik, Jan & Raymond-Jean Frontain, eds. "Introduction: The Prophet in the Poem." *Poetic Prophecy in Western Literature.* Cranbury, NJ: Associated University Press, 1984. 13-30.

Wood, David, ed. *Writing the Future.* London: Routledge, 1990.

Woodring, Carl. *Politics in the Poetry of Coleridge.* Madison: University of Wisconsin Press, 1961.

Wylie, Hal, Dennis Brutus & Juris Silenieks, eds. *African Literature, 1988 New Masks. Annual (1988) Selected Papers of the ALA.* Washington, D.C.: Three Continents Press & African Literature Association, 1990.

Yahya-Othman, Saida. "When International Languages Clash: The Possible Detrimental Effects on Development of the Conflict Between English and Kiswahili in Tanzania." In Ngara & Morrison, eds. (1989): 165-74.

Young, Peter. "Mechanism to Medium: The Language of West African Literature in English." In Anna Rutherford, ed. (1972): 35-46.

Young, Robert. "Neocolonial Times." *Oxford Literary Review* III:1-2 (1991): 2-3.

Zabus, Chantal. *The African Palimpsest: Indigenization of Language in the West African Europhone Novel.* Amsterdam / Atlanta, GA: Rodopi, 1991.

―――. "Linguistic Guerrilla in the Maghrebian and West African Europhone Novel" In Harrow, Kenneth, *et al.*, eds. (1991): 181-96.

Zacharasiewicz, Waldemar. "The Rise of Cultural Nationalism in the New World: The Scottish Element and Example." In Drescher & Volkel, eds. (1989): 315-34.

Zenzinger, Peter. "Nationalism in Twentieth-Century Scottish Literary Criticism." In Drescher & Volkel, eds. (1989):143-54.

INDEX